THE INSIDE
BATTLE

Our Military Mental Health Crisis

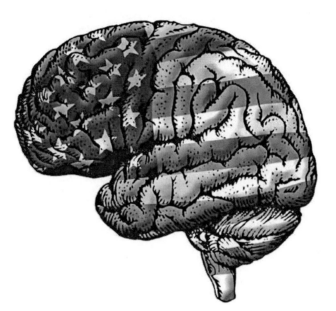

THE INSIDE
BATTLE

Our Military Mental Health Crisis

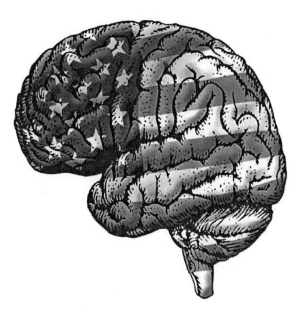

Marjorie Morrison

The Inside Battle
Copyright © 2012 by Marjorie Morrison. All rights reserved.

Published by Military Psychology Press
www.militarypsypress.com

Book design copyright © 2012 by Tate Publishing, LLC. All rights reserved
Cover design by Glenn Rico Orat
Interior design by Stephanie Mora

Published in the United States of America
ISBN: 978-0-615-70367-1
1.   Psychology/ Mental Health
2.   Psychology/ Psychopathology/ Post-Traumatic Stress Disorder (PTSD)
12.06.11

DEDICATION

This book is dedicated to
The U.S. Marine Corps for teaching me
honor, courage, and commitment

TABLE OF CONTENTS

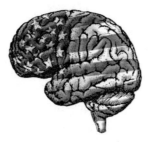

FOREWORD

By Sergeant Major Mark O'Loughlin

Mental Health Professionals tell us that self interest is the motivating factor in all human action, that human beings do things for two reasons; to move toward pleasure or move away from pain, and that Post Traumatic Stress Disorder (PTSD) is an illness of *avoidance*. I have observed during my thirty years of service in the Marine Corps, which included combat operations, that Marines (and especially Drill Instructors) will go to extraordinary efforts to ignore and conceal pain, fatigue, hunger, thirst, and injuries. They do not want to be labeled or appear as weak and feeble in the eyes of their peers and seniors. Most Marines strive to achieve and set a flawless example for future Marines to observe and emulate.

The preventive approach employed at Marine Corps Recruit Depot, San Diego, CA, where every Marine was required to meet with Marjorie, the Military Family Life Counselor, removed the stigma of talking to a Mental Health Professional. The Marine could simply sit there silent or talk about any issue that he wanted. They didn't have to avoid contact with a Mental Health Professional and as a result, were able to seek assistance for the emotional demons in their lives.

By default, issues were brought out and dealt with before the added stress of a special duty assignment, which in the past could cause a Marine to emotionally spiral out of control. Removing the stigma by routinely meeting with a mental health professional was proven, and I witnessed firsthand how well it worked with Marine Corps Drill Instructors and Officers at MCRD SD. I know it will be just as effective with all other service members.

Mark J. O'Loughlin
SgtMaj, USMC
Current Wounded Warrior Battalion West Sergeant Major
Oct 1982 to Oct 2012

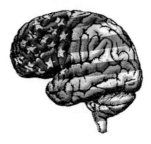

INTRODUCTION

By Debbie Ford

On Sunday March 11, 2012, as I sat down in my office to write this introduction to Marjorie Morrison's vitally important book *The Inside Battle*, a news report grabbed my attention. It was a report from southern Afghanistan about an American soldier who had gone on a house-to-house shooting spree in two villages, killing 16 people, mostly women and children. I knew there was no accident that I would hear about this incident just before writing this introduction. If only this were the first report we've heard of its kind. But of course it is not. We hear about thousands of incidents both abroad and at home where members of the military have "snapped" and not only violated the rules and protocols of the Armed Forces but have also violated the laws of humankind. This particular tragedy is not just the tragedy of the loss of lives of the villagers and not just the tragedy of yet another one of our solders driven to the breaking point where he kills innocent people but the tragedy of a mental health system that ignores and neglects these most dedicated patriots.

I can't be angry because it seems obvious to me that these incidents are bound to happen. They are terrifyingly predictable since we are sending people into such high-stress situations equipped with the uniforms and weapons but without the tools they most need -- a real understanding of themselves and how to process the experiences they find themselves in. Most of these individuals are ignorant about their emotions, not knowing why they might feel angry, irritated, upset, tearful, guilty, shameful and other emotions that drive them to want to change the way they feel. Some change their feelings with drugs. Some do it with porn. Some do it with gossip. Some do it with drugs or alcohol. However they do it, at the end of the day, they stuff their experiences and their emotions beneath the surface of their conscious minds, eating away at their self-esteem and their moral code.

As a leader in the field of personal transformation, I've always been curious how *any* of us -- in the military or outside of it—get through life without the basic knowledge and understanding of how to deal with and process our emotions and our experiences. That's why every day for the past fifteen years, I have dedicated myself to emotional education. I am a #1 New York Times best-selling author. I've taken tens of thousands of people through the transformational process of becoming complete with their past and healing the wounds that still linger in their unconscious minds. I am an expert at self-sabotage -- my own and others. I founded a training institute to educate and train thousands of people to transform their own lives and support others in doing the same. I know that there is nothing more important in this world today than to teach all men and women, especially those who will go into high stress situations, the merit of their emotions.

This is why, for the last thirty-six months, I have supported a remarkable woman in telling what I believe to be an important story. I met Marjorie Morrison when a mutual friend asked us to go to dinner. She had read some of my books and knew what I did. And I was curious about her therapy practice and how she handled certain situations. Marjorie began to tell me her story of working with the military. As she talked, I felt this tingling inside. I was both appalled and excited. I loved what I was hearing from her. It brought to life all the incidents I'd heard about over the years of the violence of our soldiers and veterans. I remembered what it felt like walking down the street in San Francisco, seeing all the homeless men with signs "I am a Vietnam Veteran. Please help me" -- men that were stripped of their dignity, lost, confused and now pariahs of society. I thought about my own family member who suffered from post-traumatic stress disorder after his deployment. I remembered the agony of his nightmares and the fear that drove him mad.

This does not have to be our reality, and Marjorie Morrison has our answer to this crisis. She is a brave and courageous woman who couldn't keep her eyes closed or her mouth shut because what she saw violated her moral code. She is a true hero who holds the well-being of each of our military personnel. *The Inside Battle* is important. It is important because we all need to understand that what affects one affects another. One unbalanced human hurts another and that person hurts someone else. Sometimes it's not just their families that get the brunt of their pain and agony but it's strangers. It takes its toll on all of us. Not only do they lose their dignity, respect and freedom, but we lose it as well. *The Inside Battle* brings us on one woman's journey to support us in waking up, showing us that it is no longer acceptable that we close our eyes and go to sleep. Marjorie Morrison has helped me to see that we have the power, the knowledge and most importantly the *responsibility* to protect each and every person who raises their hand and swears to protect our country. It is our duty as civilians to stand up and say "No more", to fight for the men and women who fight for us. We know today how to support people before the stress happens so they don't have to come home broken.

We can create a new reality for all the men and women that serve our country. Imagine if every man and woman pre and post war understood who they were, how they tick and why they do what they do. Imagine these people having the programs, processes and exercises to address their experiences. Imagine each of these remarkable individuals receiving emotional education that would allow them to come home from where they are stationed in better shape than when they left, with more skills, with an inspiring vision, feeling a part of something bigger and greater than themselves. Imagine if these men and women know that they are loved and valued by all they protect, that they are important to us, and that we are willing to give them the emotional education and the tools they need to live vibrant and productive lives.

I am excited to join Marjorie Morrison to do whatever I can to make this possibility a reality.

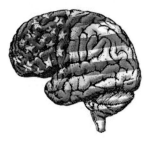

BACKGROUND

S pending time working with the incredible and inspiring
men and women in the U.S. Marine Corps has been one
of the highlights of my life. I knew very little about the
military beforehand, except what I had seen on television or in
the movies. These people were mysterious and ominous to me.
I am embarrassed to admit that my stereotypical views of them
were that they were fearless, unemotional, ruthless, and orderly
men and women with trimmed hair and fit bodies. I also used to
feel sorry for them. Every time I'd open a newspaper or turn on
the news, I'd hear about another casualty or injury of a service
member. I would wonder what motivated somebody to risk his
or her life to join a voluntary force. I imagined it must have been
sheer desperation and lack of other employment options. In one
year, I learned that everything I had believed about the military
was wrong.

These people sacrifice their lives not because they have to
but because they want to. They are educated, talented, articulate,
respectful, patriotic, and altruistic. They feel a need and desire to
protect our great country. Their lives have enormous purpose and
meaning, something that many civilian Americans have a hard
time understanding. They are part of a universal cause, which
is to serve and guard our nation, and each individual plays an
important role in that cause.

There has been much debate over the current wars in Iraq and Afghanistan. Furthermore, there is a growing discontent with regard to the harmful effect those wars are having on our service members' mental health. We keep hearing that suicides are on the rise and homicidal and violent acts are reaching unprecedented levels. We need our military to defend our country, and at the same time, we want to help them by providing them with all the tools they need to do that successfully. We as taxpayers support numerous programs that have been put in place to provide the assistance and aid that is desperately needed.

So why don't things seem to be getting any better? In 2010 Congress approved an appropriations bill that grants the Department of Veterans Affairs $4.6 billion for military mental health care, which includes treating the psychological wounds of returning combat veterans, including post-traumatic stress disorder. They matched the 2009 budget plus an additional $300 million. I don't think I can truly grasp what $4.6 billion dollars looks like, but it sure seems like an incredible amount of money, and with it we should be able to make great things happen—like reduce suicides, lower PTSD rates, and diminish domestic violence and child abuse across the military.

According to *USA Today* 7/30/2010,

> Records show that last month, the Army averaged one suicide per day among either active-duty or National Guard soldiers and reserve troops. There were 32 confirmed or suspected cases.
>
> In a few of the cases, the report says, commanders didn't realize soldiers under their control had committed suicide until long after death occurred. There are instances where a leader's lack of soldier accountability resulted in suicide victims not being found until they had been dead for three or four weeks, the report says. Gen.

Peter Chiarelli, the Army vice chief of staff said, "commanders allow infractions such as an arrest for drunken driving to go unpunished and don't refer the soldier for possible alcohol abuse treatment. Often, he states, this might by done to allow a soldier to go to war." Since fighting in Afghanistan started in 2001, 25,283 soldiers who had committed violations that could have resulted in a discharge from the Army were allowed to remain in the service, the study shows. Many of these failures were an indirect result of the wars in Iraq and Afghanistan, the study says. Army efforts have become so concentrated on training and combat that routine oversight of soldiers has lapsed, the report says.[1]

On May 11, 2009, in Iraq, an American soldier opened fire on comrades inside a combat stress clinic at a large U.S. military base in Baghdad, killing five and wounding three. A few months later in November, Ft. Hood, Texas, was plagued by the tragic and horrific massacre that we all saw on the news. An enlisted psychiatrist killed twelve and wounded thirty by opening fire on a group of innocent people at a mental health processing center. The travesties continue across the country including at home in San Diego where a young Marine in his early twenties was taken into custody for the suspected murder of his infant son. *USA Today* reported on 1/6/2011,

> The Army's largest post saw a record-high number of soldiers kill themselves in 2010 despite a mental health effort aimed at reversing the trend. The Army says 22 soldiers from Fort Hood, Texas have either killed themselves or are suspected of doing so last year at its post twice the number from 2009. That is a rate of 47 deaths per 100,000, compared with a 20-per-100,000 rate among civilians in the same age group and a 22-per-100,000

rate Army-wide. The report continues, "We are at a loss to explain the high numbers," says Maj. Gen. William Grimsley, acting commander. "It's personally frustrating." The Army had boosted staffing and psychiatric services to address the problem, particularly after the fatal shootings of 13 people on the post in November 2009. Fort Hood now has one of the largest counseling staffs in the Army with more than 170 behavioral health workers.[2]

If government spending and military mental health programs are increasing, shouldn't we see a decline in such acts? Unfortunately, I believe if we continue approaching the problem the way we are, things will inevitably continue to get worse.

Since 2001, the beginning of the War on Terror, countless additional programs have emerged. So many mental health services exist that on most bases it is hard to find one person who even knows about all the available services. Many of these programs have wonderful intentions and have been researched and devised by outstanding universities and institutions. It didn't take long for the military mental health community to discover that their myriad services were not being utilized. Now they had a new problem to deal with. How could they get military members to use them? New positions were created and filled to promote programs, and marketing materials were disseminated, but service members still were not accessing services. Blame was put on the stigma and perceived dishonor that came with seeking help. People in the military were not accessing services because they were afraid it would affect their careers and chances for promotion. On May 1, 2008, the Department of Defense changed the question on its long-standing security clearance questionnaire, which asked applicants about their mental health history. Military members no longer had to report if they were seeking mental health services.

To understand why the DOD (Department of Defense) did not get the result they were looking for, you have to understand the military mindset. I have learned that the reason I knew so little about the military before working with them is because they are a separate society that exists within our own. The very essence of being a military member is to give up your individuality and become part of the military collective whole. This process starts at the very beginning of their careers. They give up their first names, and are addressed by their rank. They adopt a stance of what the Marines call "instantaneous obedience to orders," which means you do what you are told, when you are told, because you believe that your superiors will do whatever they can to take care of you. Your life is confidential, and with the exception of perhaps your spouse, people outside the military have limited information about the work you do. The very factors that make these men and women the greatest military force in the world also make them not seek external help when they are facing problems.

In March of 2012, the *Huffington Post* reported that

> [of the] 50 percent who actually do go to counseling, 60 percent drop out—many after their first session (or during it). The reasons for this are two-fold. First, edgy war fighters with combat stress are easily spooked by well-meaning but clueless therapists who don't understand enough about warrior culture to engage them and understand them; and, two, although there are treatments that work for PTSD, that's not what most of our providers are offering. So we lose 60 percent of them right off the bat—a shame, really, because many of them had to be talked, cajoled, begged and hard-assed into giving it a try in the first place, and a one-time opportunity to do some good gets lost for good. Sadly, most therapists don't know that they have about 20 minutes to prove that they have

something to offer before that service member bolts out the door, never to return. [3]

Another issue that contributes to military members not getting mental health help is that if they go to an on-base counseling center, the notes from their sessions may become part of their permanent records. HWM, the company that hired me to work on military bases, had won the government contract that had the solution to this; they put military family life consultants (MFLCs) on installations all over the world. These MFLCs provide anonymous confidential counseling. They don't keep any notes, and there are no records. The program was devised to have licensed clinicians rotate in and out of bases every six weeks. That way the clinician, who is not called a counselor, could be seen as a safe person to share secrets with, because when he or she leaves, so do the secrets. The down side to this is that there is absolutely no continuity of care. In a DCoE blog titled "Continuity of Care Heals the Wounded and Builds Trust" written on January 8, 2010, Col. Charles C. Engel, director of the Deployment Health Clinical Center, stated,

> A growing number of doctors and patients point to something called 'continuity of care' as the single most important ingredient in your medical care. Most people find that the basics of continuity of care are so simple that they amount to common sense. But alas! We often lament just how uncommon that common sense is, and many will undoubtedly feel this is no exception to the rule.... Studies of continuity tell us that lack of continuity is associated with doctor and patient errors. High continuity leads to greater trust and confidence in your doctor, making it more likely that you will follow the medical advice you receive, and take prescribed medicines.[4]

Does it really make sense then to have a solution to mental health care be that a new provider shows up every six weeks?

I may not have all the answers, but I do believe that we are heading in the wrong direction. During my year working with Marines, I listened to and learned from these incredible men and women. With their help, I was able to devise and implement a proactive counseling program. This concept was designed by the Marines, for the Marines, and addresses and circumvents the stigma issues that are attached to getting help. We set up a program that required the Marines to see a counselor individually every three months. We also implemented mandatory and routine group sessions every three months. Essentially, every six weeks the Marines had routine access to a mental health provider. They came to rely on and benefit from these services. When every service member from the top to the bottom participates, all stigmas are removed.

It is a paradigm similar to that of your annual medical physical. In fact, no matter what type of health insurance you have, HMO, PPO, etc., you are entitled to a free routine physical once a year. Why? Because statistics show that catching illnesses and disorders early greatly improves the chances of recovery and, as a side benefit, dramatically decreases the amount of money the insurance company has to spend on you down the road.

Take the example of breast cancer. It used to be that the majority of patients diagnosed with breast cancer died from it. A lot of money was invested in finding a cure, and as a result, effective chemotherapies were developed. Unfortunately, only those patients who caught their cancer in the early stages benefited from the new treatments. The medical community shifted its course and began a push on preventative medicine. They began insisting on routine mammograms for women over forty. The number of breast cancer patients has not been reduced, but the number of deaths has decreased drastically as a result.

Unfortunately, mental health care has never been seen as proactive and preventative. It is now customary on many bases for military members to speak to a counselor once they return from deployment, to talk about any issues they may have. After a few years of this, the leadership realized that PTSD symptoms might not present right away, and as a result, follow-up sessions are often implemented. It is a step in the right direction because it is mandatory, but it is still based on the reactive model, giving service members the help they need after the fact. Why not see them before they are deployed, right after they enlist to provide them with the tools to understand how they are likely to react to stress?

Change is always met with resistance, which is exactly what happened to me during my year at MCRD the Marine Corps Recruit Depot in San Diego. As you read my story, you learn how the on-base Family Support Services counseling center was uncomfortable with my presence at the depot. My new proactive approach to counseling also put me in conflict with my employer, HWM. The majority of military mental health contracts are held by for-profit, large insurance companies, which often care more about their profits than the services they are commissioned to provide. In my eyes, my experience is just one of many examples of how this is true.

After lobbying for stronger military mental health benefits in Washington, I have become even more concerned about the future. People care, and slowly change is happening, especially in the area of resilience building, but it's going to take a long time. Unfortunately, the money that is needed to put every man and women in uniform through ongoing proactive counseling has not been prioritized. I have come to the sad realization that in the interim of waiting for public awareness, true reform is going to have to come from within. Military leaders at all levels are going to need to understand the importance of prevention. They will have to learn how to pick up the proactive counseling piece. These leaders at all levels must learn how to create meaningful dialogue with their subordinates. Talking about personal issues can be very difficult and awkward. It is my hope that this book proves the importance of pushing through the uncomfortable in efforts to create significant and lifelong change.

I wrote this book and am sharing my story because I feel strongly that I owe it to our brave service members. I am immensely grateful for all they do. These men and women jeopardize their lives every day that they are living in a war zone. They fight our battles so that we can sleep peacefully at night, yet they often can't sleep themselves. We as a country equip them with everything they need to be physically fit but have struggled to figure out how to keep them mentally fit. As a civilian, I feel I have a unique advantage to look at the pervasive military mental health problem with a fresh set of eyes. My hope is that you will not see me as a victim of the system, for I am not. I have been truly enriched and enlightened through my experiences. I am hopeful that, like me, you will feel the urgent pressure to support and if necessary fight for a stronger military mental health system.

In the following chapters, I will share with you my journey as I had the extraordinary experience of working with drill instructors in the United States Marine Corps. Through those Marines' strong values and unsurpassed integrity, I learned life's most valuable lessons: when the going gets rough, you don't quit, you are just getting started.

In this book, when I refer to the military, I am referring to the U.S. Marine Corps, the only branch of the armed services that I performed proactive counseling with. This is a true story and only the individual names, offices and contracting agencies have been changed due to privacy protection.

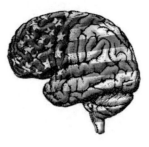

TABLES

You may find following glossary helpful with reference to the acronyms used.

MFLC	military family life consultant
HWM	Healthy Wellness Management (a subsidiary of a large well known insurance company)
FSS	Family Support Services (on-base counseling center)
POC	point of contact (military term for supervisor)
MCRD	Marine Corps Recruit Depot
Col	colonel
Lt Col	lieutenant colonel
Sgt Maj	sergeant major
CO	commanding officer
XO	executive officer
DI	drill instructor
Gunny	gunnery sergeant
BMP	basic (broken) marine platoon
Capt	captain
WFTBn	weapons field training battalion

Commissioned Officers Marines

Commissioned Officers are distinguished from other officers by their *commission*, which is the formal written authority, issued in the name of the President of the United States that confers the rank and authority of a Marine Officer. Commissioned officers carry the "special trust and confidence" of the President of the United States. Commissioned officer ranks are further subdivided into general officers, field officers, and company-grade officers. The Commandant of the Marine Corps and the Assistant Commandant of the Marine Corps are, by statute, four-star ranks.

COMPANY-GRADE OFFICERS

Second Lieutenant (2ndLt)	First Lieutenant (1stLt)	Captain (Capt)
O-1	O-2	O-3

FIELD OFFICERS

Major (Maj)	Lieutenant Colonel (LtCol)	Colonel (Col)
O-4	O-5	O-6

GENERAL OFFICERS

Brigadier General (BGen)	Major General (MajGen)	Lieutenant General (LtGen)	General (Gen)
O-7	O-8	O-9	O-10

Enlisted Marines

Enlisted Marines with pay grades of E-4 and E-5 are considered non-commissioned officers (NCOs) while those at E-6 and higher are considered Staff Noncommissioned Officers (SNCOs). The E-8 and E-9 levels each has two ranks per pay grade, each with different responsibilities. Gunnery Sergeants (E-7) indicate on their annual evaluations (called "fitness reports") their preferred promotional track: Master Sergeant or First Sergeant. The First Sergeant and Sergeant Major ranks are command-oriented Senior Enlisted Advisors, with Marines of these ranks serving as the senior enlisted Marines in a unit, charged to assist the commanding officer in matters of discipline, administration, and the morale and welfare of the unit. Master Sergeants and Master Gunnery Sergeants provide technical leadership as occupational specialists in their specific MOS. First Sergeants typically serve as the senior enlisted Marine in a company, battery, or other unit at similar echelon, while Sergeants Major serve the same role in battalions, squadrons, or larger units.

The Sergeant Major of the Marine Corps is a billet and special rank, conferred on the senior enlisted Marine of the entire Marine Corps, personally selected by the Commandant of the Marine Corps. It and the Marine Gunnery are the only billets which rate modified rank insignia in place of the traditional rank insignia.

JUNIOR ENLISTED

Private (Pvt)	Private First Class (PFC)	Lance Corporal (LCpl)
E-1	E-2	E-3
no insignia		

NON-COMMISSIONED OFFICERS (NCOS)

Corporal (Cpl)	Sergeant (Sgt)
E-4	E-5

STAFF NON-COMMISSIONED OFFICERS (SNCOS)

Staff Sergeant (SSgt)	Gunnery Sergeant (GySgt)	Master Sergeant (MSgt)	First Sergeant (1stSgt)
E-6	E-7	E-8	

Master Gunnery Sergeant (MGySgt)	Sergeant Major (SgtMaj)	Sergeant Major of the Marine Corps (SgtMajMarCor)
E-9		

MFLC
(Military Family Life Consultant)

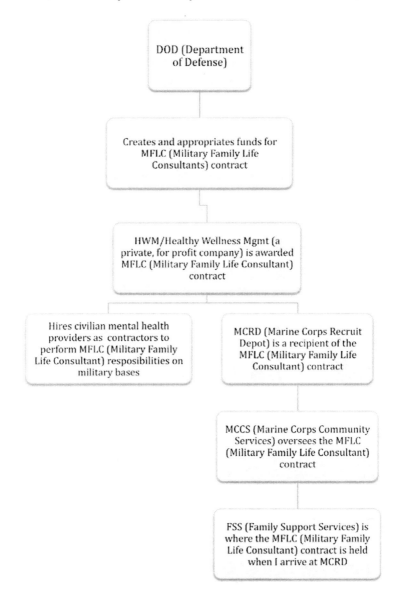

DOD (Department of Defense)

Creates and appropriates funds for MFLC (Military Family Life Consultants) contract

HWM/Healthy Wellness Mgmt (a private, for profit company) is awarded MFLC (Military Family Life Consultant) contract

Hires civilian mental health providers as contractors to perform MFLC (Military Family Life Consultant) resposibilities on military bases

MCRD (Marine Corps Recruit Depot) is a recipient of the MFLC (Military Family Life Consultant) contract

MCCS (Marine Corps Community Services) oversees the MFLC (Military Family Life Consultant) contract

FSS (Family Support Services) is where the MFLC (Military Family Life Consultant) contract is held when I arrive at MCRD

Drill Instructor Hierarchy

Drill Instructor Teams

Chief Drill Instructors (wear black belts)

Senior Drill Instructors (also wear black belts)

Experienced Drill Instructors (called "J" or experienced). Wear green belts.

New Drill Instructors (called 3rd, 4th or 5th hats-depending on how many are on a team). Also wear Green Belts.

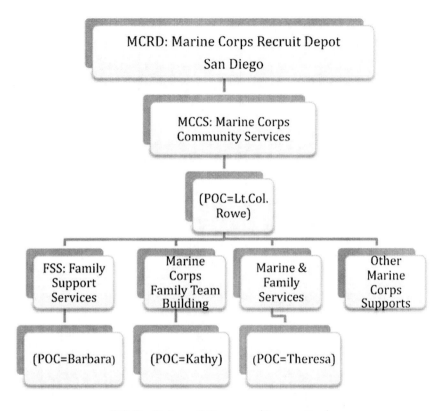

POC= Point of Contact (Supervisor)

RTR
(Recruit Training Regiment)

The RTR Commander is a Colonel
The CO (Battalion Commanders) are Lt. Colonel's
The XO (Executive Officers) are Majors
The Company Commanders (i.e. Alpha, Bravo, Charlie) are Captains
The DI (Drill Instructors) fall under each company

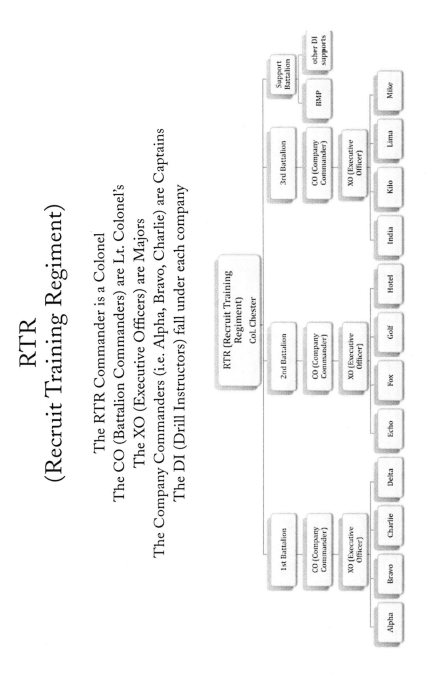

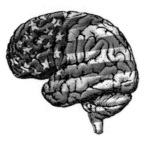

TYPICAL DAY WORKING
WITH CIVILIANS

It was a beautiful, sunny weekday morning in February, by San Diego standards, as I went through the typical routine of my day. I am a psychotherapist with a private practice in Del Mar, California. My typical client caseload was a solid mix of men, women, couples, families, adolescents, and children. I had been a therapist for enough years and therefore getting new referrals was never an issue for me. My days were typically long. I would drop off my three kids (one at elementary school, one at middle school, and one at high school) and then head to the office. A typical day looked something like this: nine o'clock, ten o'clock, and eleven o'clock sessions, followed by a thirty-minute lunch break to return phone calls, and then sessions at twelve thirty, one thirty, and two thirty. I left the office at three thirty, picked up carpools, took the kids home, and two or three times a week would go back to the office for afternoon and evening appointments. Work ethic has also never been an issue for me. I was forty years old and have been blessed with having a lot of energy. I have always felt inspired by my patients and have therefore found their growth stimulating and gratifying. Lately, things had been feeling less fulfilling. The issues appeared more superficial and everyone seemed to be in search of the quick fix. This day was a perfect example.

My nine o'clock came in and was upset because it was her birthday on the weekend and her husband had bought her a Coach handbag instead of the Louis Vitton bag that she had left hints for all over the house. She was tired of him always screwing up. He wasn't attentive and was cheap. The fact that he bought her the wrong purse was a perfect example of that. Now she was second-guessing her decision to marry him.

My ten o'clock was a television show producer who lived in San Diego with his wife and kids, but during the week stayed in LA where he worked and had a separate apartment. His presenting issue was that he couldn't sleep at night. When he was at home, his wife complained that he was never around and slammed him with a list of projects and demands that he spend quality time with his kids. When he was in LA, his girlfriend (who was a Playboy model) constantly pressured him to leave his wife. He felt like everyone wanted a piece of him. On the outside, he explained, he had the dream life, but he was experiencing what he called "inner living hell." He had tried everything to sleep. When I asked if he thought his dual lifestyle played a part in his sleeping issues, he shook his head, not seeing any connection. His doctor wouldn't prescribe him any more sleeping pills unless he sought counseling. At the end of the session, he asked me to write his doctor a letter requesting more pills.

Next came my eleven o'clock, a couple with some marital issues. He was a physician and she was an attorney. She was having a hard time getting pregnant and wanted to start fertility treatments. He didn't know if he wanted kids because he was afraid she would want to stop working, and they needed both incomes to support their lifestyle, which included a two million-dollar house. She had promised to continue working, but he wanted her commitment in a legal document. She didn't want to guarantee it because of the small possibility that once she had the child, she might change her mind. Her reluctance reinforced his fears, and they were back in the same argument cycle again.

There was no thirty-minute lunch break on this day. Instead, I had to squeeze in a crisis. A client I hadn't seen in a few years had just found out that her husband was having an affair. She was devastated. Even though they had had sex only twice in the past year, she never saw it coming. She was hyperventilating and couldn't catch her breath. Her youngest child had recently left for college, and since she had always been a stay-at-home mom, she felt as though her life had no direction. Not surprisingly, I was running a good fifteen minutes behind schedule, something I desperately tried not to let happen because of the inherent domino effect.

My twelve thirty was a twenty-seven-year-old female with chronic body pain from an unknown cause. She was in a tizzy because her mother, whom she lived with and who paid all her expenses, told her she would no longer do her laundry. That was earth-shattering news. How in the world would she get clean clothes? There was no way she could do the laundry; it would hurt too much to bend down. We talked about different ways she could possibly do it that would minimize the pain. The more I pushed, the more resistant she became. I asked if she had any suggestions to help solve her dilemma. The only thing she could think of was, if she let her clothes get dirty enough that they started to smell, her mom would start doing them again to get rid of the stench. I tried to be compassionate and suggested breaking the task into small steps. She reluctantly agreed but wouldn't commit to starting anytime soon.

My one thirty was a twelve-year-old female tennis player who was home schooled because of her rigorous training schedule.

She was initially referred because her parents had overheard her crying in the bathroom at night. She didn't like tennis anymore. She said all the fun was gone but her parents wouldn't let her quit. All she wanted to do was to go to school with other kids and have a normal childhood, like her peers on Facebook were having. I brought in her dad for the last fifteen minutes and attempted to explain the toll and pressure that the meticulous training was having on her. He told me that he had given up his career for his daughter's tennis and she was ranked eleventh in California. He said there was no way she could quit now and questioned if I understood how much time and money had been invested in her thus far. He made it very clear that my job was to help revive her interest in tennis and convince her that she needed to keep her head in the game.

My two thirty was a corporate executive who, lucky for me, was always running about fifteen minutes behind, which helped put me back on schedule. She was in the middle of a grueling divorce and was having an affair with a married man who lived in New York and happened to be her boss. She wasn't seeing me because of the relationship issues. In fact, it took three sessions before she even told me. She came to me because she didn't enjoy parenting and didn't really like her two kids. She was hoping that with some brief therapy she could learn to like them. She had a nanny who did most of the parenting, but her divorce attorney had advised her that if she didn't improve her relationship with her kids, she might lose them to their father. I explored every angle I could think of to find some redeeming qualities the children might have. When time was up, we hadn't gotten anywhere. I asked her to do some journaling, hoping that might give her some insight.

At three thirty I raced out of the office to pick up my daughter at middle school and drop off her carpool at the community theater where she was acting in a play. I made it just in time to the karate studio, where my younger son and his friends were finishing up their class and ready for their ride home. I drove them home and continued on to pick up my oldest son at his tutor's house, to which (thank God) he walked to after school. I raced home, whipped up dinner, and threw in a load of laundry. Monday nights were late nights for me, and my husband, Mike, took care of the bedtime regimen at home. I headed back to the office for a few more appointments.

My five o'clock was a new client. I met with the mom and dad, who had issues regarding their seventeen-year-old son. He had always been a perfect, straight-A student, but recently the parents had found marijuana in his room. He swore that he was holding it for a friend, but they didn't believe him. Their approach was to ground him for two months and not let him see any of his friends. Unfortunately, they were afraid that this plan had backfired because his grades had plummeted and he refused to eat dinner or spend any time with his family. He hadn't spoken to his parents in weeks, and they didn't know what to do. They also needed suggestions as to how to get the kid to come into the office because he had become so rebellious he would not do anything they asked. When I inquired if they had considered renegotiating his punishment, they both vehemently said "no way" and continued to say, "If we back down now, what next?"

My six o'clock was a college student from the University of San Diego who was experiencing panic attacks. He was going to graduate at the end of the semester and had no idea what he wanted to do. The only thing he was certain of was that he didn't want to work. He was exhausted from being a full-time student. "After all," he explained, "I've been in college for five years and I need a break." He had held only two jobs, one of them a couple of summers ago as a waiter at Chili's. He was fired because he got in a fight with the manager. The second was at the Gap for three weeks during the holidays the previous year. The thought of working made him panic, and he was considering selling the stocks his grandfather left him and traveling in Europe for a year until he figured out what he wanted to do. I did some aptitude tests with him with hopes of triggering some career interests that might decrease his anxiety and steer him in some sort of direction. He held strong that the only thing he liked was surfing, but he wasn't good enough to do it professionally.

My seven o'clock was a retired man in his early sixties. His wife was eighteen years younger than him and still working. He didn't have any friends or any real hobbies to speak of, except an occasional golf game. His one or two vodkas at night had turned into five to six vodkas throughout the day plus an occasional beer or wine. He then found himself addicted to Internet pornography. He was petrified that if his wife found out about the drinking and the porn she would leave him. He was crying so hard in the session that he actually vomited all over the floor. Luckily, he was my last session for the day. I was emotionally bored and apathetic, and I feared my abrupt comments were showing it.

My colleague was also working late. I walked in her office and plopped on her couch. We started commiserating. I asked her if it was just my patients, or were we living in a world where people had no idea how good they had it? It seemed as though people needed to have conflict and anxiety in their lives, and if it wasn't there, they created it. My colleague, who is always insightful, agreed. She told me about a couple she'd just seen. The husband had a girlfriend on the side and when his wife found out, he bought her a Mercedes to appease her. She was happy for the time being because she felt he clearly liked her more than the girlfriend because he bought her the car. I left the conversation even more disturbed. It felt like people were losing their purpose in life, and I couldn't help but wonder if it was the same for me.

I had a full day of phone and e-mail messages that needed to be returned before heading home. The first e-mail was a past patient who wanted me to write a letter so that her son could "play down" on a soccer team. I frequently get requests from parents for these types of letters because it allows their kids to play on a team with younger kids, giving them a competitive advantage. The next few e-mails were about carpools for my kids and a few patients requesting schedule changes.

The next e-mail caught my eye. It was from HWM, which is an insurance company. I got e-mails from HWM all the time because they were in desperate need of MFLCs—military family life consultants—to provide anonymous, confidential, short-term, situational problem-solving, and nonmedical counseling services to the military. An MFLC would stay on a base for typically six weeks and leave, being replaced by a new MFLC. It was my understanding that the reason for this short-term rotation was to help ensure confidentiality. Also, since these MFLCs were not part of the existing counseling staff on the bases, service members would be more trusting to talk to them.

A few years prior, in the summer of 2005, I had held an MFLC job. I'd always been intrigued with the military. I was raised in Los Angeles, in an upper middle class neighborhood. I didn't know any military kids growing up, and as embarrassed as I am to admit it, all I knew about the military was what I saw on TV. The thought of working with this population was fascinating. Then there was the added incentive that the job was in Germany. HWM had offered me round-trip airfare to Germany a weekly salary of $2600 (multiplied by six was $15,600), an additional per diem for food, a rental car, lodging, cell phone, and reimbursement for any additional expenses, including gas. It was during the summer and I could travel with the family when my contracted work was over; it was one of those "why not" type of deals.

The only down side was that I could never get HWM to return my calls. They had confirmed that I was slated for the June Europe team, but weeks had gone by without the contact person returning any of my phone calls or e-mails. Literally, the week before I was scheduled to leave, the HWM travel department finally got in touch with me to book my flight. I kept thinking, *What a waste of money!* The airfare had practically doubled since I had first committed. I remember telling the travel agent that I had booked my family's flight weeks ago and it was half the price. She said that the MFLC budget was so big that they could afford to do things at the last minute At that point, I felt pretty lucky to have landed that job; my prior experience in public mental health had always meant stretching the dollar to its fullest.

Days before I was scheduled to leave for Germany, I was informed that I would need to have a phone interview prior to my departure. This was an interesting way to do business. You get interviewed after you get the job and all travel arrangements have already been made. I was a little stressed out because I had cleared my schedule for the six weeks and all the travel plans for the family were in place. It could be a huge pain if I didn't pass my interview. Luckily the interview was only five minutes long. It was with the medical director of the program. I was expecting some questions, but instead it was more of a briefing. He wanted to make sure that I understood not to talk about my compensation with the military folks I'd come in contact with. He also said that each base would have different requirements for the MFLC, so he wanted to make sure that I could be flexible depending on where I was sent. I knew I was going to Europe, but not until I arrived in Germany would they tell me exactly which base I would be stationed at. Besides my brief phone interview, I had no idea what the job would entail. I was told I would find out all the details once I arrived in Frankfurt at the "meet and greet."

Despite the long flight, the trip to Germany was seamless. That night I met the other twenty or so MFLCs who would get sprinkled throughout the military bases in Europe. I also met a man who was going to be my supervisor. He promised the group that he would make one site visit during the six weeks and that we could call him in the interim if we needed anything. The main instructions we were given were to stay out of the way. We were repeatedly reminded that we would be guests on the base. We were to do what we were told and call the supervisor if we were ever unsure of our boundaries. I slept in Frankfurt that night and the next morning picked up my rental car. I was surprised to find that it was a beautiful BMW.

I was being sent to Hanau, which was not too far from Frankfurt. It turned out that on that base there were two MFLCs. The other one was a seventy-two-year-old man named Sam. He had a heavy New York accent and had served in the Army during the Vietnam War. Upon arrival, we checked into our on-base lodging. My two-bedroom apartment was more than spacious, with a full kitchen, living room, and cable TV. After unpacking, I found my way over to the counseling office and met the POC (point of contact), which is another name for *boss*. He couldn't have been any nicer or more accommodating. He explained that my job was to work at a summer school. School started at eight a.m. and was over at noon. Once school was over, my job was essentially done for the day. He suggested that I stop by the counseling office at noon to see if there were any clients that needed to be seen or if the other MFLC needed any help.

I found my way to the on-base school with the help of the navigation system that came with the car. I was completely surprised to find out that no one had any idea I was coming. Regardless, the administrative staff was very nice and thrilled to have me because they were short staffed for the summer. I was to be responsible for greeting the parents every morning at the entrance to the school. I supervised kids during recess and relieved teachers when they had to go to the bathroom or needed a quick break. I had an office and from time to time helped out with a few counseling issues. In my opinion, I was the most over-paid person in the world. Every day after school I'd stop by the counseling office, where the other MFLC was, to see what he was up to. He was always in the same position, relaxed in his chair with his feet up, reading the paper. I'd ask how his day was, and he would reply, "You're looking at it, kid."

Although this was also Sam's first MFLC assignment, he knew a couple of people who had done MFLC jobs previously, so he knew quite a bit. One day over a long lunch, Sam confided in me, "All the bases are the same. The soldiers won't come in to the counseling office to get help because of the stigma; they are afraid it will hurt their promotion. The base has MFLCs so they can say they have a solution to the problem, but the MFLC's office is in the counseling center and the soldiers don't really trust that it isn't going to hurt them if they come in. If they do seek help, the MFLCs (although licensed clinicians) really aren't allowed to do anything. They can't see PTSD, domestic violence, substance abuse, etc. And they can't build any significant rapport because they leave every few weeks." After I was there for a few weeks, I began to see for myself that what he said made perfect sense.

One night at dinner, the POC brought up how much money we were paid. I was concerned because the MFLC cardinal rule was never discuss your pay with anyone. Luckily, he wasn't cynical or resentful. On the contrary, he found it comical that there was so much government waste and saw the MFLC program as the perfect example. After a year of supervising the Hanau MFLC program, he came up with a summary of the typical six-week cycle: The first week the MFLCs are jet lagged, can't really focus on anything, and are always yawning and exhausted. The second week they are motivated to work and walk around introducing themselves to various offices on the base. The third week they spend most of their time researching travel opportunities and planning side trips. The fourth week they start getting bored, and the last couple of weeks, they don't pick up any new cases because they are leaving. I asked him why they continue to have the program. He shrugged and said, "When you work in the military, you don't ask questions, you just do what you are told. We were told we were getting MFLCs, and here you are."

I had an amazing experience in Europe that summer. I traveled everywhere and made over $26,000 for six weeks of work. The down side was I could count the times on one hand that I was able to work with soldiers. The brief counseling that I did do was mostly with the civilian school staff.

The following summer, I signed up for another MFLC experience. The military has a summer program called Purple Camp. It provides free residential camps to kids who have a parent deployed in Iraq or Afghanistan. The camps are one week, and the kids have a blast. I was offered a job at a Purple Camp in the Tuscan region of Italy. There would be two one-week camps with a week break in between. Just like the previous summer, it felt like too good an opportunity to pass up. My plan was to work for a week, meet my husband in Italy and travel for a week, and then work the second week. Sounded great to me. Unfortunately, as the time got closer, things were crazy at my husband's office, and he wasn't able to take that travel week off. I called HWM to see if I could do just one of the camps. To my surprise, the response was, "Why don't you go home in between the two camps?" Could they be serious? They were willing to fly me from San Diego to Pisa (not a cheap flight), home, and back again. I was informed that HWM would make so much money on my filling that slot;

the cost was nothing for them. It was inconceivable for me to imagine that there could be that much waste!

So off I went on another MFLC job. I could tell that HWM had grown considerably over the past year, and that the travel department was more efficient than the prior summer. Other than that, things were just as disorganized as before. A week before I left I had not heard one thing about my job. I didn't know any specifics about camp or what my duties would be. After multiple phone calls to HWM, I finally got an e-mail response with a phone number for the person who was to be my POC. I tried numerous times a day to reach her, but there was never an answer. It turned out they had given me the wrong number. The main thing I wanted to know was what the dress code was for camp. HWM informed me that it would be business casual. They also told me that I was on a forty-hour-a-week contract.

The camp was on an air force base just off the coast of Italy. The compensation was similar to the previous summers, with all the perks. The only difference was that this was a shorter contract, and even though I was given a hefty per diem for food, my hotel included a huge breakfast. I flew San Diego to Los Angeles, Los Angeles to Munich, and then Munich to Pisa. It took almost a day to get there, but I finally arrived at the Pisa/Florence airport. My instructions were that my rental car had been reserved and to head to the Hertz counter upon arrival. I was surprised to see how huge the line was. I waited in it for an hour and fifteen minutes. When I finally made it to the front, I was saddened to learn that they had no reservation for me. I showed my confirmation number, and they explained that my car had been reserved in Naples (wrong airport). They would have given me a car, but unfortunately they were out. Considering it was Sunday and there was no one for me to reach at HWM, I took an expensive taxicab thirty minutes to my hotel.

I arrived at the hotel only to find that they too did not have a reservation for me. Luckily, they were not full and the nice caretaker took a personal credit card from me and promised to communicate with HWM on Monday. Not a great start, but I was in Italy, so how bad could it be? I slept for a few hours and upon waking tried to call the airport regarding a car. Unfortunately, HWM had given me a German cell phone that didn't work in Italy. I took a taxi to the base to meet the camp staff for a twelve o'clock meeting which I had found out about through doing my own research. The camp staff was well seasoned and had just completed the same Purple Camp in Germany two weeks prior. The main difference was the German camp had half the number of campers. The staff was very concerned about the large number of middle school and high school children that was expected.

At that meeting I was informed that my hours would be from seven a.m. to eleven p.m. for five days. This was news to me. Five sixteen-hour days (Monday through Friday), plus I had already been there on Sunday for six hours to prep, and there was a mandatory debrief on the following Saturday when camp was over. I am a professional and certainly did not want to share my concerns with the camp staff, but this seemed a little absurd. HWM had put me on a forty-hour weekly contract, and the base was expecting me to work eighty-plus hours that week. I politely asked if the other staff members were expected to adhere to the same schedule. That is when I found out that the entire camp staff had been put on what they called double duty. It was explained that they were being paid for an eighty-hour week and would make two weeks pay for the one week of work. They were told that the counselor (the MFLC) was on the same contract. I explained that I was on a forty-hour-a-week contract, but that I of course would do whatever was needed. I was jet-lagged and exhausted, and it was brutally hot outside. I decided it would be more appropriate to talk to HWM about the schedule than to involve the camp staff. I had to call them anyway to figure out the car, hotel, and phone situation.

As I was leaving the base that day, the camp director told me I was expected to dress in shorts and t-shirts, to fit in with the camp staff. They said they had informed HWM of this because the last MFLC had packed all the wrong clothes. I had brought only one pair of shorts; all the rest was business clothes. Luckily, I had a couple of free hours that evening and was able to find a store to buy some more appropriate clothes.

It took two days for someone from HWM to get back to me. When someone finally did, he told me that I needed to stick to forty hours and that I should flex my time, the contract was a weekly salary not hourly. He also explained that I should buy some German minutes to put on my phone and that I could expense the phone card. At that point, the whole thing felt like a lost cause. I had already put in over thirty hours, and it was only Tuesday. I had also learned that you couldn't buy German cell phone minutes in Italy. I had taken four taxis to and from the airport to get a rental car, and I never was able to use my phone for communication.

This assignment clearly needed two MFLCs. There was no way to flex my time and not work the full camp day. There were countless situations that kept popping up that required interventions. These kids had all kinds of issues going on. For starters, every one of them had a parent deployed. I remember meeting with a fourteen-year-old girl who had terrible night terrors. Both of her parents were deployed, her father in Iraq and her mother in Afghanistan. Her uncle had died in Baghdad four months before. These kids had to forego having a parent at home; the least I could do was make a sacrifice and help them during that week. This could be their only opportunity to get help with their problems. There was always a line of kids that needed or wanted to be seen. I found it impossible to leave, even for a few moments to get lunch. I got back to my room at midnight every night and had to leave at six thirty every morning to get back to the base. HWM had no idea what they'd sent me into.

The camp finally ended on Friday night, and the buses departed for the airport at one a.m. I had to stay there until the last bus left because there was a suicidal teen that needed supervision. I returned to my room at two a.m. and, before collapsing, calculated that I had worked ninety-six hours that week. The next day at the wrap-up, the POC awarded me a special coin and thanked me profusely for all my hard work. He was very grateful to me and shared that his previous experience with MFLCs had not been positive. He'd found them to be somewhat useless, typically older, retired clinicians looking for travel opportunities. Although I was exhausted, I'd had a great experience and really felt that I was an asset to the camp. I'd been able to do some good work and thought the kids and I all benefited from the experience. On the other hand, I was so excited to go home. I might have been in Italy, but I never saw one thing but my hotel bed and the base.

That afternoon I checked in at the airport only to find that my airline reservation had been cancelled and all the flights out of Pisa were booked for the next couple of days. I was so tired; I decided to try my fate at standby. I got lucky; there was a no-show, and I was able to make the flight to Munich. I was hopeful that the rest of my reservation was okay. Unfortunately, once I arrived in Germany, I learned that HWM had booked my flight for the previous day. My HWM itinerary had the wrong date. How could I have left a day earlier even if they had printed it correctly? Camp would not have been over. Regardless, because I hadn't showed up, they considered me a no-show and cancelled all my connecting flights. In the end, I flew multiple flights standby and twenty-eight hours later returned home, without luggage.

I e-mailed the head of HWM, explained my week, and requested that if I were to go back, they needed to hire an additional MFLC. I never got a reply. I ended up getting a terrible flu with a very high fever, and there was no way I could return for the second Purple Camp. I felt really bad but knew it would be a bad idea to fly across the world. I did, however, ensure that they were able to find a replacement. I promised myself that that would be the end of my MFLC career. In Germany, there were two MFLCs and no work, and in Italy I was slammed doing two people's jobs. HWM just seemed way too disorganized. After my return, I still received weekly emails from HWM. They were always posting some type of job opportunity. The company's disorganization did not seem to stop it from growing. For a year and a half, I deleted every e-mail I received from them. After a day like today of what felt like meaningless and superficial work, one of their emails caught my eye. Perhaps it was the combination that I was feeling disgruntled with the lack of depth in my practice and that this e-mail was personally addressed to me. Apparently MCRD, the Marine Corps Recruit Depot in San Diego, was looking for a local MFLC provider. For a brief moment, I was intrigued. Within a minute I remembered how frustrating it had been to be a MFLC in the past, and I hit the delete button.

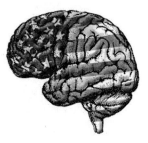

RECRUITED
TO THE MARINES

That night I happened to see a special on TV about the toll that the wars in Iraq and Afghanistan were taking on our military. The program stressed that there was a shortage of clinicians and horrifically explored what the aftermath of all of this was going to look like in a few years. The ongoing psychological trauma of war is profound, and when you complicate that with multiple deployments, the emotional consequences are huge. Lying in bed, I couldn't help thinking about our men and women in uniform. I briefly wondered if I should consider being an MFLC again. I reminded myself that I had a thriving full-time practice that I couldn't possibly just abandon for six weeks. I also doubted that the experience would provide me with what I was looking for. The MFLC program was so convoluted that the Marines probably were not even utilizing it. I decided to pass on the opportunity and went to sleep.

The next morning on my way to the office, I received a call from HWM. It was a recruiter who wanted to talk with me about MCRD (the Marine Corps Recruit Depot). Apparently the POC at the base was very difficult. She was unhappy with the MFLC program and had been threatening to cancel it. HWM didn't want that to happen because the base at Miramar Air Station was dropping the MFLC program, and Camp Pendleton refused to pick it up from the beginning. Without MCRD, there wouldn't be any MFLC representation on any of San Diego's Marine bases. The recruiter went on to explain that the MCRD (Marine Corps Recruit Depot) wanted its MFLC to stay two rotations (twelve weeks) and they'd like the position to be filled by someone local. She stressed that HWM needed to put someone clinically strong in there because they were having significant problems with the entire Marine Corps and they didn't want to lose another Marine base.

I don't know why I didn't say no. I wanted to, but instead I asked if she could give me a few days to think about it and promised to get back to her. Later that day, I called a friend who was a "career MFLC." That is what they call someone who travels around the world as an MFLC and rotates in and out of a variety of bases. I was curious as to how the program was going and if it had possibly gotten any better in the past few years. I think she summed it up perfectly. She described the trick to being a good MFLC is to be as mediocre as you can. You can't do too good of a job because then you are either seen as a threat to the on-base counseling center staff, who may feel like you are in direct competition with them, or if they like you, they hold future MFLCs to your standards and give HWM a hard time about who they are sending in after you. If you do a bad job, then the MFLC supervisor has to deal with the base. The perfect MFLC is the one that they never have to hear about. She then went on to say that I would need to expect that HWM would not support me in any way. I'd be completely on my own. I had found the same to be true in my two past experiences. You never hear from the supervisor while you are on a job, and if you need help, getting someone to return a phone call is almost impossible. She was also familiar with the particular situation at MCRD (Marine Corps Recruit Depot). She had heard that the POC (Point of Contact/on base

MFLC supervisor) was really difficult and hadn't liked any of the MFLCs in the past. Every indicator told me to stay away.

I reminded myself how well things were going in my life. My private practice was booming, with referrals coming in on a daily basis. Why in the world would I leave that for three months to work on a base for a pathetic company that strives for mediocrity, under a woman with a bad reputation? But I kept thinking about the Marines and how incredible it would be to work with them, help them, and learn about their issues. Counseling Marines had to offer more meaningful work than what I was doing in private practice. It was as though I had already made my mind up to do it. All my logical reasoning was countered by my ridiculous and insatiable sense of adventure.

That night I decided I was going to take the MFLC job. I thought for sure my husband would tell me I was nuts, but he didn't. Instead he encouraged me to go for it, reminding me that if I didn't like it I could always quit. That was even after I told him that the compensation wasn't so great. HWM had lowered their hourly wage over the past few years and since I was local, I wasn't eligible for the per diem, car rental, lodging, or cell phone. I was going to be making considerably less money than in my private practice and HWM was going to be saving a lot of money by having me, as a local provider, take this rotation.

I had a month to figure out the logistics. I went through my caseload to decide which patients might be able to come in every few weeks instead of every week. My colleague said she could take the high-need patients, and I figured I could work two nights a week and every other Saturday to continue seeing the rest. I hired a college student to help with the after-school driving to get the kids to their activities. I was preparing to put in three months of long days and wanted to make sure I'd have minimal interruptions.

The night before I started, I sat the family down, and we had a talk. I told them they had been lucky that their mother was able to work and still pick them up from school every day. I explained that this was important work that I was going to do. These Marines were risking their lives for our safety and working with them over the next few months was going to be my way of giving back. I needed everyone to pitch in, help and be supportive. Everybody was in agreement, and I was ready to start the adventure.

I had lived in San Diego for fifteen years and had never been to MCRD. I had probably passed it a hundred times without even noticing it was there, I had no idea where it was. It turned out it was right by the airport. The current MFLC, Carol, a woman in her early sixties, met me at the gate. Apparently, under a new protocol, each MFLC had two days with her successor before leaving the base to help with the transition. Carol was very pleasant and immediately informed me about the politics of the office. She explained that the MFLC program was housed in FSS, the Family Support Services office, which is also the on base counseling center. They are the place where Marines are sent if they are mandated for counseling for committing domestic violence, had anger management issues, or were required by their command to get help. Family Support Services cases were documented and went into the Marine's career file.

She continued by explaining that most Marines do not use the MFLC program because they associate the Family Support Services office with getting in trouble. She said she had worked with a few spouses but had pretty much spent her entire six-week rotation doing remedial tasks for the Family Support Services staff. She added that her only saving grace was that the MFLC didn't have to see people in the office. She would escape whenever she could and go for long walks just to get away. She unfortunately confirmed that the POC, Barbara, was incredibly difficult. She also added it was a close competition between her and Gretchen, the gatekeeper or intake coordinator, as to which was worse. Apparently Barbara had a bad temper and would scream and yell, but whenever the officers came around, she would quickly change her tone and could pour on the charm. Carol had more issues with Gretchen because she was not as transparent. I learned that Gretchen was always seeking Barbara's approval and would constantly report to Barbara everything that was going on. Carol was relieved that she stayed off both of their radars but warned me about Gretchen. She described her as "your worst high school nightmare," the type that would lie about others just to make herself look good. None of what she said bothered me too much. It sounded like typical office politics, and every office had theirs.

Carol loved San Diego and really enjoyed the trips she took on weekends and all the restaurants. Other than that, she had a very limited amount of information to offer. The infamous Barbara wasn't going to be in the office that day, but I got to meet everyone else. The first person I met was Gretchen. She was approximately forty years old, the same age as me. She held a bachelor's degree in social work and was considered the "gatekeeper" in the office. She saw everyone that came in and then referred them to the various counselors. The other two counselors were both master's level and were licensed behavioral health clinicians. I was a little surprised that Gretchen didn't have the same credentials, but my brief experience with the military had taught me that they followed their own guidelines. It's my understanding that only in the military can an unlicensed bachelor level mental health clinician see patients in the same capacity as someone licensed in the civilian world. Gretchen would be the one to determine which cases would be referred to me. If someone came in on his own and the case didn't require documentation, she would send him to me.

On Carol's last day, we took a tour of the depot. She explained that all recruit training west of the Mississippi happened here. Recruits are the young adults who have chosen to become Marines. They were at MCRD for boot camp. One of the Marine Corps drill instructors that we met explained to us that MCRD is where young men [There are no woman recruits in San Diego, they are at Parris Island in South Carolina] are transformed into Marines. It is a combination of shared hardship and tough training that creates the comradeship and standards of conduct so strong that Marines will let nothing stand in their way.

Recruit training lasts three months. Once they graduate, the trained Marines are sent to other bases to prepare for their future in the corps.

Carol knew very little about what went on at the depot. She knew that there are twelve companies, companies A to M. Every week a company graduates a group of recruits (approximately 500), and every week a new company starts the training cycle. Everything that goes on at MCRD was highly confidential, and as an MFLC, you couldn't ever work with the recruits. Family Support Services didn't work with the recruits either; they were off limits to all outsiders until they became Marines. The majority of people that work on the base are Drill Instructors, but Carol clarified that I would have very little contact with them. I remember reading that "Drill instructors have notoriously been known as the scariest S.O.B. a recruit ever meets, and the last person he or she ever forgets." They had very intense training schedules and, in addition to not having time, weren't the type to come in for counseling. The people Carol had worked with were mainly civilians who were employed at the depot and wanted free counseling.

We continued our tour around the base. It always amazed me how inclusive military bases are. This base was located on the San Diego Bay. It had boat rentals, parks for kids, restaurants, a food court, even a Starbucks. There was a home store that looked like a Macy's and a few clothing stores. You could buy designer purses, watches, makeup, jewelry, or shoes. There was a hardware store, an electronics store, a ticket office, a library, a bank, a liquor store, a grocery store, a childcare center, and a recreation center that included a bowling alley, arcade, movie theater, and tavern. The gym was incredible, with every machine imaginable and a variety of classes available all hours of the day, from spinning to yoga. They had everything they could ever need right there on the base. Being there, you could understand why the civilian and military worlds are so separate. The military is self-sustaining, and does not need the outside world. It even has its own school system. If you wanted to go to college, there was a satellite university on the base where you could take classes. There was something so comforting and safe about this lifestyle. What was I thinking? There is nothing safe about this lifestyle!

We continued our long walk, and Carol pointed out the recruiter school. This is where Marines go to school to learn how to be recruiters. She knew very little about it and sadly reported that Gretchen and Barbara held a tight leash on her, controlling whom she could and couldn't talk to. It sounded so counterintuitive to me. They sent us here to do anonymous, confidential counseling, but they put us in a Family Support Services center, which was viewed as pejorative and most wouldn't go in voluntarily. I asked her if that bothered her, and she replied, "It's a game; you have to learn to play it or you will lose in the end." She knew MFLCs who had been fired from the program because they pushed their way around bases. I knew she was right because I had heard the same type of stories. Why should Carol take the time to learn the nuances here? After all, she was only going to be around for six weeks. I left that day with mixed emotions. I hoped I had made the right decision.

I was a little anxious going back to the base for day two. Barbara would be there, and I didn't know what to expect. I calmed myself on the drive by remembering that I'm the type of person that can get along with anyone. Needless to say, I was not at all prepared for what I walked into. After putting my things down in my office, I introduced myself to Barbara. She was in her late fifties or early sixties.

I lightly knocked on her door, which was half open. "Barbara, I would like to introduce myself to you. My name is Marjorie, and I am the new MFLC."

She looked at me and retorted in an escalated tone, "What do you mean, new MFLC? I cancelled that program. I don't want a new MFLC! I have written endless amounts of e-mails to HWM, and no one ever replies back to me!" She continued on her rant, "It is nothing personal to you, but there is no supervision from these MFLCs. They are like loose canons on the depot. They don't report to anyone, they are a liability to me, and I just can't handle it right now. I'm dealing with some personal issues, and I need to minimize my stress. I'm sorry, but you will have to go back to wherever you came from."

I believe it was at that point that she asked me to leave her office and shut the door. I heard her mutter behind the door that now she had to call HWM again and that she really didn't have time for this!

Okay, now I'm really screwed, I thought. I'd completely given up my practice for three months and hired a nanny. I tried to stay calm and walked back to my office. I should have known something like this would happen. I called HWM, which was similar to calling a black hole; no one ever answered. I left five messages in a two-hour span. I didn't receive a return phone call, but I decided to go back to Barbara's office and attempt to talk some more. I explained that I lived locally and was not visiting

San Diego to vacation. I also explained that HWM had made an exception on her behalf and was allowing me to stay for two cycles, which was three months, because it sounded like the six-week turnover was part of the problem. She still clearly wasn't happy, but she did apologize for the outburst and clarified that it wasn't my fault; she was just really frustrated with HWM.

According to Barbara, HWM had come to the base a couple of years earlier to sell the program with what she called "their dog and pony show." Ever since then, she had had little contact with them. She didn't have any notification that I was coming and was incredibly concerned that there was no oversight on the program. Reluctantly, she agreed to have me stay. She made me promise that I wouldn't wander around the base unsupervised. She shared a story with me about how an MFLC a few cycles previous went into the general's building and asked to speak with the general to introduce herself. Barbara explained that in the military that is completely out of line. I had to pledge that I'd be very careful whom I would speak to. She reminded me that it was serious and confidential business that went on here and that I was to stay out of everybody's way. I was relieved that she was letting me stay, yet concerned. This was not starting out great, and I knew if there were any mess-ups, I was out of there. It was like three strikes and you're out, but I was starting with two strikes and I hadn't even done anything yet. All I had to do was follow the rules and stay on Barbara's good side and all should be okay.

For the first few days, I did everything I was told. I wasn't sure if there was some dialogue between Barbara and Gretchen, but Gretchen kept close tabs on me. She gave me projects like helping her prepare for classes by stuffing goodies in giveaway bags and sorting out supplies in the storage room. She had me clean out the files in the office I was in. It was quite the project; it had been years since the drawers had been organized. It didn't really matter how long it took because I didn't have anything better to do. Every once in a while she'd asked me to see someone, but they were civilians seeking for assistance. The MFLC phone rarely rang. I'd ask from time to time if I could pass out some MFLC business cards, but Gretchen didn't think it was a good idea. She did let me out one afternoon to hang posters. The signs promoted the MFLC program with the phone number on them. I didn't think it would generate any traffic, but it was worth the try.

The other counselors in the center were very nice. Like typical mental health professionals, they appeared to genuinely care about their jobs and took them very seriously. They all seemed busy, and I certainly didn't want to burden them with my boredom. They had a steady flow of referrals, and because their cases all needed to be documented, I couldn't be of any assistance. If I was going to do any clinical work with Marines, I either had to market the MFLC program or hope that Gretchen would send some people my way.

Friday finally came. It felt like the first week took forever to end. How was I going to handle eleven more weeks of nothing to do? Pulling into the base, I noticed huge crowds of people and cars everywhere. I was reminded that Fridays were graduation days, when the recruits officially became Marines. The new Marines' family members had traveled from all over to come watch. I never imagined the graduation to be such a large event. There were well over a thousand people. There is a giant parade deck that spans the width of the depot. During the week, I'd noticed platoons practicing there. The parade deck was another one of those "off limits" places. No one can walk across it; you have to go all the way around to get to the other side. One side of the massive concrete area was open to the parking lot, and long rows of bleachers lined the other side. In the middle of the bleachers is a viewing stand. This is where the VIPs and the higher-ranking officers and families sit. There is an area that is lined with red rope adjacent to the viewing stand. That is where the drill instructors from the graduating company stand.

I really wanted to attend the graduation. I remembered Carol, the prior MFLC telling me that she went to one, so why couldn't I? HWM allows you to attend events if it is for outreach purposes. I figured this could be considered an outreach; maybe I'd find someone who needed counseling. Luckily, Gretchen wasn't in the office because it was doubtful that she would have let me go. Barbara was in her office working on her computer. I poked my head in and asked if it would be okay for me to attend the graduation. Thankfully, she said okay.

I made my way through the masses of people and nestled myself among them to watch the big event. The crowd got quiet as the chaplain came out and led us in the national anthem. A massive American flag flies right in the middle of the parade deck. On this perfect San Diego day, the wind made the flag flawlessly smooth. Every man and woman in uniform stood at parade rest (with their hands in fists at their sides), and together, everyone sang. I put my hand over my heart and sang along. I was surprised at how choked up I felt.

After everyone was seated, the graduating company, which on this day was Lima, began to parade the new Marines. They marched in perfect unison, moving up and down the deck. The discipline it must take to learn how to do that is profound. Drill, which is what the marines call these movements, is part of the rich history of the corps. I learned that from the elderly retired Marine sitting next to me. He explained that teaching the new Marines these moves is a way to link them to the history. Every step is calculated, and they move with precision. The repetition of practicing this over and over trains them to take their time and think about every move they make. It makes sense, considering in combat the wrong move could cost them their lives.

A man, whom I later found out was Colonel Chester, got up and spoke about what the last three months had been like for these Marines. This man exuded leadership. I'm not sure if it was the way he looked, talked, or moved, but he was obviously important, and I felt important just being in his presence. He reminded us that when the recruits left home they were boys, and now they were men and part of the strongest military force in the world. I found the speech to be profoundly moving. The hundreds of new Marines were lined up silently marching along the parade deck. The man in front of me, clearly a proud father, started to cry. A woman next to me had her hand over her mouth and kept saying "Oh my God!" I've never considered myself an extremely patriotic person, but all of a sudden, I felt a tear stream down my face. I felt so proud to be American.

As I watched the proud new Marines march past me, all that kept running through my mind was *Wow!* I sat there wondering how in the world could they transform these guys in just three months. I wondered what they actually did during that time. I fantasized about the lives they left behind. Were they happy, sad? What prompted them to join the Marine Corps? Were they scared about getting deployed? Were they excited to have completed recruit training? Was it harder or easier than they thought it would be? All I knew about the military were the comments I'd heard in my social circle, which were things like "Oh those poor kids, they are going straight to war." I never really thought about what type of person joins the military. Now I was curious, really curious. The next thing I knew, there were cheers from the crowd and families were rushing toward their new Marines. I felt paralyzed. I just sat there and watched. In the middle of the parade deck stood a bunch of Marines with wide-brimmed hats. I had already learned that those were the infamous drill instructors. From time to time I have used the expression *drill sergeant* when referring to someone who is very strict. Now it was all coming together. These drill instructors, otherwise known as DIs, are the ones responsible for turning these young men into Marines.

Every once in a while a significant event happens in your life that has a profound impact and changes you. That graduation was one of those times for me. All I wanted to do was learn about these people. I couldn't help but see some similarities. They trained for three months, and I was going to be on the depot for three months. I just had to make my three months at MCRD mean something. There must be something that I could do to be of assistance to these amazing and mysterious men.

I went back to the office and looked for someone, anyone, to ask my questions. Few people were around, and those who were had their doors shut. I went back to my office and started thumbing through papers that lined my desk.

I drove home that day in a state of awe. I hadn't had an opportunity to work with a Marine yet, but I was hopeful I was going to find a way. It was the end of my first week, and I already had learned more about the depot than my predecessor. I had a feeling that next week was going to be a better week.

Monday morning of week two felt a lot smoother than the prior week. My goal for the week was to work with at least one Marine. Carol had mentioned before she left that when she arrived at the depot, the prior MFLC had done a small group with some new Marines called BMPs. She explained that the BMPs were "broken Marines" (the real meaning is Basic Marine Platoon) who'd gotten hurt during training. They were able to graduate, so they were Marines not Recruits, but they were not healed enough to move on to the next level of training, which for most at MCRD grads was at Camp Pendleton. Carol had tried to get this group up and running, but no one ever showed up, so she gave up. She'd suggested that I give it a try. I had nothing better to do, so I wanted to try my luck.

No one in Family Support Services knew where the BMPs were, so I decided to try my fate and find out on my own. I started walking down the corridor. There were two drill instructors walking toward me. Did I dare ask them? Would that be considered "out of line"? Would I get in trouble from Barbara if she found out I stopped them to talk to them? She'd warned me over and over again about not bothering the Drill Instructors, often reminding me how busy they were. I decided not to chance it; I didn't want to get in trouble. As they were about to pass me, they stopped and asked if I needed some help. I must have had a lost look on my face. I apologized for taking their time and quickly asked them if they knew where the BMPs were.

They both smiled and said, "Of course, ma'am. They are housed in the opposite direction. Let us walk you over there to show you." I graciously thanked them but said that wouldn't be necessary. They insisted upon it, turned around, and walked me to the complete other end of the corridor. The whole time I couldn't help but worry that someone from Family Support Services might see me. During the walk I described to the drill instructors what I do on the depot.

I explained that I was an MFLC and there to provide anonymous, confidential counseling. One of them asked if I saw spouses. I was excited to hear that question, and I enthusiastically answered, "Of course." He mentioned that this duty had been very tough on his wife because he was never home. He'd just gotten back from being in Iraq for nine months, and his wife was hoping she'd see him more. Since he got to the drill field, he was almost never home.

The drill instructors took me inside the support battalion building and introduced me to Gunny Banks, who was in charge of the BMPs. I thanked them and gave them the MFLC number in case they ever needed anything. The one who had shared his marriage situation said he was going to have his wife call. As they left, Gunny Banks welcomed me and invited me to sit down. I talked to him about the idea of starting up the BMP groups again. He was very supportive and asked if I wanted to do one that afternoon. I was thrilled and nervous, but I reluctantly agreed, revealing that I knew very little about BMPs. He didn't seem to mind and suggested that I ask them to teach me. He said that Marines love to talk about what they do. We chatted for a while longer when he asked me where my office was. Before I could even finish getting the words *Family Support Services* out of my mouth, he shook his head with disgust.

"I hate them in there. I went there to get help because I was having a hard time controlling my anger. They enrolled me in anger management classes, and for three months, I had to attend every week. They also told my command. I had to go in and report to my first sergeant about my progress every couple of weeks. Never again will I do that. I suppose you are going to go back and tell them that. It's okay if you do. They know how I feel. I've told them repeatedly."

I explained to Gunny Banks that although my office was there, I was under a special type of contract, and I didn't have to report anything unless a Marine was a danger to himself or others. At first he was reluctant, but then he started talking. He told me all about his last deployment in Iraq and that since he had been back he had had a hard time controlling his anger. We talked for about an hour. I mostly listened and gave him some basic anger management techniques. I was afraid that his initial complaints would fall under PTSD, and as an MFLC I was under strict guidance to refer out anyone with PTSD. I was also not to see people who had an open Family Support Services cases. I wanted to maintain his trust, but I had to ask some qualifying questions. I found out that his Family Support Services case was closed and that he had been screened for PTSD and determined not to have it. As far as I was concerned, he was a perfect case for me to work with. We talked for a while more and scheduled a time the next day to meet at the Starbucks on base.

That afternoon I had my first BMP group. I didn't have time to do any research before starting, and I had no idea how it would go. The group was scheduled for 1400; I walked in ten minutes early. Gunny smiled and said, "They are waiting for you."

Surprised, I replied "Already?" It was then that I found out that Marines are always early, and on time is late. It was later explained to me that punctuality in military units often could be considered a matter of life and death. Also, being late sends the message that my time is more important than yours, and in the Marine Corps everyone is treated equally.

Gunny Banks escorted me into a room where approximately twenty Marines were seated. As soon as we entered, they all rose and spoke in unison, "Good afternoon, ma'am." I don't recall ever having experienced that level of respect before. I walked through many rows of chairs to the front of the room. There stood what was referred to as the "throne." It was a table with a smaller table on top. Gunny asked me to have a seat and then he excused himself to do some work. There I was, sitting on a throne amongst twenty Marines. For what felt like forever, I was speechless. I absolutely couldn't think of anything to say. Thankfully, I somehow miraculously remembered the therapist golden rule, "When you don't know what to say, ask questions. People love to talk about themselves."

I decided to go for honesty. My opening went something like this: "Hi guys. My name is Marjorie Morrison, and I am an MFLC, which stands for military family life consultant." (We are not allowed to say we are therapists. No idea why, but it is another one of those MFLC cardinal rules.) "I am here to do anonymous, confidential counseling. I will not share anything that we talk about unless you are a danger to yourself or someone else or reveal domestic violence, child abuse, or sexual abuse. This is my second week here, and I know very little about the Marine Corps. I'd love it if each of you could tell me a little about yourself." Panic came over me as soon as I finished. *What if they don't like sharing? What if they don't want to talk, and I'm putting each of them on the spot and making them share?*

The first Marine started. He stood at parade rest. "Hello, ma'am. My name is Private Miller. I am from the state of Oregon. I have a torn ACL and recently graduated from India Company. Is that all you wish to know, ma'am?" I wasn't expecting him to be so formal. I motioned to him to take a seat. I asked Private Miller if there was anything special about himself, hobbies, etc., that he wanted to share with us. He replied that he loved cars. His dad was a mechanic, and he could rebuild just about any engine. I then asked him what led to his decision to join the Marine Corps. He answered that he had tried a few college classes at a community college but that he couldn't keep his grades up. He had a hard time finding a job in his hometown. He and a buddy met with a Marine Corps recruiter, and the rest was history.

A Marine from the back of the room raised his hand. "I hope I am not interrupting, ma'am, but may I please address Private Miller?" I nodded. He asked Private Miller where in Oregon he was from. It turned out the two Marines were from neighboring towns. They joked about rival high schools and had a good laugh. I asked him if he'd like to go next. I then told all the BMPs that they didn't need to stand and did not need to call me *ma'am*.

I learned a lot that afternoon, including that quite a few of them were drug addicts and came into the Marine Corps to turn their lives around. One-third of those in the room were in gangs prior to enlisting, and many spoke about growing up in broken homes. Some BMPs had been there for months and had more complicated injuries, while others were only going to be there for a few days. These young men were the newest additions to the Corps. Their only experiences as Marines thus far had been in recruit training.

After that day, I really began to realize what a wonderful opportunity the military is. It provides options for people who may not have many choices. It gives them a life of discipline and a steady paycheck. Yes, I knew they have to go off to war, but they seemed excited about that. They were patriotic and didn't see war as a burden, but more of an honor. Many of these young adults had resorted to criminal acts to sustain their drug use or just to survive. Had they not joined the Corps, they may have ended up in jail. Instead they are now proud to be part of this great organization.

The next morning I poked my head into Barbara's office to tell her I'd had a group with the BMPs. I was anxious to let her know how well it went and that the group lasted over an hour and a half. I should have expected her reply, which was concern that an hour and a half is too long for them to be pulled from their responsibilities, and I should make their group shorter next time. That hadn't entered my mind. Gunny Banks had seemed pleased that the BMPs were so engaged with the group. He had said that they had very few things to do during the day. The majority of them had fractured bones, which made physical activity almost impossible. They'd sit around and get depressed because the Marines they went through recruit training with had moved on. Even if she was right, I got the message that Barbara wasn't happy for me that I was having a small success. I got the feeling that she saw me as a burden. She knew that there was no supervision from HWM, and she was burdened with so much work, she simply didn't have the time to oversee me.

After leaving four phone messages to HWM since I started at MCRD, that afternoon I finally received my first return phone call. The woman who called introduced herself as Sylvia. She apologized for not getting back to me sooner but explained that she had been going through a really tough personal time and was working on limited hours because she was on a partial stress leave. She added that the MFLC program was growing so fast that she couldn't keep up with all the work. I told her what had happened with Barbara when I arrived on the depot. She didn't sound at all surprised. She had heard numerous stories from past MFLCs about how difficult it was to work in Family Support Services offices. I asked her the logic behind putting anonymous counselors in that type of setting. She had no clue. I asked Sylvia to please call Barbara to touch base with her. I explained that it felt like Barbara was holding her dislike toward HWM against me. Sylvia was honest and admitted that she didn't think she would have time to call her but would send a follow-up e-mail. She spent the rest of the conversation telling me how difficult the Marine Corps had been to work with because the conflicts between the counseling centers and the nature of the MFLC program. It seemed to me that no thought had gone into where the MFLCs were placed, and housing them in Family Support Services was a conflict of interest for all parties.

Things were still going pretty slowly at MCRD. More than sixty new Marines now attended my BMP group, the highlight of my week. I saw a few spouses, and every once in a while, Gretchen would give me a referral. The majority of my time was spent trying not to get in anyone's way and heeding the advice to stay off the radar. It amazed me that they were paying me to do virtually nothing! I couldn't help thinking about all those MFLCs who had come from outside San Diego. They'd gotten the $2,000 a week, a car with reimbursed gas, a per diem for food, plus a hotel suite with kitchen. I remember the prior MFLC Carol had said she was able to pocket the extra $100 a day she got for food, because her hotel provided breakfast and dinner. This was the best job in the world if your goal was to get paid and barely work.

I was slowly getting to know the counselors in Family Support Services. Doug was the most senior counselor under Barbara. He was an incredibly kind, gentle man in his fifties. He seemed to genuinely care about the service members, which was refreshing. Gretchen sort of carried the attitude that all Marines were abusive and some of them had learned restraint while others hadn't. Being new to the military culture, I believed that what she said held value. Doug taught the anger management classes. Even though the majority of the Marines were mandated to attend, I think they got a tremendous amount out of Doug and his curriculum. I don't know how he did it, but he had the perfect personality to endure Barbara. He was easy-going and didn't seem to take it personally when she went on her rants. He was also very nice to me. He would tease my newfound love for the military by telling me to "be careful not to drink too much of the Kool-Aid on the depot." The other counselors in the office were very nice also. They had a tough job there. It was complicated and stressful. They had to protect the spouses and families from domestic violence. They had a tremendous amount of paperwork and incredible amount of liability. They all had a tough job, and I didn't envy them.

I became obsessed with the Marine Corps. I spent every free moment studying them. Doug, the head counselor, was practically the only one who appreciated my passion. Sadly, truth be told, I wasn't putting my newfound knowledge to much use. Gretchen continually used me as her glorified assistant. Every day I was tasked with some project that she needed help with. It typically involved counting and ordering materials and then stuffing the materials in individual bags. On the days that she had classes, she would have me follow her to hand out the bags of reading materials. It wasn't uncommon to see Marines throw away the bags as they exited the class.

I was doing very little clinical work. I had a couple of interesting cases. One was helping a couple handle issues dealing with a porn addiction. The Marine husband had gone to his spouse asking for help, reporting that he was spending hours a day looking at porn on his cell phone. I complimented him on his strength for asking for help and reassured him that typically that is the hardest step. I also supported the wife in her strength throughout this, pointing out to both of them what a strong relationship they had. I searched for information on the military and pornography addiction. It turned out that it is fairly common. Apparently, the obsession starts while service members are deployed in Iraq or Afghanistan. They have free time, are lonely, and are afraid for their safety. When you string those emotions together, it makes sense that they might find a release in viewing pornography. Similar to someone with a chemical or substance addiction, porn addicts tend to replace important relationships and commitments with Internet sex or other forms of pornography. When they return home, they may have unresolved issues from deployment, and porn may continue to act as a release. Unfortunately, as with all unhealthy vices, when you don't deal with your emotions, eventually they are going to rear their ugly heads and get in the way.

One of the biggest obstacles I had to deal with was where to see people. If the referral came from Gretchen, I would see the Marine at the Family Support Services. The problem there was that everybody had to sign in. The whole premise behind the MFLC program was that it was anonymous and there were no records. It was very difficult to earn the Marines' trust when they had to sign in. I brought it up to Barbara once, but she adamantly replied that for security purposes, they needed to know everyone who was in the building. It wasn't her idea, just another one of those rules that don't make a lot of sense for the MFLC program. I circumvented the issue by using an empty office upstairs in the depot library. The librarians didn't mind me using it, and the Marines seemed more receptive to coming in to see me if they didn't have to go into the Family Support Services office and sign in.

The following Saturday night I was at an engagement party and happened to meet a sailor. Before my time at MCRD, I probably would have thought nothing of his military life; now I wanted to hear everything about it. Luckily, he didn't mind my insistent questions and was happy to share. He was a captain in the Navy, which I learned is equivalent to a colonel in the Marine Corps. He had been in for twenty-one years and was starting to think about retirement. I was really excited to share with him that I was working at MCRD. I started out by telling him my usual line, "I provide anonymous and confidential counseling." He was intrigued and asked me more questions. We weren't more than three minutes into the conversation when he learned the truth about me and how I was just another example of taxpayers' waste. The Marines were not going to access my services for a variety of reasons. I was a glorified free assistant for the counseling center. The sad part was that the military members really did need help, and I wanted to give it. I picked his brain trying to find some way to push through the broken system.

He shared with me a tragic story about a recent suicide on his base. He said that helpful programs surrounded this sailor, yet no one knew he was having a tough time. He asked me the simplest question: "Aren't most people who are depressed isolated?" He concluded, "I don't see those people as the type that are going to reach out and get help. They are alone." Sadly, I agreed.

I couldn't sleep that night. I kept thinking about what he'd said.

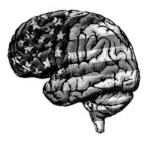

TAKING RISKS,
FINDING SUPPORT

I'd been at the Marine Corps Recruit Depot for six weeks, and I would be the first to admit that I was a waste of taxpayers' money. That week I was determined to take some risks. It wasn't going to be easy because the Family Support Services had such a tight hold over me. They were afraid that I may not have clinically sound insight and, without proper supervision from my contractor, could be seen as more of a liability than an asset. There had to be a way to reach more Marines, and I had to figure out how. I decided to consult with Doug, one of the Family Support Services counselors, for two reasons. First, I trusted his advice, and I was optimistic that if anyone could, he would lead me in the right direction. And second, if I got in trouble for "talking" to Marines, I at least could say that I discussed it with Doug first. My instincts proved to be right. Doug was very helpful and supportive. He appreciated my passion and suggested that I go to each battalion and ask to see the XO (executive officer). He did stress that they were very busy men, but he thought they would most likely take a few minutes to chat with me. I told him that Barbara had sternly warned me against wandering around to offices uninvited. He suggested that I take some business cards and treat it as outreach. I loved the idea, except that I didn't have any business cards. HWM had promised for weeks that they would send cards with the MFLC number on it, but to date there were no cards. That night on my way home from work, I stopped at an office supply store and bought some generic business cards. I went home and printed up one hundred cards that said military family life consultant with the phone number.

The next day, I ducked out of the office around lunchtime. I wrote on the sign-out board that I was doing "outreach." I began by walking down the long corridor that lined the parade deck. On my right I could hear drill instructors yelling cadence to a platoon of recruits. I couldn't make sense of the words, but the drill instructors would shout and the recruits would, in response, march in perfect unison.

The first door I passed was drill instructor school. I had been in there once with Gretchen when she taught a class. The door had a sign on it, reading, authorized personnel only. I stood there for a while, but the sign intimidated me. I decided to keep walking. After all, Doug had specifically said go to the battalions. I noticed my heart was pounding. I walked a bit farther to a door that read, 3rd Battalion. I kept hearing Barbara's voice in my head, "We once had an MFLC that walked right into offices all over the depot. Like she had a given right to wander around. You do not have liberty to walk wherever you want. You must be invited to go into people's offices. These are busy men and women, and they don't want to be bothered." I took a deep breath and walked into 3rd Battalion. There were a few offices with doors open, but nobody was inside any of them to direct me. I peered around the corner and saw a door that said "XO." The door was wide open, and I poked my head in. There was a gentleman sitting behind the desk. I apologized for bothering him and introduced myself. I explained that I was the MFLC and gave him some cards. He thanked me, introduced himself as Major Smith, and promised to pass a card to his boss, the CO (commanding officer). He assured me that they would call me if they needed anything.

I walked out and drew another deep breath. Okay, that wasn't so bad, but I also didn't get anywhere. I was going to have to be a lot more aggressive. I didn't know what I was looking for, but I knew I wanted more than "we will call you if we need anything." I knew enough to know they wouldn't be calling for help. The next door that I approached was 2nd Battalion. I was determined to figure out a way to bring mental health services to them.

What I didn't know walking through those doors was that I was going to meet someone who shared that vision with me. Like 3rd Battalion, the entryway was quiet. I assumed that the layout of the battalions were all the same, so I peered around the corner and made my way to the XO's office. As I approached the open doorway, the man sitting behind the desk stood up and introduced himself. "I'm Major Anderson. Can I help you?" I introduced myself, and he asked me to have a seat. I briefly explained that I was contracted to provide anonymous counseling. Just like everyone that I had encountered thus far, he had never heard of the MFLC program.

We hadn't talked for long before we both realized that we shared common goals. We both wanted to reach out to the Marines and help them access services. The refreshing thing about Major Anderson was that he brainstormed with me for a while. I told him about the groups that I was doing with the BMPs. He said he liked groups because they took the individual stigma out of getting help. After approximately thirty minutes of dialogue, he asked me what I thought about doing a group like that with the drill instructors at the beginning of their new cycle. He clarified that they pick up their new recruits on Fridays, but the prior week they are at the battalion in classes all day. He would be willing to ask the battalion commander if he would support carving out some time for a group. I thanked him for his time and openness and left. I had been there for more than forty-five minutes, which was a long time to be away from the office. I decided to save going to 1st Battalion for another day.

I had barely made it back to my office when Major Anderson called to tell me that he had talked to the CO and gotten the green light. I hung up the phone and wanted to scream. I was so excited! I was finally not only going to get an opportunity to work with Marines, but drill instructors! I'd had so little exposure to those men, just a couple of minutes at the end of Gretchen's classes to brief them on the MFLC program. Although the BMPs were Marines, their only experiences were in recruit training. The drill instructors were real Marines. They were commonly considered the best of the best! I went down the hall to tell Barbara the great news. She could see how excited I was and smiled. She even complimented me for achieving more than any of the prior MFLC. It was a good day, but I still had to nail that first group.

The next day I shared my exciting news with Gunny Banks. He reassured me that the drill instructors would react as favorably to the groups as the BMPs had. He thought the format of the BMP groups was outstanding and suggested I do exactly the same thing. He loaned me the Tom Ricks book *Making the Corps.*[5] That book was one of the greatest gifts I've ever received; I read it in two days. It was perfect because it helped me understand recruit training and the unique issues that drill instructors dealt with.

I also learned that 2nd Battalion had had a horrible situation a couple of years earlier. A sergeant drill instructor had terribly abused recruits and was sentenced to prison. As a result of that public case, there was a big push on the base not to abuse recruits. This had caused some inherent conflicts because historically the role of drill instructor had always been somewhat abusive.

The following week I headed over to 2nd Battalion to meet with the drill instructors from Hotel Company. I received very little direction from 2nd Battalion on how I should conduct the group. They gave me full autonomy. Major Anderson (the XO) escorted me into the DI classroom, which was filled with more than thirty men in uniform. This group looked very different from the BMPs. These men exuded confidence. They were the legendary drill instructors, among the top 10 percent of the Marine Corps, chosen after a rigorous selection process. One of the main qualifiers for getting into DI school was having had multiple deployments. These Marines had been around, and for a woman with limited military exposure, this was an intimidating bunch.

I started to feel sick. Was my format from the BMP group going to work with them? What if nobody talked? I think Major Anderson must have felt my nerves because he broke the silence.

"Gentlemen, listen up. This is Marjorie Morrison. She is a counselor who is here to talk with you. Unlike the folks at base counseling centers, Marjorie is not required to take any notes, and with the exception of a danger to yourself or another, she will keep all conversations confidential. I know that to many of you, counseling represents a sign of weakness. I used to feel the same way, but one day that all changed for me. It was on September 11, 2001. I was the duty officer for the Marine barracks that day and was delayed at Henderson Hall." I sat there intently listening to his every word. "I went to visit a friend who had an office that overlooked the Pentagon. He was informing me about what was going on at the World Trade Center in New York. We were saying that it had to be more than a coincidence that there were two accidents at the same time, when we heard a plane outside. I remember commenting to my friend that I didn't think that plane belonged there. Someone from down the hall started yelling, 'Oh my God, they are going to fly into the Pentagon!' At that point we looked out the window, and we could see the remnants of the plane crash. I remember the clear blue sky had literally turned red. I was half a mile away from my office, which was in the Pentagon. I later found out that the plane crashed less than a hundred meters from my office! The mental health folks gave us numbers to call if we needed to talk to anyone. I was a tough guy and didn't need to talk to anyone. It wasn't until I came here to MCRD, which is situated right next to the airport, that I realized I had a problem. Every time I'd hear a plane landing, I had a visceral reaction. I finally went and got help. It was one of the best experiences I ever had. Nobody is too strong to get help. Be respectful and open minded to Ms. Morrison. She only wants to help." He looked at me with a smile and a wink and walked out of the room.

Wow! I now understood why Major Anderson was advocating for me to work with the drill instructors. I couldn't possibly have asked for a better introduction than that! There I was, alone with a sea of men in camouflage uniforms. The room was set up in rows, which gave it a classroom feel. The environment did not feel conducive for group cohesion. I asked if the men wouldn't mind forming a circle. Without a second of reluctance, the thirty drill instructors and the company officers formed a large circle. I had no idea how this was going to turn out, but I could not have asked for a better setting. On the other hand, starting out with regular Marines and not drill instructors may have been less daunting.

Somehow my mouth opened up, and I found my voice. I barely remember what I said, but it was something along the lines of, "I'd like to meet each of you and learn a little bit about who you are: how long you've been a drill instructor, what some of the challenges have been, what you have learned that you'd like to share, and anything else that you'd like to add." This was a risky move and quite possibly could have turned into a complete disaster. One thing I had going for me was that they had given me an hour and thanks to Major Anderson's talk and my rearranging the classroom, I was down to forty-five minutes left. Forty-five minutes, I could get through that.

I asked if anyone wanted to start, I wanted to avoid going in a circle because I didn't want it to feel like kindergarten. Finally, after what felt like an eternity, a man spoke up. He introduced himself and stated that he was in his fourth cycle. This was his first cycle as a senior drill instructor, and he was excited to wear the black belt that the senior DI's get to wear. The company had just had a few weeks off in between cycles, and he was surprised how much he had missed coming to work. He was excited to be back. He was married and had a two-year-old daughter with another on the way. His wife was due the week of graduation (in three months), and if things went according to plan, he would be grateful for how the timing worked out.

Phew, it was a perfect opener. The man sitting next to him went next. His story was a little different. He was also on his fourth cycle, but he had been moved around from one company to another. He started with Golf Company where he did two cycles, was moved to Fox Company, and then switched over to Hotel Company. He had just found out the day before that he was getting moved again. He didn't know anyone in the company and felt a bit out of place. I could tell what he was really trying to say was that he was frustrated that he had been moved around a lot. Anybody else would take this opportunity to complain, but not a Marine. These men do not complain; that would be considered selfish. These men were here for the greater cause, and this DI was going to show up to duty wherever his commander told him to. I asked him to take this time to introduce himself to his new company, to take a few moments and let them know a little about him. I could tell he was embarrassed, but he participated in the exercise anyway. It turned out that he lived in the same complex with a few other DIs in the company. They agreed to chat after and discuss carpooling options.

Next, another DI from the back of the room spoke up. He welcomed the DI who had just spoken and told him how lucky he was that he was now part of Hotel Company because they were the best. He offered his support and let him know that he had a similar experience and that if he needed anything to please let him know. He was one of the more senior DIs in this company and would be happy to help acclimate him.

So far this was going quite well. The next Marine was a new DI, and this was his first cycle. He shared that he was scared that he wouldn't be able to measure up. He had been preparing for this first cycle for months, and now it was finally here. He was worried that he wouldn't be able to earn the recruits' respect and didn't want to let his team of drill instructors down. Now the dialogue was getting started. A DI from the other side of the room spoke up. He reassured him that everyone feels that way his first cycle. He went on to say that the first cycle is by far the hardest and as long as he was prepared to work hard, he'd be okay. The Marine next to him spoke up. "The most important thing you can do is learn from us. So many new DIs think they know how to do things the right way, and they don't learn from each other." I was beginning to see from the dialogue how the hierarchy in the company worked.

Each company is broken up into platoons. Each platoon, depending on the size of the recruit class, has approximately seventy-five recruits. The platoons have teams of drill instructors. The "senior," the most seasoned drill instructor, takes the role of the parent and doesn't do much disciplining with the recruits. He is seen as the one the recruits can trust and talk to. The senior wears a black belt; the other drill instructors wear green belts. Typically the senior has had five-plus cycles. Beneath him is the next most experienced drill instructor, often referred to as the "J."

He is the lead green-belt instructor. Under him is the third hat, and depending on how many DIs are on each team, there may be a fourth or fifth hat. Those DIs are considered the "heavies," and they do all the yelling, screaming, and disciplining.

Now the dialogue was starting to flow. Drill instructors were reaching out to each other, offering support and encouragement where needed. New drill instructors were recognizing that they were not alone in how they felt and that all the new guys were equally anxious about the unknown. The green belts had their own issues and concerns. They wanted to make sure that the new hats did what they were supposed to because they wanted to keep the senior hats out of their business. The biggest concern was not getting in trouble. If you got in trouble, you got "sat out" and couldn't work while the situation was being investigated. From what I was learning, almost anything could get you in trouble. The biggest "no-no" was touching a recruit. The DIs needed to instill fear in the recruits and could do it by yelling and screaming but could not physically touch them. I was informed that 2nd Battalion really drove this point home. The DIs were under a lot of pressure not to do anything wrong.

Before I knew it, the door opened and my time was up. I was about to wrap it up when the company commander spoke up. His name was Captain Teagan, and up until this point, he had remained relatively silent. "Gentleman, I think this was an outstanding exercise, and I am happy to see such great camaraderie amongst you. I hope you will join me in thanking Ms. Morrison. I'd like to suggest that she visit with us again in the middle of our cycle to see how things have progressed." He continued, "I can tell from how you are treating each other that we are going to have an outstanding cycle. Let's look out for each other, stay professional and focused on the task at hand, and we will grow as people and Marines in the process."

I was thrilled at how the group had gone. I followed Captain Teagan into Major Anderson's office, where he reported that the group was incredibly successful and helpful. They both thanked me and scheduled me in for later in the cycle. I thanked Major Anderson before I left the office. It was his idea to do the groups, and he set the perfect stage for me. He knew his men would benefit from counseling, and he also knew that if we didn't think about things from a different angle and try a different approach, things would never change.

I smiled all the way back to my office. That went much better than I could have ever possibly expected. Second Battalion wanted me to do groups for every company during pick-up week, and Hotel Company wanted me to come back and do another group in six weeks, halfway through their cycle.

When I got back to Family Support Services, everyone's door was open, but nobody was around. I asked the receptionist what was going on. She reminded me that it was the weekly staff meeting. I was told from the beginning that I would not be able to attend these closed-door meetings where the counseling staff discussed highly sensitive issues. I was disappointed that there wasn't anyone I could share my story with. I decided the most productive thing to do would be to enjoy my high and make an attempt at meeting the XO in 1st Battalion. I had tried a few times but had never found anyone in. I was hoping I would have the same success as in 2nd Battalion and that they would decide they wanted groups also.

I marched into 1st Battalion with a lot more confidence than I'd had when I initially went into 3rd Battalion. It was hard to imagine that only one week had passed. The XO wasn't in, so I poked my head into the CO's office. This was the lieutenant colonel's office, and I had been warned about not bothering them. The XOs are the supposed gatekeepers, and they decide what gets taken to the colonel. By this point, I'd had a number of failed attempts to reach the XO, and I was feeling pretty confident. I lightly tapped on the lieutenant colonel's door, which was slightly ajar. I was surprised that Lt. Col. Adams asked me to come in and have a seat. I was learning just how courteous and respectful Marines are. They treat people with dignity and reverence. I couldn't help thinking how productive our general society would be if everyone in the outside world treated each other like that.

I introduced myself to Lt. Col. Adams, who, like everyone else I had met, had never heard of the MFLC program. There had been an MFLC at MCRD for two years. I shuddered to think of all the wasted money! I explained that I was interested in doing more to bring services to the Marines and that I didn't want to sit in an office and wait for them to come in. We both knew that likely wasn't going to happen. We talked for quite a while and it turned out that he too also shared my sentiments. I told him about the group I had just done in 2nd Battalion. He didn't seem too interested in the idea of groups. I wondered if it was because there is sort of a competition between battalions and he didn't want to appear as though he were copying 2nd. On the other hand, he wasn't quick to kick me out of the office and kept me talking for quite some time. I could easily understand why this man was in a position of leadership. He asked deep questions and really analyzed my responses.

We agreed that the goal was to bring services to the Marines and show them how easy it is to talk to someone. He was a progressive thinker. He looked me dead in the eye and asked if I was willing to try something different. I was up for his challenge. He wanted me to meet with every drill instructor one at a time, for ten to fifteen minutes during pick-up week. That would give the drill instructors a chance to meet me. During that time I could give them my contact information and have a brief talk with them. They could ask me questions if they had any, and I could schedule a follow-up appointment if necessary. I loved the idea.

Gunny Banks was right about Marines. If you don't know what to do, ask them and they will help you figure it out. What a day! I had a fantastic group with the drill instructors from Hotel Company, and I was now going to have thirty one-on-one meetings with the DIs in Alpha Company the following week.

I was anxious to talk to Barbara and fill her in on what had been going on thus far with the drill instructors. She either didn't care, was genuinely too busy to talk to me, or was overwhelmed by the liability I caused her. I believed it to be the latter, but I could never be sure. One thing was very clear to me, Barbara had very little time to commit to me. I always got the feeling when I approached her that I was wasting her time. It felt like I was allowed to stay there as long as I stayed out of her way. I briefly explained to her that I would be spending two days the following week meeting with the DIs one at a time, being careful not to go into too much detail or take up too much time. She cautioned me about getting too busy and then excused me from her office. Funny, she was worried about me becoming too busy, and all I wanted to do was become busy.

The next week I started my experimental one-on-one sessions with the drill instructors of Alpha Company. The sessions went surprisingly well, even though I didn't get as exciting an introduction as I did from Major Anderson. I also wasn't nearly as nervous as I had been before the previous week's group. I personally thrive in one-on-ones and find myself in my element there. Initially, as expected, the Marines were a little uncomfortable but they loosened up very quickly. I think at first they didn't know what to expect. I met with them in the chaplain's office, which was perfect because it was a warm, comfortable environment. I pulled them out one at a time, and they missed about ten to fifteen minutes of whichever class was currently taking place. They hear the same classes every three months, so many of them were happy to have an escape.

The majority of the DIs had a lot to share. I asked them questions like: How's life? Are you married? How is that going? How is work? Being a therapist, I was well trained on reading body language, and I knew when I'd touched on an area that needed further probing. The sessions were very informal and for most that seemed to be perfect. I learned a lot and found common threads of concerns that all drill instructors seemed to share. Some of them used the opportunity to get very personal while others were reserved.

One drill instructor shared a war story with me about an enemy fire attack. He lost two men that day, and he still couldn't forgive himself. He kept reliving the event over and over again in his head. I was surprised to hear that he had never shared the story before. He was visibly shaking and teary eyed while telling me the story. After lengthy discussion he thankfully recognized the importance of talking to someone further about his potential PTSD symptoms. We sat together and made a referral for the MTF (medical treatment facility). I marveled at his strength and how much he had kept inside for all this time.

After two days, I had seen every one of the drill instructors for at least fifteen minutes. There were only two DIs out of the thirty that were remotely difficult. I couldn't get them to open up. They answered with one-word answers and clearly were very uncomfortable. It didn't seem to matter what questions I asked or what I brought up; they weren't going to share anything with me.

At the end of the second day, I went into Lt. Col. Adams's office to report how it had gone. I told him that everyone appeared to open up to me but two of them. I started to talk about those two Marines when he stopped me and exclaimed, "You will never be successful here."

I was stunned. All of the drill instructors had seemed to get a lot out of those sessions. Even though I couldn't get two to talk, the other twenty-eight had had a lot to say. In fact, a few of them had talked for over a half hour. A bunch of the DIs had asked me very personal questions. I felt confident that I had truly helped many of them. I'd provided the DIs with referrals to a variety of resources, depending on what their issues were.

I started to argue my point; I had gotten this far, and I wasn't going to quit easily. He interrupted. "Listen, you will never get one hundred percent. If you focus on the two you didn't get, you will never get anywhere. You need to focus on the other twenty-eight. That is an outstanding success ratio. If you can accept the fact that you will never reach perfection, but strive for it anyway, you can be successful." He went on to tell me I should feel proud.

He also shared that he had pulled a few of the DIs in after they'd met with me to get a sense of how it had gone. He wanted me to know that he didn't ask them to share anything personal, but wanted some overall, honest feedback. He informed me that the ones he'd asked all had found it to be beneficial and helpful. "If you can handle that there will always be a few that you won't be able to reach," he said, "I'd like for you to come back in three weeks when Delta Company picks up." I thanked him and promised that I would try to focus on the positive. I am a driven person, and always strive for perfection. On the other hand, I saw his point, and I really appreciated his advice.

I was getting a little nervous because in a couple of weeks my twelve-week contract would be up, and I was finally getting momentum. If I had six more weeks, I was confident that I could get a strong program up and running. The battalions would see the benefit of mental health services, and future MFLCs could step in and continue the work. That afternoon, I asked Barbara how she would feel about me asking HWM if I could stay an extra six weeks. She supported the idea, mostly because every time a new MFLC came, it took up more of her time. I called HWM every day for a week. Luckily the following week I received a response that HWM would make a special exception for me and allow me to stay for an additional six weeks. I continued sending new referrals in my private practice over to my colleagues. My husband was becoming increasingly nervous about all of this. He appreciated that I wanted to make a difference but was very concerned that I could be jeopardizing my career to make that happen.

Things were definitely picking up for me on the Marine base. I had my weekly BMP group, which, depending on the week, had anywhere from sixty to seventy Marines in attendance. My work with groups in 2ⁿᵈ Battalion had grown as well. I met with the company as a whole during their pick-up week and then met them again halfway through their cycle. I continued to do the one-on-ones during pick-up week for 1ˢᵗ Battalion. As a result, Marines were getting more comfortable with me and started contacting me for private sessions. I was finally starting to feel productive.

In the middle of every three-month recruit training cycle, the companies moved forty-five minutes north to Camp Pendleton for a few weeks of field training. There is a Marine Corps Recruit Depot battalion there called Weapons and Field Training Battalion. Second Battalion wanted me to go there to do their mid-cycle groups. I wasn't sure how that would work with my HWM contract. I was told that Camp Pendleton never picked up the MFLC program. I had heard it was because other Marine bases had issues with HWM and they didn't want the aggravation, but that was all hearsay. There was no cost to the base for having an MFLC, so the fact that they didn't want it said more about how convoluted the program was than anything else. When I shared 2ⁿᵈ Battalion's request to Barbara, I pitched the idea that I could spend the day there providing MFLC services to the Marine Corps Recruit Depot Marines that were stationed there. Surprisingly, Barbara was supportive of my going up there one day a week. It was refreshing to hear her not be negative with me. I could never tell with Barbara if she was burnt out on her job or if she just had a bad temper.

Spending a day at Camp Pendleton would be something new and exciting. Camp Pendleton is a huge base, equivalent to a city. I thought MCRD was all-inclusive, but this place had everything. It was about thirty-eight miles north of MCRD. It was a massive base, sprawling over approximately 125,000 acres. More than 38,000 military family members occupy base housing complexes. More than 6,736 housing units are available for Marine families, plus two hotels that offer temporary housing. The base has a self-sustaining water supply, sewage treatment plants, with its own telephone and electrical systems. It has five public elementary schools, a comprehensive naval hospital to meet all medical needs, its own Subway, Wendy's, Pizza Hut, Dominoes, and McDonald's. The first time I visited Camp Pendleton, I thought I had made a wrong turn because I drove into a strip-center shopping complex that looked exactly the same as a civilian one. There was a safe feeling on the base. Security was very tight, and people in uniform were all over the place. I had imagined that I'd feel a little frightened at a place like that, but I felt the opposite. Everybody had a job to do, and they performed it with the utmost professionalism and dignity. Situated on the Pacific Ocean and surrounded by the mountains, it appeared a nice place to work or live at.

Weapons and Field Training Battalion (WFTBn) was happy to have me. The XO and CO were both excited to have their own mental health provider. They heavily promoted the MFLC program by sending e-mails to all the companies. They also made a point to introduce me to everyone and encouraged all Marines to take advantage of my services. They did everything they possibly could to help remove the stigma. I was amazed at how supportive they were.

I was starting to get really good at understanding the unique stressors that drill instructors experienced, and I was beginning to be able to separate normal complaints from what seemed to be greater concerns. I had also realized that to make the most of the groups, I needed to break the drill instructors up into smaller groups. I started doing green belt groups and then senior groups. My second week at Pendleton, I held a group with the green belt DIs from Golf Company. They complained about how the seniors were never around, so the green belts had to do all the work. Experience working with DIs had taught me that this was not okay behavior. Had I been the typical MFLC who was only there for six weeks, I would have missed the significance of this. I was glad this behavior came up in our groups because it was the first time the green belts had discussed the situation with one another. There is an underlying culture in the military to not share things with people, to keep it inside. It is a complicated value system that I believe starts during recruit training. Many Marines believe that a true Marine does not tell on a fellow Marine. The good thing about group interaction is that participants have the opportunity to see that they are not alone in their experiences. I encouraged them to rely on one other and support each other.

Later that day I met with the senior drill instructors from the same company. They had their own set of issues with one of the chiefs (the top two DIs in the company). I shared with them that I was concerned with the level of discord I was feeling in the company. I persuaded them to talk to their first sergeant about their issues and told them that I was going to share some of my concerns with the company commander.

I met with the Golf Company commander, Captain James, later that day. He had just taken over the company a week prior. It was not unusual for me to touch base with the commanders and provide nonpersonal feedback. I never gave specifics but tried to give them a sense of how things were going. I shared with him that the drill instructors appeared very disgruntled and that I was worried that the heightened tensions in the company may potentially trickle down to the recruits, making them quite vulnerable to recruit abuse. The next day, the company commander called me to tell me that there had been a physical fight between the chief and one of the senior drill instructors. He thanked me for the insight and said that as a direct result of my intervention, he was able to get the drill instructors to give him honest feedback about what was really going on. He wanted me to know that four of his men had come to him separately to thank him for providing the company with my services. I was very relieved that the DIs benefited from the experience and the command benefited from the feedback.

The next day the battalion commander contacted me and thanked me. He was also grateful for my insight and felt that my early intervention had helped avert a potential disaster. He informed me that he had sent an e-mail to Lt. Col. Rowe regarding my services. I was grateful that he had done that because I had never met Lt. Col. Rowe. He was Barbara's boss and was the head of MCCS (Marine Corps Community Services). Later that day I received a copy of the e-mail:

Lt. Col. Rowe,

I wanted to provide you some feedback on another of the great things you have done for us. I am amazed at how far you have brought the Depot in just 18 months.

I submitted the attached AAR to Col. Chester and the RTR on the subject of Ms. Morrison, MFLC.

I recommended her/MFLC to ALCON in the RTR. Ms. Morrison is invaluable in gaining insight into unit morale, challenges, and has a great rapport with the Marines. Thanks again for the support of this great program. Semper Fidelis, Pete.

Very respectfully,
Lt. Col. Peter. R. Davis, USMC
2nd Battalion, RTR
San Diego, CA

UNITED STATES MARINE CORPS
SECOND BATTALION
RECRUIT TRAINING REGIMENT
MARINE CORPS RECRUIT DEPOT/
WESTERN RECRUITING REGION
SAN DIEGO, CALIFORNIA 92140-5540

IN REPLY REFER TO:
1000
CO
15 Jun 08

From: Commanding Officer
To: Commanding Officer, Recruit Training Regiment
Subj: AFTER ACTION REPORT

Company: F
Class: 2108
Week/T-Day: 5/T-27
Annex: Z
Number: 0000

Topic: MFLC Session

Subj: Hotel Company After Action Report

Discussion: Marjorie Morrison is the Marine Family Life Counselor supporting 2d Battalion. She has led "team building" focus groups with the drill instructors of Company F. The purpose of the group is to teach drill instructors to depend on each other for strength and support. She describes the sessions as focused on building "synergy and cohesion." If a drill instructor is having a difficult time, either personally or professionally, she encourages him to rely on those in their company for advice and encouragement, instead of carrying the burden alone.

Ms. Morrison meets with the drill instructors during Pick-Up Week, during Grass Week, and at the end of the cycle. She meets with the whole company together, and then meets with the green belt drill instructors and the senior drill instructors in separate groups. The group discussions have been very well received and drill instructors often ask for additional sessions.

Company F had a change of command at the conclusion of Phase One of cycle 21-08. During his first week of command, the new company commander realized that one of his chief drill instructors did not have a good working relationship with his senior drill instructors. However, it was not until after Ms. Morrison met with the company's drill instructors that he became aware of how severe the problem was. Ms. Morrison reported that the company's green belt drill instructors were experiencing anxiety that is normal among new drill instructors, but that they were generally supporting each other. However, she reported that the senior drill instructors were the most depressed and disgruntled drill instructors that she had ever met. She told the company commander that the source of the discontent was the same chief drill instructor. This vital piece of information confirmed the new company commander's suspicions and enabled him to take appropriate action to fix the situation, such as more determined efforts to mentor the chief drill instructor. Ultimately Ms. Morrison's insight proved prophetic when the same chief drill instructor was involved in an inappropriate physical altercation with another drill instructor.

Recommendation: Ms. Morrison has developed an excellent rapour with the drill instructors she counsels. She has greatly enhanced the ability of drill instructors to build strong teams that provide each other with strength and support during the rigorous recruit training cycle. She is also an extremely valuable asset for the command because she provides crucial information on the morale of the unit and suggestions on how to improve it. Ms. Morrison's focus sessions should become scheduled events on the training schedule and an additional session should be added to third phase.

As my work with the Marines increased, tensions in the Family Support Services were rising. A couple of weeks prior, Gretchen had referred a young couple to me. They were in their early twenties and came for help with their fighting. The Marine explained that they had gotten in a fight and his wife had thrown a book at his foot. His toe hurt, and he couldn't do his daily physical training. He had gone to his command and requested the day off from running. After hearing about the fight with his wife, the command sent them to Family Support Services for marital counseling. They'd had an initial session with Gretchen after which she sent them to me. Typically if command sends a Marine over, it is a reportable situation and not one that I would be allowed to see. This situation was different. The Marine was a victim of his spouse's violent outburst. This wasn't a typical domestic violence case and Gretchen (the Family Support Services gatekeeper) had sent them to me, so I went ahead and saw them twice. The third time they came in they got into a fight in front of me that caused me concern. I quickly realized that they were going to need much more intensive ongoing therapy than I could do as an MFLC. I was allowed to do only short and brief counseling.

Later that day I stopped by Gretchen's office to let her know that I thought the couple needed a higher level of care and would need an in-house referral to someone in the Family Support Services. When I reviewed the case with her, she first appeared lost and could barely remember the couple. Immediately after she became furious with me and was angry that I had ever worked with them in the first place. She had a temper tantrum shouting at me that I had no business seeing a domestic violence case. After the daze and confusion from the outburst passed, I realized what was going on. She was worried she would get in trouble for having had referred them to me because they were a command referral. In hindsight, I probably should have argued with her and not taken responsibility, but at the time it didn't seem worth it. I had a Marine waiting for me at the library, and I was running late. Instead I apologized for the misunderstanding. I felt bad for the Family Support Services counselors. They had so much paperwork, and their liability with every case must be overwhelming.

I knew Gretchen didn't like me, but I never expected the next series of events to occur. While I was gone, Gretchen met with Barbara. I don't know what she told her, but I imagine it was that I had screwed up and had seen a domestic violence case two times before letting anyone know. I do know that she claimed the couple never told her that their command had sent them in. I find that almost impossible to believe because it was literally the first thing they told me when they stepped in my office. Needless to say, when I came back, I was not prepared for Barbara when she came storming into my office. She screamed at me that I had no business doing counseling if I didn't know what a domestic violence case was. It's hard for me to remember everything she said because most of it was so cruel that I tuned it out. I do remember hearing that I'd lost all my credibility and that she could no longer trust that I could do the right thing. She went on to say that this was a perfect example of how having me on the depot was a liability for her, one that she was not willing to accept. She let me know that she was going to call HWM and ask for my contract to be terminated and that she was dropping the program.

I had heard that threat from my first day on the depot. It was amazing to me that one day I was getting praise from the Marines for my work, and the next day I was getting terminated for a misunderstanding that I didn't feel completely responsible for. I am not a confrontational person; in fact I'm more of the pleaser type. Perhaps that was my downfall. I had tried so hard over the past months not to make Barbara mad. I had never had anyone yell at me like that before. Instead of sharing my side of the story, I found myself tongue-tied and started to cry. Sadly, I fell silent. I wasn't sure if I should pack up my things that very moment and leave. If only I had some support from my contractor, but I knew better then to expect support from them.

HWN has a solid reputation of not defending their MFLCs and terminating their contracts with any single complaint from the base. Frustrated, I packed up my stuff but decided to leave everything in the office, optimistic that I would have a better idea of how to handle things the next day.

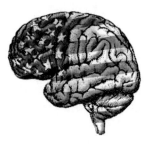

TRIUMPH AND SUCCESS

Sylvia, my old HWM supervisor was no longer there. The new one was Donna, and I called her on my way home from work. This was the first time I'd had to use her cell phone number, which she gave out for emergency use only. Lucky for me, she answered on the first try. I explained to her what had happened in Family Support Services. Her opinion was that it sounded as though I was a scapegoat. She told me that although I worked under Barbara and she was my POC, she wasn't allowed to fire me without discussing it with HWM first. Barbara hadn't had contact with HWM in over a year and wouldn't know who to discuss it with. There had been two or three changes in contact persons at HWM just in the few months I was there. How was Barbara supposed to keep up with the changes if no one ever contacted her? I hoped that Donna would call Barbara to smooth things out. I knew that a big part of the problem I'd had with Family Support Services from the beginning came from the lack of support they received from HWM.

Unfortunately, Donna said she was too busy to call Barbara. They were short staffed, and she was leaving for Japan the following day. The best advice she could give me was to go over Barbara's head and talk to her superior, sharing with him my side of the story. I was confused; Family Support Services couldn't fire me without HWM's consent and HWM didn't have time to call

Family Support Services. What was I supposed to do? The only positive I could see in the situation was that Barbara's superior was Lt. Col. Rowe, the person that 2nd Battalion had recently e-mailed about me.

I couldn't sleep all night. I didn't like the advice to go over her head, but then again I couldn't think of any better options. The next morning I showed up to work at the usual time. I had planned to speak to Lt. Col. Rowe (Barbara's boss and the head of MCCS) but thought it would be a good idea to warn Barbara first. I wasn't sure this was a smart move, but I always try to treat people the way I want to be treated. If someone were going to go to my boss, I'd want a heads-up. I also didn't want her to feel that I was going behind her back. There was a part of me that sympathized with Barbara. She was an overwhelmed and busy person, but in her defense, she had been up front about that from the beginning. I was on a short leash; one wrong move and I was out of there. I was much more disappointed in Gretchen. She was very insecure, and she threw me under the bus to cover for her own negligence. I was also disgusted at how poor HWM was at providing support to both sides.

To put it nicely, Barbara was less than pleased with my decision to go over her head. Once again, she got angry with me, and this time accused me of not understanding the hierarchy in the military. It also proved to be poor timing on my part, because Lt. Col. Rowe was scheduled to spend the morning in meetings with Barbara and would be hearing from her first. Regardless, with a lack of other options, I decided to go ahead with the plan. I found my way to Lt. Col. Rowe's office, but he couldn't see me until afternoon. I didn't know exactly how to handle the situation. I certainly didn't want to get Gretchen in trouble. As much as I felt this was her fault, if I placed the blame on her, ultimately it would just make me look bad. I decided to go with honesty and just give Lt. Col. Rowe the facts. He could decide if they were grounds for firing me.

When we met, I explained that I was referred a case directly from Family Support Services and saw them twice before I asked to have them transferred. I clarified that I never would have seen the couple if I thought I wasn't supposed to and that I apologized for the misunderstanding. I also shared with him how far I had come with the Marines and how much they were utilizing the MFLC services since I had arrived. I assumed that Barbara had gotten to him first and had already told her side of the story. Lt. Col. Rowe did not look up at me once during the whole conversation. He kept his eyes glued on his desk. I imagined this meant that he had no interest in my story. He finally looked up and started to speak.

He informed me that Barbara had an issue with the MFLC program since its inception. It had been her idea to pick up the program in the first place, and she had been very disappointed with the follow-up she had received from HWM. I already knew that, but the next part surprised me. Although Barbara did not want to be responsible for MFLC program anymore, he had heard from many marines that RTR (Recruit Training Regiment) was benefiting from my services. He wanted to move me to another department. Until he figured out the best place for me to go, he suggested that I temporarily work under Marine Corps Family Team Building. It was a short meeting, and he had to get going. He asked me to get in touch with Kathy, the POC of Marine Corps Family Team Building and that she would find me some office space and in the interim sign my weekly time cards.

This was more than I ever could have hoped for. My office was going to get moved, which was a real positive since I knew Marines had such an aversion to being seen at Family Support Services. Later that day I introduced myself to Kathy, my new POC. She was in her forties and quite a remarkable woman.

Over the years, she had worked very hard to build up Marine Corps Family Team Building. She was married to a Marine and really wanted her program to be an asset to the depot. She had a reputation for having a lot of passion toward her work, and I was thrilled to be part of her program. She did warn me that she was overloaded and didn't think she would be able to devote much time to me. I didn't feel that I needed much supervision; I was just happy to get away from the politics at Family Support Services. I left Donna at HWM a message to report what had happened. I knew better than to expect a return phone call.

It was now the beginning of July, which brought about a lot of change on the depot. All four battalion commanders (1st, 2nd, 3rd, and Support) were rotating out, and new battalion commanders were coming aboard. That is the way the military works. No one stays in one place very long. I was a little concerned and sad about this transition. I had gotten to know the existing battalion commanders quite well. I was doing individual sessions for 1st Battalion, groups for 2nd Battalion, attending all of the family events for 3rd Battalion, and doing BMP groups for Support Battalion. I had become very fond of the leaders and was worried about the stability of my counseling program when the new leadership took over.

It is very difficult to measure success when you are a therapist; you have to be creative. I had no way to track accomplishments in the individual sessions because I hadn't been on the depot long enough to see the Marines on rotation more than once. It was also difficult to gauge the true benefits of the groups. The only way I could evaluate if I was making a difference was by the Marines' willingness to seek services or talk with me. I had worked hard to earn their respect, and it was starting to pay off. The drill instructors knew that I understood their world. I studied recruit training, watched the drill instructors in action, analyzed them, and learned from them. I was finding that wherever I went, DIs would stop me to chat. Some would ask me questions about how to handle a situation, while others would just want to share a personal story in continuation to what they had told me in a one-on-one.

A few months earlier, I'd known very little about the military. Now I knew that these men not only needed help, they deserved it, and we owed it to them. One day during my mandatory one-on-ones, a Marine lingered after our time together ended. This is what typically happened when a Marine had something he wanted to get off his chest but didn't know how to start. I finally asked him if there was something he wanted to tell me. He started sobbing, sharing with me that ever since he'd come back from Iraq he'd found himself unable to control his emotions. Every night he woke up around two a.m. crying. He was an infantry-man and had recurring nightmares of the bloodshed he'd seen. I sat with him for a while until he felt better, then explained that he needed to get professional counseling to talk about his issues. After some coaxing, he agreed. He said talking to me was easier than he'd thought it would be. He felt confident that he could do it again. He didn't want to see someone on the depot because he was afraid it might hurt his career. I gave him the numbers of Military OneSource and TriCare, which both provided free counseling for military members.

He promised he would call, but that wasn't enough for me. I had heard this story too many times to hope he would make the call. I picked up my cell phone and had him schedule the first appointment in my presence. I then had him call his wife and tell her when he'd scheduled the appointment. That way I knew someone else was aware of the appointment, which made his commitment and accountability to show up more likely. This type of situation was becoming more and more commonplace for me.

Although each of the Marines' stories was unique, the overall issues were the same. Many of them had things they were struggling with, and they didn't know how to get help. They knew there were a multitude of programs available, but they were never going to make that call. When they sat with me, it was easy and natural. Because everyone did it, from the company commander down, they were not singled out. Often Marines would cry in session and then comment that they felt so much better afterward. I can't even imagine what it would be like to carry the burdens and secrets that they did. Now that I was beginning to truly understand recruit training, I understood that because of how these men and women were trained, things would have to be really bad before they ever admitted that they needed help. This was an organization that demanded excellence; weakness, whether mental or physical, was looked down upon. I believed in my purpose on the depot and was determined to have the program continue even with the new leadership.

I decided it was worth the effort to stop by and share my concerns with Col. Chester; he was the most senior officer in the Recruit Training Regiment. I was still paranoid about walking into people's offices, but now that I wasn't under Barbara, I was feeling more confident. I knew that Col. Chester was aware of the work I was doing, mostly because he would see me on a daily basis walking around the depot. I knew he was a busy man and probably hadn't even thought of how the change of command would impact the newly found proactive MFLC program and me. I was curious to see if he had any suggestions on how I should handle things with the new commanders. I would have called him first, but as a temporary contractor, I didn't have access to the depot data base and did not have his phone number. I was very nervous about just showing up but felt the visit was warranted.

The Recruit Training Regiment (RTR) building was intimidating. There were "restricted access" signs everywhere. I timidly entered the building and made my way down the hall to the front office. I announced that I was there to see Colonel Chester. Of course when asked if I had an appointment, I had to reply "no." The Marine behind the desk said that Col. Chester only saw people by appointment, but he would ask if he had a few minutes to talk to me. While he was gone, I was so nervous; this felt like a bold move. The Marine came back a few minutes later and said that Col. Chester would see me.

I walked in and immediately apologized for not calling and scheduling a visit ahead of time. He smiled and asked me to have a seat. I should have known that he would be accommodating; all the officers I had encountered thus far had been incredibly respectful. I gave him a brief overview of the services that I had been providing to Recruit Training Regiment. I told him about the BMP groups and the unique issues they were dealing with. I told him about the 2nd Battalion groups and how I was meeting with the drill instructors a few times during their cycles. I informed him of how the Marines were starting to trust me and open up. I also told him about how the individual sessions in 1st Battalion were going and how beneficial proactive counseling was proving to be. I shared a few generic stories about Marines and how they'd been able to get help with their issues before the problems escalated. I told him how I was proud that the stigma of mental health issues was decreasing and that reluctance to see me was almost nonexistent. There's no stigma when everyone does it, especially the leaders. I expressed to him my concerns about the trends I was seeing with the DIs and how the pressures of their demanding schedules were affecting them.

He appeared impressed. I don't think he had realized how much I knew. He took me into what he called his "strategic planning room." I sat at the long boardroom table as he drew me diagrams on the white board. He showed me his vision for drill instructor teams and shared the obstacles that were getting in the way. We talked some more and brainstormed.

I couldn't help but reminisce in my mind about the first time I had seen Col. Chester. It was at that first graduation I attended. When he entered the parade deck, the entire audience fell silent. We all knew we were in the presence of a leader. As far as recruit training goes, he was the "top dog," reporting directly to the general. This man was no-nonsense. He strived for perfection from his men and women and would settle for nothing less.

I tried to give him concrete examples of how I felt the MFLC program was helping both the drill instructors and the companies. The individual sessions were helping the DIs with their personal issues and the groups were helping the companies bond and grow as a collective whole. He concurred that he had received great feedback on my work. He shared with me that recently a company commander had told him a story about one of the Marines. He had said that one of his drill instructors had shared with him that he had seriously been contemplating taking his own life. Talking about his personal problems with a stranger was something he would never have done. But since he had to go through the mandatory process of talking with me, he was somewhat forced to share what was going on with him. The company commander told Col. Chester that as a direct result of the proactive sessions, I'd helped him get the assistance he needed. That Marine was taking some time off now to get better. Col. Chester assumed I knew exactly whom he was talking about. We both knew better than to discuss names because confidentiality was an utmost priority for me. Truth be told, I had no idea whom he was talking about. I'd had similar situations happen quite often.

Col. Chester decided with me that he would like all of the drill instructors to have proactive one-on-one sessions. They all deserved to meet with a counselor every few months. He also wanted to have all of the companies partake in the groups. We talked for a while more to figure out logistically how I could make all of that happen. He asked me to meet with every drill instructor during pick-up week and then do groups with every company during the middle of their cycle. I knew that would be a huge undertaking, but I also knew how amazing it would be to be able to expose all five to six hundred drill instructors to mental health counseling.

I figured that this would be as good a time as ever to explain to him that I would have to leave in a month for six weeks. I had stretched my six-week contract as much as HWM would possibly allow, but after I took a six-week break, I could come back for another rotation. I was hoping this news would not affect his decision to make the MFLC services mandatory across the depot. I knew better than to ask HWM if I could stay another cycle, but leaving while I had so much momentum was going to be very tough. As I expected, Col. Chester wasn't pleased with the news. For a brief moment, he even considered taking everything off the table. He stressed the importance of consistency and said this rotation thing went against the very nature of an effective program. He felt strongly that I was successful with the drill instructors because I understood them and the unique issues they faced. I explained that I already knew HWM wouldn't let me stay but that I'd be more than happy to volunteer my time for the six weeks. I didn't care about not getting paid; the only thing I cared about was continuing to get desperately needed mental health services to these Marines.

What I didn't tell him was that I had no idea if I would be able to keep up the demanding pace. This was a lot of Marines I was committing to seeing. On the other hand, hard work has never been an issue for me, and the opportunity to bring mental health services to all these Marines was so profound that the outcome seemed more important than the details.

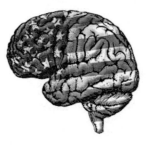

BATTLING BUREAUCRACY

T he next day I received a call from HWM. They wanted to inform me that they were going to start a weekly phone conference with all the MFLCs working on Marine bases. This was exciting. It would mean that once a week I would have some support and a direct contact at HWM. John was now the new supervisor; my previous contact, Donna, had been promoted to a higher-level position. John was very nice and right from the start admitted that he knew almost nothing about the military and the MFLC program. The first conference call was a disappointment. The majority of the MFLCs had very little to offer. They reported things like "I was really excited because I met a captain this week and he let me brief him about the program" or "I had two sessions this week with Marines." The most common issue was regarding the difficulties they were having with the staff in the counseling offices. It was almost always revolving around the same issues I was having—they didn't trust the MFLCs. From my perspective, understanding how little oversight there was, I could understand their fears.

I felt a little guilty. My situation had gotten so much better since I was not working out of the Family Support Services office. When I'd first arrived at MCRD, I'd spent most of my day trying to figure out how I could get in front of a Marine. Now I spent all day, nonstop working the Marines. I was averaging getting in front of over one hundred Marines a week.

Mondays I would always have two groups, along with individual and marital sessions at my office in the library. The BMP groups were heavily attended. I was often told that those one-hour groups were the highlight of their week. They were enjoyable for me as well. These new Marines had not been deployed yet, and their issues revolved more around the anxiety of the unknown.

I also had a handful of drill instructors with whom I was doing extra individual work. The majority of their issues grew from disturbing incidents that had occurred while they were deployed or relationship problems. Most weren't comfortable talking about their war experiences with their loved ones, but they couldn't get the images out of their minds. Many carried around significant guilt that they had killed innocent women and children. Others struggled with the sheer brutality of the bloodshed they'd observed. Feeling emotionally out of control and drinking excessively were common complaints. Nightmares, night sweats, flashbacks, and melancholy were issues that almost every one of them struggled with.

My Tuesdays and Wednesdays were spent meeting with the drill instructors for the mandatory individual sessions. They were in classes all day, and I would pull them out one at a time for about twenty minutes each. I had to make sure that I completed sessions with all thirty of them from each company during their two days of instruction prior to the new cycle starting. The days were long. I'd start around seven a.m. and would be lucky to get out of the depot by seven p.m.

Although each and every Marine was unique, the problems they were all dealing with were uncannily similar. They all really welcomed the opportunity to talk. I think the best way to describe it would be that the majority of these men carried invisible wounds. They had sacrificed everything to defend our country. They'd left their spouses and families for six to twelve months at a time. Many were home for only a few months before they were sent back again. Still, they never complained; that was not their style. This was a voluntary force, and they were part of the brave and the proud. Nine out of ten of them would go back in a heartbeat. They had a sense of purpose and were determined to do their job well. On the other hand, the repercussions were huge! They carried so much guilt and shame, and they had no idea what to do about it. They didn't think anyone else felt the way they did, and they were embarrassed about their feelings.

After meeting with multiple Marines week after week, I really began to understand the underlying mental health issues. Many, many Marines would share stories about how they'd lost men under their command, in either Iraq or Afghanistan. They felt tremendous guilt and couldn't help thinking that if they had done things differently a Marine would still be alive or would not have gotten so critically injured. Many talked about hearing screams from an enemy who was shot; they couldn't get the sounds out of their heads.

The thing that amazed me more than the stories was that these men had never shared their feelings before. It took me a long time to understand why that was. In my private practice in the civilian world, people couldn't wait to share their stories. The military is a very different climate. Everyone can tell a Marine to go talk to somebody, even his command can tell him to do it, but unless everyone else is doing it (like in this program), most would never go voluntarily.

I was also starting to recognize that different men exposed to the same circumstances related to similar events differently. It had nothing to do with strengths or weaknesses but more with the predisposition of their personalities. By listening to their stories, I could tell what type of coping methods they used to handle their stress. When tensions mounted, some became introverted and withdrawn; others resorted to angry outbursts and engaged in chronic marital fights, while others turned to alcohol. Even the Marines who were not having negative ramifications from their behaviors still reported having negative urges and had to learn ways to cope. I used a lot of time during the individual sessions to do psychological education, tailored to individual issues. For example, I talked to the Marine who'd punched a hole in the wall the previous week about anger management and gave him techniques to utilize, instead of acting out. With a Marine who didn't feel like he could relate to his family anymore because they could not understand what he had been through, I talked about communication skills and tried to help him comprehend the implications of continuing to withdraw.

Thursdays I was at Camp Pendleton. I did green belt groups, senior drill instructor groups, groups with the series commanders and chief drill instructors, and lastly groups with the first sergeants and company commanders to go over themes, concerns, and issues in the companies. The groups became a powerful part of my work. Once I recognized the common issues these men were dealing with, I could help them see that they were not alone. All it took was for one DI to open up, and the dialogue would start to fly. In the groups the men came to realize they were all struggling with similar issues and they needed to help and support one another. Those who were not dealing with those issues still had a lot to offer by sharing and supporting their fellow Marines. A side benefit of the groups was that team cohesion became a lot stronger, which led to greater job satisfaction and helped minimize the stressors. Having the groups with every level of the company seemed to help with communication and helped eradicate personality issues that could lead to unnecessary work tensions and frustrations. After completing all the Thursday groups, my Camp Pendleton work was not done. I received numerous referrals from both the chaplain there and the Weapons and Field Training Battalion office. I typically had back-to-back sessions scheduled for the entire afternoon and into the evening.

Fridays were also long. I went to every weekly company recruit graduation. These events never lost their magic for me. They were a culmination for the drill instructors, and I wanted to be there to show my support to them. I also found them to be very inspiring. I was now always invited inside the red rope where the drill instructors would stand. Sometimes I would sit in the viewing stand. The Marines always made sure I had a seat, which made me feel valued and appreciated. These ceremonies were often the highlight of my week. My Friday afternoons were spent in more private sessions and doing paperwork for HWM.

Although my days were long, the work was tremendous. I no longer wondered if I was making a difference—I knew I was. Every once in a while I talked to someone who was opposed to a proactive counseling approach, saying you shouldn't force someone to talk. I didn't agree. I truly saw how well it was working. After doing it for three months, I couldn't believe that every military base didn't do it this way. It was not about forcing someone to share his feelings; on the contrary, it was providing the opportunity to talk while removing the stigma of having to ask for it. I was just starting to really get momentum at MCRD (Marine Corps Recruit Depot), and the thought of rotating out made me incredibly anxious. What if the new MFLC couldn't keep up with the intense pace or didn't understand the complex issues these men were dealing with?

After one of our weekly conference calls with John from HWM, I stayed on the line and asked him if there were any way

I could stay at the depot and not leave for the upcoming six-week rotation. I knew that he wouldn't have authority to make a decision, but I had to hope that he would properly share my story with his chain of command. A few days later John called to tell me that I would not be able to stay. He said that HWM had to maintain the integrity of its contract with the OSD (Office of the Secretary of Defense), and technically I shouldn't have been there for more than twelve weeks. I already knew that—it was what I had been told from the beginning. I also knew my leaving was definitely not what was in the best interest of the Marines

Now that there were weekly telephone conference calls, I had an opportunity to meet the other MFLCs who were working at other bases. I found out that one base, Quantico, had two MFLCs who never rotated out. Parris Island also had a special situation and kept their MFLCs for longer cycles. My problem was that I didn't feel like I had anyone on the depot advocating for me. My POC, Kathy, was so busy it seemed like every time I went to see her I was bothering her. I had learned after my experience with Barbara not to bother anyone unless it was a necessity.

I did receive confirmation that I would be coming back to MCRD after the six-week break. I didn't want to make waves at HWM, but I really didn't want to leave. How could someone new come in and grasp all I had learned with just a two-day turnover? I desperately wanted the program to continue without interruption in the coming months. Volunteering my time on the depot seemed like the perfect alternative. A new MFLC was coming to replace me, but the two of us could work together. I didn't mind not getting paid, and I knew with two MFLCs we could really get this program up and running smoothly. It felt too new and vulnerable for me to walk away at this point

The next day I ran into Lt. Col. Rowe (the head of MCCS— Marine Corps Community Services) on the depot. He asked me how things were going. I of course shared my enthusiasm but also told him of my apprehensions about having to leave for six weeks. I shared with him my idea of seeing if I could volunteer my time during the six weeks so I wouldn't have to leave. I also assured him that if I couldn't, I would be back at the end of the six weeks for another three to four and a half months. He had a very concerned look on his face, which reinforced my fears that this required break might not be perceived well. He asked if there was anything he could do. I explained that it was a contractual issue and there wasn't anything that could be done about it. He said he was going to e-mail HWM anyway on his own to ask about possibilities. A few days later I received this e-mail message from Donna at HWM:

Hi Marjorie...

Some really nice words from Col. Rowe about you and the work you are doing at MCRD.

Wanted to be sure you saw my response to Col. Rowe as he was asking about the possibility of you extending and, as we previously discussed, it was already stretched one rotation beyond OSD guidelines and cannot be further stretched. I am confident that you will ensure the base that the work HWM does on the whole is quality work and a new consultant need not breed any anxiety.

Please let me know if you have any questions. I can be reached at the cell phone number below.

Thanks,
Donna J. White
Manager, Clinical Operations
Military and Family Life Consultant Program
HWM Governmental Services

The e-mail communication between Lt. Col. Rowe and Denise, which she forwarded, read as follows:

Donna,

Wanted to find out if we here at Marine Corps Recruit Depot SD have any options of keeping Ms. Morrison on, as she has been providing some very useful services to the Marines, particularly in the Recruit Training Regiment (RTR). She has set up a number of support groups which she leads and the feedback from the commanders has been excellent.

Respectfully,
Lt. Col. T. E. Rowe

Good Afternoon Lt. Col. Rowe,

I am thrilled to hear about how well Marjorie is doing on her assignment at the Marine Corps Recruit Depot. She certainly is an asset to HWM and we love to hear about differences the consultants are making on bases we provide consulting services to.

As you are aware, our guidance on rotations (durations and lengths) comes from OSD. The current guidance is that consultants are not allowed to do more than 2 consecutive rotations at any one location. There was an exception made just recently for Marjorie to stay one additional 45-day rotation which started on 6/29 with the understanding that she would break once that is completed.

That being said, we are already working with Marjorie to bring her back after the 45 day break and will staff her as much as we are able (and she is willing) within OSD guidelines.

Thank you so much for the support you provide to the MFLC program. The next consultant will overlap with Marjorie for a couple of days so Marjorie can bring the person up to speed on everything and Marjorie will also be creating a transition report as well for the new consultant to use as a guide to the goings on while Marjorie is on break.

Please let me know if you have any questions or concerns.

Thanks,
Donna J. White
Manager, Clinical Operations
Military and Family Life Consultant Program
HWM Governmental Services

I was a little irritated that they never addressed the issue of my volunteering my time in the e-mail exchange. I already knew and understood that the contract did not have the flexibility for me to stay on. Later that week I saw Col. Chester at a change of command ceremony. I told him that I had struck out with my attempts to stay during the six weeks. I reassured him that I had formalized the program to my best ability and intended on explaining things in great detail to my replacement. Regardless, he was upset and found the whole thing to be ridiculous. I wanted to agree with him but remained professional. The problem was that as a result, he wanted to forget the entire program. He wasn't comfortable having a stranger coming in and talking to all of his Marines. He insisted that he send a letter to my supervisor asking for a special circumstance so I could stay. It was frustrating because I felt that if HWM were doing what was in the best interest of the Marines, they would let me continue to work with the drill instructors.

I had been very meek thus far but decided it was time to try being a little more aggressive. I left Donna a number of messages over the following week. I reported to her that I knew Quantico did not rotate out their MFLCs and all I wanted was for her to listen to my case before making her decision if I could volunteer my time over the six-week break. I truly did not want any compensation during the six weeks; I just wanted to keep the program going. Finally I received a return e-mail from Donna.

Hi Marjorie,

First off my apologies for not getting back in touch with you earlier as I know you left me a message yesterday in addition to today. Between business travel and keeping up with everything I have going on unrelated to the travel, I often find myself with very little time and you always say in your voicemails "no rush" and so I always think I will call when I have a chance but I find those chances are few and far between.

I will ask our directors their thoughts on your request to volunteer during your break and find out who they would like this letter you mentioned the base will be writing to be sent/copied to at HWM. The people I want to touch base with are all out of the office on business travel the remainder of the week so Monday would be the earliest I could get a response on this for you.

I know they do believe that part of being an effective MFLC is to allay concerns about the rotating nature of the program so no doubt they will question why there would be such a sense of panic given how great of a job you do out there.

Please let me know if Monday is early enough...if not, please forward/direct to me and I will forward on.

Have to join a conference call…

Thanks.
Donna J. White
Manager, Clinical Operations
Military and Family Life Consultant Program
HWM Governmental Services

I never heard back from Donna, but the next week I gave her a call. She explained that the MFLC program had a new boss and he felt very strongly about the MFLCs rotating out every six weeks. She gave me his number but said she was doubtful that he would let me stay on the base, voluntarily or not. I called him later that night. I was surprised he answered, but he didn't listen to one word I said. He interrupted me, telling me, "There is a new sheriff in town, and from here forward, no MFLC will stay at a base for more than one rotation." He clearly did not care about my circumstance. One thing I now knew for sure, in my case HWM did not have the Marines' best interest in mind. It was beginning to feel like all they cared about was keeping the contract and of course maintaining the profits for the company. He made me promise that I would not go on the base during my rotation off and said if I did, I could be putting the entire MFLC program in jeopardy.

I couldn't let this setback get me down. After all, I knew upfront the limitations of the MFLC contract. I had been at the depot for almost four and a half months, and they did extend the contract for me once already. I had to figure out a way to make this program run as seamlessly as possible so that the new MFLC could pick up where I left off.

My last week before the six-week break brought a surprising new obstacle. Bravo Company was having their pick-up. Bravo, which had a reputation as the best company on the depot, had already done a cycle of my individual sessions, so having me come in it was nothing new to them. It was the new battalion commander's first week on the depot. When I came in the morning to get started, he stood in front of the entire company and said, "Marines, you don't have to go in and see her. By a show of hands, does anyone have a problem they need to talk to her about?" It was no surprise that nobody responded. He shrugged his shoulders at me, saying, "We don't need you here." I was shocked and humiliated. This was the first opposition I'd had from any of the Marines since I had been on the Depot. As I walked from the room, the company commander followed me. He was harsh, cold, and very abrupt. He said, "I am the company commander here, and I will take care of my Marines. If they have any issues, which I highly doubt they will, they can talk to me and I will help them." I really didn't understand where this was coming from. I could have seen this happening in 2nd or 3rd Battalion because they were just getting stated with the one-on-ones. I certainly didn't expect it from a 1st Battalion company. I tried talking with him to understand this newfound animosity. It felt personal to me, but I wasn't sure why.

I went into the brand-new battalion commander's office. He had just taken over the command, and I hated to burden him with a problem. On the other hand, I really didn't know what to do. He was very nice and said that he had been directed by Colonel Chester that every drill instructor was to partake in the program. I really wanted this for the Bravo Company Marines because I remembered that three months earlier they had been dealing with a lot of stressful issues. What I didn't find out until later that day was that the Bravo company commander was a very good friend of Gretchen's from Family Support Services.

The time for my six weeks' rotation came. I expressed my concern to John at HWM about getting a strong person in to replace me. After a lot of begging, I was able to get the contact information for the new MFLC prior to his arrival in San Diego. His name was Gary, and I felt very fortunate to have him be the one to replace me. Gary had been a Marine, and although he was in his sixties and had been out of the corps for many years, he truly understood the Marine culture. The trust and bond that I had to work tirelessly to achieve with the drill instructors was there for Gary from the get-go. I didn't have to go into great detail regarding DIs because Gary had been through recruit training himself.

Luckily, Gary loved the program. He really embraced the notion of proactive counseling. When you tell most people that the Marines were required to come in for counseling, they assume that they wouldn't want to do that. I told Gary that about 95 percent of them loved coming in. During our few days of overlap, Gary heard many of the drill instructors say that seeing me was their favorite part of pick-up week because it felt like a huge stress release. We made an executive decision not to do groups with a company unless the company specifically asked Gary to do them. Our reason was that the groups were very complicated. You really needed to be able to speak the drill instructors' language and understand the depth of the issues they were talking about. If the facilitator didn't understand them, the issues could go right over his head and things could get very chaotic.

I spent so much time prepping Gary on the program, I practically forgot to mention the situation with Family Support Services. I guess it was because it felt so trivial and irrelevant compared to discussing the content of the work. I really didn't want to leave the depot. I did not want to share that sentiment with the Marines; that would be unprofessional, and I knew better than that. On the other hand, I found it very difficult to explain to the company and battalion commanders how the contract I was paid under was structured. The truth was without that MFLC program I wouldn't be there, so we all had to adjust. One of the many good things about the Marines is that they are used to change. Every two to three years a Marine is pulled out of whatever job he or she does and moved somewhere else. In addition, to them six weeks is nothing, and they knew I'd be back in no time.

Ultimately, the transition was pretty seamless. The "new sheriff" at HWM had instructed me that I was not allowed on the base during the six-week rotation in order to stay in agreement with the OSD (Office of Secretary of Defense) contract. I didn't intend to get them or me in trouble, so I passed the baton to Gary. One hitch was that I found out the day before I left that Kathy wouldn't be my POC at the depot anymore. Lt. Col. Rowe (from Marine Corps Family Services) was moving the program to Marine and Family Services. It still fell under his responsibilities, but he felt it was the best place to house the MFLC program. The director of that program was Theresa, and I had just met her for the first time right before I left. She seemed really nice, but I felt bad for both her and Gary that no continuity had been established.

I drove off the base with mixed emotions. I couldn't have asked for a better replacement than Gary. He was awesome, was excited about doing quality work, and had really bought into the proactive counseling approach. I also could really use some time off. Since I had been at MCRD (Marine Corps Recruit Depot), it was not uncommon for me to work ten to twelve hours a day. I was getting a lot of flack at home about never being there. My private practice had dwindled down to four or five cases that I would see on Saturdays. The thought of six weeks off sounded divine.

As I drove off the base, I called Gary. "I promise I won't call you every day, but I threw so much stuff at you, I want to make sure you understand to stay out of the way of Family Support Services. They don't like me, and consequently, they probably won't like you either."

He said, "No problem," but I could tell he was on complete overload.

My plan was to spend the six weeks learning as much as I could about the Marine Corps. I intended on reading books about recruit training, about being in war, about the value system of Marines, and anything else I could get my hands on. Everywhere I went, I found myself talking about the military. I was so enamored with this culture. It felt so rich. There was something so compelling about the way they go through life. It is as though, because they are part of the greater good of our country and because they are each an integral part of the institution, they have a vital purpose for their lives. As a result, I was learning that they do not suffer from the same type of generic depression that civilians do. We are always searching for our purpose. We are unclear of what our life contribution roles are and often find ourselves wanting to make a difference but not knowing how.

These men and women had issues, for sure, but they were different from civilian issues. These Marines had a tough exterior, and it was going to take more than someone posting a flyer for them to get help. In my pre-military life, people would come into counseling because they couldn't get their toddler to eat vegetables or they were afraid their eight-year-old had anxiety because he had four nightmares in six months. A Marine would go on three difficult deployments, have terrible nightmares, feel that he had lost control over his emotions, and yet in many cases would choose to drink his problems away rather than seek help.

So why were we approaching mental health services for the military the same way we were approaching them with civilians? I was excited to have some time to do some good research. I had a lot to learn.

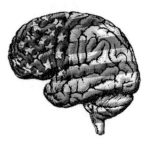

WHERE HELP IS FOUND

I began my six-week break by doing basic research. I was curious what was really going on in the military mental health world. Through my countless hours of initial reading, I found the same information everywhere. Suicides in all branches of the military were rising at an alarming rate. I learned that 72 percent of Marines who killed themselves in 2009 had deployed to a combat zone. [6] The counseling programs in the military were plentiful, and the military was trying to put the word out that seeking treatment was the right thing to do. But there was an inherent disconnect between saying it and it actually happening. The language that was used around the squadrons and the platoons was often still very derogatory with regards to seeking help. Even if they do ask for help, the on-base counseling programs are bogged down with referrals. On July 3, 2008, *TIME* magazine reported,

> "The scope of the problem is becoming enormous, the latest predictions show upwards of 20 percent of combat veterans are coming home from Iraq and Afghanistan with posttraumatic stress disorder (PTSD). As recently reported in TIME, the military is prescribing antidepressants to troops downrange to help blunt the psychological effects of combat. "There's just a tremendous need for counseling," says Paul Rieckhoff of Iraq and Afghanistan

Veterans of America. "The [Department of Veterans Affairs] psychological-counseling program is overwhelmed. The suicide rates for returning vets are just off the charts." [7]

I learned that less than 50 percent of the military reporting mental health issues sought assistance. [8] Despite the large sums of money put toward researching how to best handle these issues, the problems continued to rise. Longer deployments meant more time that military members were exposed to traumatic events. In addition, they were away from their families longer, creating more personal stress. The more I read, the more discouraged I became. There were countless articles on new programs being created. Didn't the leadership understand that the majority of military members probably weren't going to utilize them?

I remembered what Gunny Banks had said when I was first getting started. He had told me that if I needed any questions answered, all I had to do was ask a Marine. He was so right. It was the Marines who suggested the mandatory individual sessions, and it was the Marines that came up with the concept of the groups. All I did was facilitate their ideas. I wondered if the people that put military mental health programs together were talking to the folks on the ground about what types of services were needed? If they were asking the right questions, I assumed they would have figured out that perhaps they should be adding more proactive programs and less reactive ones.

If a service member in any branch decides that they want to get help, access for mental health/behavioral health/psychological health is routinely available through several venues at all bases. First, there is the Family Support Center; different branches of the military have different names for it. At MCRD they have it under the MCCS (Marine Corps Community Services). There are behavioral health clinics at every base, and they have sub-stance abuse clinics, regular mental health counseling and/or psy-chiatric medication management, and Family Advocacy.

There are also chaplains' offices, which can provide support and direct individuals to other care. TRICARE (the military health program) also allows up to six visits for counseling or mental health evaluation for active-duty families without a refer-ral from their primary care manager. Finally, Military OneSource offers twelve free confidential counseling sessions without need-ing to go through command or medical channels.

The problem is many of the programs require documentation, and if this information ends up in their permanent military file, it could affect their opportunity for advancement. The Marine Corps states this on their website:

> A fear Marines have is that their Commander will have complete access to their mental health records. However, confidentiality is maintained for most Marines who self-refer to Mental Health. In cases where information is released, the cases either involve mandatory reporting or the unit leadership was solicited to be a resource for the member (with the Marine's consent). [9]

To explain the concept of "mandatory reporting", the Army states on their website

> Sexual Assault is the most under reported crime in our soci-ety and in the military. While the Department of Defense prefers complete reporting of sexual assaults to activate both victims' services and law enforcement actions, it rec-ognizes that some victims desire only medical and support services and no command or law enforcement involve-ment. The Department believes its first priority is for victims to be protected, treated with dignity and respect,

and to receive the medical treatment, care and counseling that they deserve. Under DoD's Confidentiality Policy, sexual assault victims are offered two reporting options- Restriced reporting and Unrestricted reporting.-

Restricted reporting is described as an option recommended for victims of sexual assault who wish to confidentially disclose the crime to specifically identified individuals and receive medical treatment and counseling without triggering the official investigative process. Service members who are sexually assaulted and desire restricted reporting under this policy must report the assault to a Sexual Assault Response Coordinator (SARC), Victim Advocate (VA), a healthcare provider or chaplain. This policy on restricted reporting is in addition to the current protections afforded privileged communications with a chaplain, and does not alter or affect those protections. Healthcare providers will initiate the appropriate care and treatment, and report the sexual assault to the SARC in lieu of reporting the assault to law enforcement or the command.

Unrestricted reporting is described as the option that is recommended for victims of sexual assault who desire medical treatment, counseling and an official investigation of the crime." [10]

The Marine Corps website reports the same information adding that,

Some Marines incorrectly believe mental health information is entered into their Military Record. Mental health information is recorded in the outpatient medical record and the appropriate mental health file but not the Military Record unless they are found unfit or unsuitable for duty. [11]

The problem I found is all it takes is one person who feels that they were unjustly documented to tarnish the views for others to have confidence that it will be kept confident. I remember a Marine officer who told me his story about how he went to the substance abuse center on the depot for help with his alcohol issue and was told his treatment would remain confidential. He later found out that his commander was notified. It was not put in his permanent file and his leader was most likely notified as "a resource," but it still left the Marine with a negative experience.

One of the ways this is circumvented is by providing programs that are put in place to augment the on-base services. The two largest are the MFLC (Military Family Life Consultant) program that I am contracted with and the Military OneSource program. Military OneSource is considered the best-known program for both service members and their families. It is a free service with a 24/7 toll-free number staffed by trained consultants. Military OneSource also offers access to a wide range of financial, legal, moving, and home repair services. It contracts with licensed mental health providers to provide service members, and their families, free counseling, and psycho-education services. Active-duty service members, reserve component members, and deployed government civilians and their families are eligible.

The problem with both of those programs is that a counselor is only allowed to see V-codes. What that means to a non-clinician is best described in the e-mail below, which I received from Military OneSource's contractor, Ceridian.

Dear Ceridian provider,
The *Ceridian Affiliate Provider Guide* has been recently updated with important information concerning the Military OneSource (MOS) Scope of Practice.

Please read through the guide to update yourself with the most recent MOS guidelines.

The following breakdown is an overview of issues that are deemed appropriate or inappropriate for short-term, solution-focused EAP counseling services for *Military OneSource referrals only:*

Appropriate issues for short-term, solution-focused, problem-solving counseling services include, but are not limited to, subclinical (V-Code) issues such as:

- Relationship issues, parenting skills, communication

- Relocation, academic or occupational problems

- Anger management, grief, stress, adjustment, deployment, reintegration, separation

- Phase of life, decision-making, life skills, coping skills and interpersonal skills

- *Inappropriate* issues for short-term, solution-focused, problem-solving counseling services include, but are not limited to:

- Post -Traumatic Stress Disorder (PTSD), Traumatic Brain Injury (TBI), and any mental disorder, (Axis I or II other than V Codes) identified in the *Diagnostic and Statistical Manual of Mental Disorders*, Latest Edition

- Chronic or multiple issues stemming from underlying conditions that are more ingrained or severe, including substance-related disorders

- Active suicidal/homicidal thought or intent or other threats of harm to self or others

- *Inappropriate* situations include:

- If Client is working with a mental health professional (in individual, couples, family or group counseling) or prescriber of psychoactive medication (such as Zoloft, Prozac, Ambien, etc.)

- If Client has a history of recurring in-patient mental health treatment (hospitalized more than one time for mental health issue)

- If Client has an open case with Family Support Services, Victim Advocate, Sexual Assault Response Coordinator or child protective services (this includes if a mandated report or Duty-to-Warn report is indicated)

- If Client is requesting a formal evaluation, assessment or treatment regarding fitness for duty, return-to work-recommendation, medical-leave documentation/recommendation and/or court-ordered counseling/treatment

- In the event a client presents with an inappropriate issue or situation that is out of scope, as identified above, please assist the participant with a referral and warm hand-off to the appropriate services

- Referrals for active duty may be made to base mental health treatment facility or TRICARE

- Family members of an active-duty service member would be referred to TRICARE

- National Guard/Reservist and/or family member would be referred to community resources or through their private insurance

- Once the referral is made, the MOS EAP case is closed

Although the scope makes sense from a program stand-point, it is very limiting from a practical standpoint. The MFLC program is very similar, according to the IIWM website: "MFLCs provide informal support and outreach for Service Members and families. MFLCs work exclusively with V-codes; they do not diagnose or treat mental disorders."[12] (Mental disorders are referred to military mental health resources or other professional resources.) So essentially, if a service member is experiencing PTSD or any other diagnosable issue, they must go through the military system. The biggest concern with this is not that it gets reported in the file (we refuted that earlier); it is that it is still based on a reactive model. The person is not going to seek help until there is already a problem. We now know that the longer a problem exists the harder it is to recover from it.

In addition to the two nongovernment programs I mentioned above, there are quite a few more available. These programs vary greatly from base to base and also by different branches. Some of these are run through the government and others are not. I will go into more detail about additional programming in the chapter: "New Trends in Preventative and Resiliency." Below are a few of the larger, non-government run programs.

- Give an Hour: www.giveanhour.org: This is a nonprofit group founded in 2005 to develop national networks of volunteer mental health providers to meet the mental health needs of the troops and families affected by the ongoing conflicts in Iraq and Afghanistan. They provide counseling to individuals, couples and families, and children and adolescents.

- The Coming Home Project: www.cominghomeproject.net: Started in 2006, this nonprofit organization provides free counseling and retreats for service members and their families. It is based in Northern California but has a referral network throughout the United States.

- The Soldiers Project: www.thesoldiersproject.org: This is a private, nonprofit group of volunteer licensed mental health professionals who provide free counseling and support to military service members and veterans.

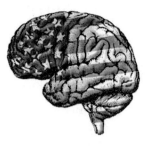

RECRUIT TRAINING EFFECTS

A week before I had left the depot for the six-week break, one of the battalion commanders had invited me to watch the beginning of the recruit training process. What a treat that was for me! I arrived at the depot the middle of the night and stood there amongst a group of drill instructors and officers waiting for the buses loaded with recruits to arrive. I'm not sure what I had expected to see, but I was surprised to find how young the new recruits looked. They looked scared, confused, and dazed. Some of them had been awake for twenty hours or more, since they had reported to their military processing stations the day before.

"Now" is the first word that they will hear. This is a reminder that for the next three months they will be locked in the present. They will not be told anything in regards to their schedule. They will be told to march, and they will find out the next thing to do when they stop marching. I was informed that they are brought in at night to add to their nervousness, exaggerating fear and intimidation. Within a few minutes, the DI shouts out a welcoming speech and demands instant compliance to orders. Simply getting through three months of boot camp will consume all their mental and physical energy. However, at this initial point, the corps wants only to disorient the arriving recruits, not shatter them. The job is to strip them of their civilian ways before building them into Marines. Every drill instructor they meet will talk to them the same way. Nothing is considered theirs, not even the right to be called "Marine." They are simply "recruits" and will have to earn the title and right to be called Marine.

Once they get off the bus, they stand on rows of yellow footprints painted on the asphalt. The footprints, four to a row, eighteen rows, are so closely packed that you cannot tell the newcomers apart from one another. Watching them standing there practically heel to toe, with their faces barely visible, they look like one mass. There was no more individuality for this new batch of recruits.

Shortly before the bus arrived, I stood on a pair of yellow footprints. It had a completely different feel for me when I stood there alone in comparison to these recruits standing there with their bodies smashed together. I asked one of the company commanders what a typical recruit class was comprised of—in other words, who were these kids? He explained that the majority of them are eighteen and nineteen years old, with a few of the men in their twenties. The youngest is typically seventeen and the oldest is twenty-seven. Most of them come to the corps without strong prospects in the civilian world. They are, with a few exceptions, from the bottom half of the American economy. "They are mostly poor kids with lousy educations," chimed a DI who overheard our conversation. "This is their chance to achieve excellence."

There is no sugar coating the experience a recruit will go through on their journey to become a Marine. I watched the recruits as they attempted to follow the drill instructors' orders and march to the next spot. I knew that in just a few weeks that march would be much sharper, with an emphasis on every movement. The hallway I stood in was lined with posters and signs. I read each one as I walked through the cold, dark hallway: "We promise you sleep deprivation, mental torment, and muscles so sore you'll puke. But we don't want to sugar coat it." Another read, "Nobody ever drowned in sweat." The next one read, "Pain is temporary. Pride is forever." I continued down the corridor reading them one at a time. "The deadliest weapon in the world: a Marine and his rifle." "Marine, your best friend, your worst enemy." "The most dangerous place is between a Marine and his country." "Marines fear only God. No others." "It's not an attitude problem. We are that good." "To err is human, to forgive is divine. However, neither is Marine Corps policy." "Some people spend an entire lifetime wondering if they made a difference. The Marines don't have that problem."

When I looked up, I could no longer see the recruits. They had officially begun their processing which starts immediately with the removal of all contrabands (tobacco, food, cards, cologne, etc). This initial receiving of recruits lasts four disorienting days. They go through physical exams, including medical and dental exams, urinalysis and HIV testing. If any illegal drug use is found in the urinalysis results, they are immediately expelled. They will receive the infamous thirty-second "cranial amputation" haircuts designed to remove individuality.

During this initial phase, they learn about the chain of command, weapons safety, saluting, standing interior guard, and how to break in boots. They receive an unloaded rifle and are taught how to handle it. The recruits are required to carry their rifle with them wherever they go to emphasize its importance. All Marines are trained first and foremost as warriors and are all considered equally suited for the work. The stripping of individuality happens in many different ways. The most obvious is how the recruits are addressed as "Private" or called by their last name only. They are not allowed to speak unless spoken to, and "Sir" or "Ma'am" is an obligatory part of every answer they give. Recruits are forbidden to use the word "I" to refer to themselves. Instead, they refer to themselves in the third person, saying, "This recruit requests…" and so on. I once read a story about a recruit that swat a fly from his face. This type of behavior is not permitted, and the drill instructor held a funeral for the insect to drive home the message of concentration and self-discipline. Marines should not be bothered by something as trivial as a small insect.[13] I remember a drill instructor tell me during a one-on-one session that he made a group of recruits click a pen open and closed thirty times to hone in on the concept of paying attention to every fine detail of their actions.

A few days later, I was able to observe the IST (initial strength test). This is given to be sure that the recruit is strong enough to handle the grueling training ahead. The minimum requirements are that they must be able to do two pull-ups from a dead hung, forty-four sit ups in two minutes, and a one and a half–mile run in under thirteen minutes. For females it is different, but they do not have females at the Recruit Depot in San Diego. The female recruits go to Marine Corps Recruit Depot in Parris Island, which is on the coast of South Carolina. By the end of recruit training, the recruits can do these basic tasks in their sleep.

Drill instructors are no longer allowed to touch recruits, meaning they need to discipline them in other ways. One of the more common methods they employ is called "IT" standing for incentive training or incentive torture. There are strict regulations of the use and durations of IT exercises, but the drill instructors have this spelled out for them in their Recruit Training Pocket Guide, which they carry with them at all times. Recruits spend the majority of their time marching and drilling, much of it designed to train them to act as a team. When I would first watch them practice, I couldn't understand what the point was. The majority of the new Marines were going to go into combat, so why so much emphasis on drill? I later came to find out that drill teaches discipline, develops team spirit, provides combat formations, and is used to move units around in an orderly manner.

There are three phases to recruit training. Phase one is divided into three four-week phases. The focus is on physical conditioning, self-defense, and close-order drilling. They take classes on USMC core values and history and learn general military skills, bayonet techniques, customs, and courtesies. As they move toward the middle and end of phase one, they begin a more detailed instruction, including first aid, physical training, weapons handling, USMC history and terrorism awareness, circuit course, inoculations, confidence course, USMC leadership course, Uniform Code of Military Justice, senior drill instructor inspection, series commander inspection, and initial drill evaluation.

Phase two is weeks five though eight, where the emphasis is in combat water survival and weapons marksmanship. The first "swim week" takes place along with the Marine Corps Martial Arts Program testing and a five-mile conditioning test. The recruits at San Diego Marine Corps Recruit Depot head up to Camp Pendleton for a few weeks where they work on their shooting skills. At the end of phase two comes "team week," which features an obstacle course and ten-mile conditioning march that emphasizes team skills.

During phase three, weeks nine through twelve, the focus shifts to basic warrior skills. They learn about weapons training and night firing, they go through a combat endurance course, basic field skills, final drill competition, final physical training test, rappelling tower, company commanders inspection, defensive driving course, land navigation, and the military operations in urban terrain (MOUT) movement course. The last week is culminated by the famous crucible, which is a fifty-four-hour, no-rest intensive test of the recruits' new skills. It is a grueling experience where the recruit is challenged above and beyond his limits. It involves strenuous physical activity combined with food and sleep deprivation and mentally challenging exercises. The recruits travel forty-two miles carrying their full combat gear, sleep no more that eight hours, and eat less than three MREs (Meals Ready to Eat). While they are doing this, they must solve over thirty problematic exercises and challenging obstacles. As the crucible continues, teamwork becomes essential, with recruits helping each other when they need it. They learn that they become stronger as a unit when they all contribute to their success. When it is over, the recruits have a "warriors breakfast" and an emblem ceremony. This is the moment when recruits actually receive the name Marine and see their families for the first time in three months. It is held a day before the big graduation.

The research I was doing helped me realize just how important the understanding of recruit training is. As one can see, the transformation that occurs during that three-month time is very calculated. Recruits learn to rely on their drill instructors for instruction of their next move. They learn to trust the institution and to think as a collective whole and not as an individual. I now understood why Marines may not feel comfortable going outside of the system to ask for help, even if it is an on base counseling center. They have been trained to rely on their superiors to take care of all their needs. So why would they go talk to somebody else if their superiors are the ones who are supposed to take care of them?

Because Marines are trained to be self-reliant and to complete the mission at all cost, it is unacceptable for many of them to ask for help or to receive assistance when offered. My research has shown me that historically, this has been the major barrier to receiving care and continues to be the case with present-day veterans. The underlying meta message is very clear: a strong Marine will not need to go outside command for anything. Although this wasn't spoken, it was implied. When people become Marines, they are giving up large pieces of their personal identity. They drop their first name and are called by their rank. They are taught "instantaneous obedience to orders," which ultimately means they have to trust those with authority. One has to believe that the institution has their best interest in mind and that if they obeyed orders they would be protected as best as possible.

I also now understood just how much the Marines really cared about each other. The drill instructors did not treat any single recruit differently—"equal opportunity for all, special privilege for none." These men were transformed into a strong working unit. Starting in recruit training they learned how to depend on each other. Watching how this occurred was a truly magical experience. New Marines would share that when a new task was assigned, they could depend on their new brothers to help them accomplish it. By the same token, they knew collectively that they could depend on the corps, and in return the corps depended on them to defend our nation. I no longer wondered why such a spirit of brotherhood was absent in our civilian world. We could do so much more as a nation if we also collectively ignored race, color, religion, and economical status.

The Marines also took leadership very seriously. They worked hard to earn the trust of their men and genuinely wanted what was best for them. The problem I found was that they didn't always know how to help their subordinates if they were having a hard time or not working up to their potential. I was beginning to understand why the commanders liked my individual and group sessions so much. I helped them gain insight into their companies. They wanted to know what was going on with their men. They had no other way to obtain that information. I would teach them how to effectively talk to and elicit candid conversations with their Marines.

I now understood why Bravo Company was initially concerned with my groups. The commander adamantly discouraged his men from going outside of the company to get help. If they had a problem, he wanted them to go to him or the first sergeant for help. From there, they would come up with a plan. Now I was beginning to see the underlying nuances of being a strong Marine. One of the most poignant things I read that helped drive this point home for me was by Dick Schading, former sergeant, U.S. Marine Corps, called "Being a Marine."

> It is hard to explain what it is to be a Marine to someone who is not one. The title "Marine" is not just a word. It's like a living, breathing Corps: a warrior spirit, which connects you with all the rest of the thing, from its historic past to the present, that cannot change for those that will follow in the future. The Corps is a place where honor, tradition, pride, and an inability to fail are not just words or obscure concepts but rather a reality that lasts a lifetime.
>
> The Corps is a place where lifelong friends are made, and sometimes lost, at very young ages. November 10, 1775, will always be a Marine's other birthday for one who has earned the right to call anything associated with the Navy (except the Corpsman) rude and demeaning names.
>
> Among the wonderful life lessons learned from the Corps are the facts that taking pride in what you do and how you appear are not character flaws. Working until a job or objective has been completed is expected and is the right way it should be done. Never giving up on friends, jobs, or anything else is keeping with the training and tradition of the Corps and becomes a part of your character forever.
>
> One of the less-than-wonderful lessons learned from the Corps is that you cannot give up on friends, family, or relationships, even when it's the logical thing to do.

Failure, by one's self or by friends and loved ones, is not just an obscure concept, but a crushing experience that is extraordinarily hard to deal with. In combat, errors or mission "failures" sometimes equates to death. Simple mistakes cost lives in the blink of an eye or the flash of an M16. The losses of my young friends so long ago are still very hard to come to grips with, and not preventing these losses are still considered personal failures.

It is said that Marines are made at Parris Island. It is true that the training and fine edge are put on there, and the formal induction into the Corps is begun at graduation with the awarding of the title United States Marine, but I think that the warrior heart and soul of a true Marine are there from birth.[14]

Being a civilian, I know I do not truly know what it means to be a Marine, or any service member for that matter, but throughout my research, I was gaining a lot more insight. The sense of brotherhood and sisterhood was thick, and going outside for help could be seen as breaking that bond. I now understood with more clarity why the proactive counseling programming was working as well as it was. If everyone participated in it, it removed the stigma, and because I conducted the sessions in the battalions, it could be viewed as staying within the system.

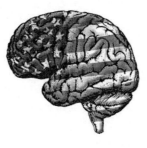

GROWING PAINS
AND MORE PROGRESS

I felt I made good use of my time away and learned as much as I could about the military during my break. I had very little interaction with my replacement, Gary. One time he did call very upset. He had received a referral from a battalion commander and had seen a Marine who supposedly already had an open case at Family Support Services. He went to Barbara to let her know that the case had been referred to him and he wanted to know how she wanted him to proceed. This was exactly how he was supposed to handle these types of conflicts. She apparently got really angry and yelled at him. Amongst the many criticisms she threw his way, he was most concerned when she said, "This is a perfect example of why we have to get rid of the MFLC program. I have a friend at Marine Corps headquarters that oversees the MFLC program, and I've been waiting for a reason to call her to yank the program from our depot."

Poor Gary was very disturbed and afraid that because of him the whole program would be terminated. He was also perplexed because he felt he was doing the right thing by going to her to ask advice. He was sure that he'd put the MFLC program in jeopardy. I wasn't at all surprised that he'd had a run-in with Family Support Services. It was so hard to stay off their radar. The Marine who was seeing Gary hadn't even told him that he had previously been seen in Family Support Services. This type of thing actually happened often. A Marine would go into Family Support Services and might not have a good experience for one reason or another, so he wouldn't go back. I never thought it was anything personal with the counseling staff there; it was just the way the system was set up—it can be somewhat punitive. If the Marine has an open case with Family Support Services, as an MFLC we are not allowed to work with them. If the case is closed, then we are able to see them. It sounds complicated, but the reason behind it is if the case needs to be documented and the MFLC provides anonymous, confidential counseling, there could be a complicated, inherent conflict. The programs are not supposed to be working against each other. In theory, they should complement each other. Poor Gary. He was completely shaken up.

I always try to find the positive in a situation, and the good that should have come out of Gary's experience was that John (the supervisor at HWM) could have seen that it wasn't only me that was having issues with Family Support Services. I could understand that Family Support Services would be concerned having a licensed therapist on the base seeing every single drill instructor and not having to tell anyone anything that we heard (with the exception of "duty to warn"). I imagined that they were worried and did not know if we were using good judgment. However, the proactive program was working and I was going to serve the Marines the way they wanted, bringing counseling to them and utilizing the program that they devised. I was simply the vehicle in articulating the services into a comprehensive, structured approach.

Despite the run-in with Family Support Services, Gary had an incredible experience during his six weeks. He marveled at how well the program flowed. He admitted that initially he had been apprehensive about forcing Marines to sit through counseling, but he'd found that they really enjoyed the opportunity to talk. Gary confirmed that they felt empowered and important that he was taking the time to talk to them. They were eager and wanted to share their experiences with him, in a safe and comfortable setting. He must have told me ten times that if this was how the infamous drill instructors responded to proactive counseling, every military member should respond just as positively. He loved the approach and, like me, was amazed that it wasn't used everywhere and all the time.

Despite some small fires that needed putting out upon my return to MCRD, it was good to be back, and I was ready to swing into action. My second day back I had my weekly conference call with John and the other Marine Corps MFLCs. The calls were always the same. John immediately wanted a quick and brief overview of our week. While each MFLC spoke, I could hear John clicking away on his computer. I got the impression that he was more concerned with getting his report done than providing support. The conference calls were almost the exact same, every week. The average MFLC was on a base for only six weeks. The first two weeks they were busy meeting all the key people. By about the third week, they would report that they had seen a few Marines. Occasionally they would be really excited because they got in front of a captain. Some MFLCs did regular groups and commented on those. Most had issues on their bases with the counseling centers, very similar to my experiences. When it was my turn to speak, I felt a little arrogant. John liked us to report in numbers, for example: I saw five individuals and two couples and did a group. My reports sounded more like *I saw thirty-six individuals, did five groups, worked with four couples, and attended four base events*. It was always the truth, although it may have sounded exaggerated to the callers on the other end. It was frustrating for me that so many of the bases, including Parris Island (the East Coast recruit depot), had two MFLCs. At MCRD, there was one MFLC and we most definitely had enough work for two people.

At the end of the conference call, John said, "Marjorie, could you please stay on the line?" I had no idea what he wanted to talk with me about. I had heard him do that to other MFLCs; I guessed this day was my turn. It turned out that John had received a call from Gretchen over at Family Support Services. She felt it was her responsibility to tell him that I had colluded with command and that I didn't keep things confidential because I sent command e-mails. She included that it was the only reason the commands liked me. He went on to say that he'd discussed Gretchen's call with Donna (his supervisor), and together they had determined that this was a situation of mere jealousy. They'd decided not give it any credence. They'd come to this conclusion because somehow, whatever Gretchen had said, actually made me sound good and reinforced to them that I had a good relationship with command. The frustrating part to me was that HWM never asked me what type of things I shared with command. I knew better than anyone that I walked a very fine line every time I spoke to a commander about his men. I'd even sent a blind copy to Donna every time I sent any type of e-mail. I was hyper-vigilant about not crossing confidentiality boundaries. I was becoming increasingly annoyed at HWM, considerably more than the folks at Family Support Services. They never took the time to listen and learn about the program that had been created and the work that was being done. Every time I'd try to talk to John with more detail, he'd reply that he hoped to have time to listen someday. They truly did not have a clue what I was doing and it was not for lack of me trying to explain. I loved every opportunity I could get to share specifics about the proactive counseling program that had evolved.

John did ask me to no longer communicate with anyone on the base via e-mail. I found this so incredibly frustrating. I liked sending weekly or biweekly e-mails. I had no one overseeing me, and I felt that it was imperative for me to have some accountability as to how

I was spending my days. Also, I was receiving useful information from the Marines, and in many instances I felt it was helpful for the command to know. I knew that the Marines almost never put anything in writing. I did not expect return e-mails. My e-mails were for informational purposes only. Never once did Donna respond to the blind copies I sent her with any feedback, either positive or negative. This is what a typical one of my e-mails looked like:

Lt. Col Cooper and Sgt. Major Simpson,
   I wanted to briefly touch base with you regarding my work with 1st Battalion. Last week I had the opportunity to meet with Charlie Co during pick-up week.
   I met with every DI (except for three) for approx. 15-20 minutes each.

Observations:

-   Tremendous sense of "family."

-   They are very supportive of one another.

-   A few of the experienced DIs expressed that they focus on the "big picture" and that they keep that vision in their heads during the cycle to help them when they get stressed or exhausted.

-   The Chiefs are outstanding and very enthusiastic about the cycle. They get along and communicate well with one another. I will be meeting with them and the Series Commanders in the coming week.

Concerns:

-   They are a young Company, and like other Companies, they are moving up very quickly. The J's each equally expressed concern and apprehension about the new billet and their own lack of experience.

- 2 or 3 DIs are returning from early quota and were used to things the way they used to be, which involved hazing, both of recruits and new hats. There was concern that they would have a hard time adjusting to the new ways and the new schedule!

Overview:

They are a great Company. Across the board, they have a great attitude and I expect that they will have a good cycle.

I also met with the Company Commander and the 1st Sergeant.

Observations:

- They had only known each other for one week.
- At first they were very formal with one another.
- After the first 10 minutes or so, they began to open up and share their thoughts and opinions with one another.
- The 1st Sergeant knew almost everything about each of the DIs. It was very impressive, and I wouldn't doubt that it has a lot to do with their overall sense of family.
- The Company Commander is very eager to learn.
- There was no apparent tension.

I missed Alpha Company yesterday at Epson Range. I was hoping to do groups with them while they were on Grass Week. I just received the Company Commander's e-mail and I will see if we can arrange something on Monday.

Please let me know if you have any questions. Have a great weekend.

Marjorie

From: Cooper Lt. Col. James M.
Date: July 25, 2008 5:27:01 PM PDT
To: Marjorie Morrison
Subject: RE: 1st Battalion MFLC Update

Marjorie,

Thanks for the insight and time you spent with each of the Co "C" Marines.

Let me know if you are not able to coordinate a date/time with Alpha Co.

R/Jim
Lt. Col. J.M. Cooper, USMC
1st Battalion, RTR

Here is another example:

From: Marjorie Morrison
Sent: Friday, July 25, 2008 13:35
To: Becker Lt. Col. Linda A; Trimm Maj. Robert
Cc: Chester Col Craig T
Subject: Support Battalion MFLC Update

Hi. I'm sorry I have not had the opportunity to see either one of you this week. Next week I will make an effort to stop by.

This week I have had the opportunity to have a very good group with the BMPs. There has been a trend in our meetings to discuss ways to improve their overall image on the Depot and to figure out ways to try and keep themselves from being bored. During our group today, we came up with some suggestions.

- They LOVED the financial class they took. Unfortunately, they had to leave half way through for drug testing. Many of them reported that they have not spent any money since the class. They would like to be able to take it again and sit through the whole thing.

- They also liked the Weapons class they had this week.

- They would love to take a language class. They have so much free time and would like to learn the language spoken in Iraq and Afghanistan to help them when they get to the fleet.

- They would like to get their qualifications to use the 9 mm pistols.

- They would like to volunteer in the community and help with kids (i.e., the boy scouts)

- They would love to have an MOS tour.

They feel that if they had the opportunity to see the fleet it would motivate them to continue to get better. They suggested perhaps a Fleet Day.

They would like to spend time at Camp Pendleton and feel that will help them get "out of their slump."

Everything they do is based on negative reinforcement. They would like to try and make it more positive. This is what we came up with:

There are 4 squads. The Squads can engage in healthy competition to earn points that would give them privileges.

Some suggestions of how they could earn points:
    Field Day
    Completed MCIs
    Cleaning Squad Bay
    Working parties
    Checking in on time (accountability)
    Volunteering

Rewards could be:
    Liberty on weekends
    Barbecues

We could implement new programs such as:
    BMP of the month
    Ribbons, etc.

Perhaps an article could be submitted to the Chevron on the BMPs to help promote an image change.

These are just a few suggestions. Please feel free to contact me if you have any questions or concerns.

Have a great weekend,
Marjorie

From: Becker Lt. Col. Linda A
Date: July 25, 2008 2:18:25 PM PDT
To: Marjorie Morrison
Subject: RE: Support Battalion MFLC Update

Thank you Marjorie, some excellent inside information and I appreciate your feedback so we can chart some courses forward.

Have a great weekend, and hope to see you next time you have a free moment on the Depot.

Thanks again!
Lt. Col. Becker

Lt. Col. Linda A. Becker, USMC
Commanding Officer, Support Battalion
Recruit Training Regiment
Marine Corps Recruit Depot

Someone must have showed Gretchen a copy of one of my e-mails. I really didn't understand her issue about colluding with command. I saw it as working with command. When there are helpful information and trends, doesn't it help everyone to provide feedback?

Unfortunately, there was no point in trying to explain this to John. No more e-mail communication for me. With HWM it was always best to walk on eggshells. It felt like they had no investment in any MFLC. We were contractors who could be terminated for any reason. The message I always got was that a good MFLC was one they didn't have to deal with. I never got the impression that there was any emphasis on sound clinical and counseling skills. They needed you to stay off the radar and not cause any strife. The whole thing was beginning to have more clarity to me. HWM is a for-profit company, and if the military for any reason is not happy with them, they may lose their multimillion-dollar contract. The stakes were high for them. The way I saw it, the stakes were a lot higher for the service members who risked their lives every day.

I asked John if there was anything he could do to help mediate the situation between me and the Family Support Services. I was confident with even the smallest amount of interaction, things could improve. His reply was as expected: "You just need to stay out of their way." He felt that HWM's involvement at that point would cause more harm than good.

I decided that there was no way I could make significant, long-term headway with the Marines if there was animosity with Gretchen. I couldn't have someone undermine me, let alone someone from Family Support Services, which is the on-base counseling center. The next day I decided to go into Family Support Services and have a talk with Gretchen. There had to be a way to clear the air between us. If HWM was not going to help me, I would do it myself. I was prepared to do whatever it took. After all, we should both have had the same goal, which was to provide the best mental health counseling to the Marines that we could.

I had contemplated bringing her a Starbucks coffee, and all I could think of as I walked out of her office was *Thank God I didn't*, because had I brought her one, she would have thrown it at me and I'd be wearing the coffee. Needless to say, the conversation did not go well. I used the approach that I often recommend to my clients. Start with a positive, give the correction or feedback, and end with a positive. I told Gretchen that I thought she was a wonderful clinician. I shared with her I had spoken to drill instructors who had talked to her and found it very helpful. I apologized for the misunderstanding with the domestic violence case that occurred months prior. I asked if we could put it behind us so that we could move forward and work toward bringing quality services to these outstanding Marines.

I am not a confrontational person. In fact, I have always been the type that avoids conflict at all costs. Once again, those skills did not help me at all this time. She literally screamed at me, "I don't like you—never have and never will!" She continued, "Not everyone loves you here. I happen to know a company commander and somebody else that doesn't like you." It sounded like a tantrum you'd expect a middle school child to have. It felt to me that she was having a popularity contest and was excited to have some Marines on her side. It reminded me back to the days of my private practice. *Why are we wasting our time worrying about stupid things?* I thought. *Does she not understand that the suicide rates in Marines are climbing at an unprecedented speed? Does she not know that the Marine I had seen earlier that morning woke up with his sheets ripped because he had clawed them with his toenails during a night terror?* I was giving up on Gretchen; it was now clear to me we were never going to be able to reconcile.

I now had the sense that Family Support Services had divided forces between us. It felt incredibly unprofessional and embarrassing. The funny thing was that before Gretchen started not liking me, she used to bad-mouth Barbara to me all the time. Now I gave her and Barbara something to have in common; they both saw me as the enemy. Sadly, the talk got me nowhere; the only thing I accomplished was that I now knew just how venomous her hatred toward me was.

I walked out of the office and took a few deep breaths. I reminded myself that my intent was to work with the Marines and I had no problem sending them to Family Support Services if they needed a referral. My office wasn't there anymore, and unfortunate as the situation was, I didn't really need her validation to continue with my work.

Despite the setback with Family Support Services, things were going great. I was seeing even more drill instructors that would call me for follow-up sessions in addition to the mandatory one-on-ones. Every one of those Marines had had at least one, if not multiple deployments. Many of them shared the same complaints. One of the most common was difficulty sleeping. They would report that they would wake up with the bed sopping wet because of terrible night sweats. Recurring nightmares regarding killing or witnessing death were very common. The more comfortable a Marine was with me, the more he would share. A number of them reported having dreams that they killed their spouses, fellow Marines, and sometimes even children. They would feel such shame sharing those horrid visions that it almost always brought them to tears. I'd always keep in mind that Marines had not only been heavily deployed during Operation Iraqi Freedom; they'd been sent into some of Iraq's most volatile areas, and they suffered 25 percent of the casualties, though they made up only 16 percent of ground forces there. What amazed me was how, in the right environment, it was so easy for them to share their feelings with me. One day, two different spouses came up to me individually at a company event to tell me that their husbands were like new men since they had "bared their souls" in session.

A few sessions with these guys appeared to make a huge difference. They were getting used to seeing me, and they knew the routine. Each time they would open up more. Since the MFLC program was anonymous and confidential, they felt safe and didn't worry that they might be hurting their careers.

Every week the number of Marines I was working with increased. I was doing individual sessions with drill instructors, about twenty-five to thirty a week, doing groups, and seeing Marines in my office upstairs in the library. I was so busy, yet enjoying every minute of it. The more I got to know and learned from the Marines, the more I wanted to help them and give back. I had achieved what I had set out to do and felt that at least with the drill instructors at the Marine Corps Recruit Depot, I was helping them change the way they viewed mental health services. I always used the analogy of getting a routine medical physical. You go to the doctor when you are healthy for a "check up" to learn how your physical health is doing. This program was the same, yet looking at the mental health instead. When they saw it from that perspective, it made sense.

Things were also going quite well at Camp Pendleton. I'd gotten to know the command there because I was there every

Thursday doing groups. I typically made time to stop into the command headquarters to see how and where I could be of assistance. My main points of contact there were the chaplain and Lt. Col. Wood, who was the XO of the battalion. They would often express frustration that they wanted their own MFLC and didn't really want to share me with MCRD. I tried to support them as much as I could, but I was getting stretched pretty thin.

Below is an e-mail I was cc'd on written by the Weapons and Field Battalion Chaplain to a contact at Marine Family Services with regards to augmenting my services:

From: Rumley Lt. Stuart S.
Date: October 25, 2008 2:30:24 PM PDT
To: Crane CIV Samuel
Cc: Wood Lt. Col. Jason L. , Marjorie Morrison
Subject: MFLC Question IRT WFTBn (MCRD) Edson Range Camp Pendleton

Sir,

I hope all is well. I wanted to ask you if it would be possible for Weapons Field Training Battalion to have its own Military & Family Life Consultant? It has been great to have Marjorie Morrison here for our Marines to be able to go to in order to get the help they may need. She has been great to work with. The need is there. I just wanted to see what the possibilities were. Thanks for the time and consideration. Take care.

LT Stuart S. Rumley
Command Chaplain
WFTBN (MCRD)
Edson Range, Area 31

From: Crane CIV Samuel
Date: October 27, 2008 8:00:33 AM PDT
To: Rumley Lt. Stuart S.
Subject: RE: MFLC Question IRT WFTBn (MCRD)
Edson Range Camp Pendleton

Lt. Rumley,

I am pleased to hear that the Weapons Training Battalion has benefited from the MFLC program. The MFLCs are intended to be temporary, situational augmentation to the installation's Marine & Family Services counseling capability, vice permanent full-time plus ups. However, whenever Ms. Hardy and Ms. Brown (CPEN's Marine & Family Services Director and Counseling Center Director respectively) or Ms. Kahn and Ms. Rosita (MCRD San Diego's Marine & Family Services Director and Counseling Center Director respectively), whoever supports your battalion, determines their internal assets are going to be unavailable to meet your needs, they can request MFLC augmentation through me and it will be provided. The company for which the MFLCs work, under the terms of the contract with OSD, provides the MFLCs on rotations of various lengths (30, 45, 60, or 90 days depending upon availability and need) so you may not always have Ms. Morrison, but you will always get a licensed clinician to provide short-term, solution focused consultation to the Marines and their families.

Samuel Crane
Marine and Family Services Branch Head (MRR)

I took this as a positive for me in HWM's eyes because they had tried to sell the MFLC program to Camp Pendleton and they had previously turned it down. I found it interesting that the program was seen as an augmentation to existing on-base counseling centers. I knew from my weekly conference calls that the majority of MFLCs out there were not doing brief counseling. In fact, most of them did very little counseling the whole six weeks they were there.

My clinical work with Marines grew even stronger over the following weeks. Third Battalion started adding some extra groups. They had me meeting with the series commanders and the chiefs together as a group during pick-up week. They felt that this helped the cohesion within the upper management of the company. They also had me meet with the company commander and the first sergeant together at the end of pick-up week. This was the final layer, the highest level of the hierarchy of the company. I treated it like marriage counseling. Together we worked on issues that could get in the way of the upcoming cycle. It also gave me the opportunity to provide them with any feedback from having met with everyone in the company. I never shared individual stories, only trends. For example: "It sounds like you have four or five guys whose wives are expecting this cycle and another two or three have new infants. There seem to be concerns about getting the necessary time off. Also, your experienced drill instructors have had to move up quickly and don't feel they have the experience base that they need, so overall the company is feeling a little insecure." At this point, I had a great frame of reference and could see the differences in the companies. It wasn't too long before First and Third Battalions wanted me to do the same groups for their companies.

Every week I was getting busier and busier. Never once did I say *I don't have time*. I knew it was such a victory just to have Marines ask me for mental health services, the last thing I wanted to do was turn them away. At any rate, the days kept getting longer and longer. I'd think back to the MFLC that I replaced who said, "You won't ever see the drill instructors; they are too busy to talk to anyone," and how Barbara sternly warned me about talking to the battalions because they didn't have time and couldn't be bothered. Now, I walked in the battalion doors, and the commanders always eagerly awaited my visits to chat.

Wherever I went on the depot, Marines stopped me and told me stories about whatever was going on in their lives. In order to maintain the MFLC integrity, I was never allowed to take notes. Since I worked with over five hundred drill instructors, I could never remember their individual stories, but I would nod my head like I remembered because I never wanted to hurt their feelings or have them feel unimportant. I was always open to talking with them and genuinely loved hearing their stories, whether good, bad, or just an update.

Some of my favorite comments were about how after seeing me and realizing how easy it was to talk to someone, they were going to counseling for themselves or with their wives. One story stands out in my mind. I was at the convenience store at Camp Pendleton and a drill instructor came up to me, asking, "Do you remember me?" I hated when they did that because I'd often feel trapped.

"Of course I remember you," I replied, "but please refresh my memory. Which company are you with?"

He reminded me that he was with Bravo Company. He continued, "My whole company feels that our company commander shafted us. We've all talked about it. We liked coming in to see you. My brother is a DI in Kilo Company, and those guys get to see you a couple of times a cycle. We wish we could meet with you like all the other drill instructors get to do on the depot."

I apologized and said, "You can always come see me in my office if you want to talk."

Bravo was the only company in the depot that I didn't work with because the commander felt he could take care of his men himself. I knew that the company was about to have a change of command and the new commander that was taking over was coming from Delta Company. He knew me well, and I didn't anticipate a problem once the change took place and was optimistic that I would begin doing the one-on-one sessions with them again. I felt it was the ultimate compliment; the one company on the depot that didn't have the individual sessions felt left out and wanted them. In my mind that was a true sign of a successful program.

I'd started going to the companies' initial drills that were on Saturday mornings. It was the first time the DIs marched with their recruits. The drill instructors' families came because it was an opportunity for them to see what their husbands, boyfriends, sons, etc., had been doing for the past month. The commanders liked me to go because the families were there, and they liked me to be visible to them. Monday mornings, I went to whichever company had their final drill that week. I also went to every graduation on Friday mornings. I loved these, and they were one of the highlights of my week. One week when I was five minutes late, a few of the drill instructors and an officer texted me asking where I was, telling me they were nervous I wasn't coming. It was little gestures like this that showed me that they had started seeing me as one of them. They trusted me, and I was honored to be a recipient of that trust.

A few days later, after a routine meeting with First Battalion commander, I was cc'd on an e-mail in regard to the upcoming Bravo change of command. Lt. Col. Cooper informed me that it was his intent that every drill instructor was to see me. When the new commander took over, they would be instituting the one-on-ones just like everyone else. Aside from the long days, things were going better than ever. I had pretty much avoided any mishaps with Family Support Services. The only drawback was that since I had minimal supervision, it felt like no one really knew how much effort I was putting in. It was a bizarre situation because Theresa (my POC) completely trusted me and let me do my thing. She was always complimentary and supportive of my work, but she also really didn't know the extent of what I was doing every day. I'd stop in on Fridays to "check in," but that was about it. Each company knew what I was doing for them, and each battalion knew what I was doing for them, but there really wasn't one person who knew everything that I was doing. To make the situation more complicated, because of the nature of my work, everything was confidential and I wasn't allowed to share it with anyone. Suffice it to say, I was working on the notion that hard work pays off and "what goes around comes around."

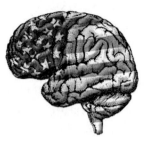

TYPICAL DAY WORKING WITH MARINES

At this point, my workweek had changed drastically from back in the days of my private practice working with only civilians. I still marvel every day at the strength of the Marines. Their bravery encompasses every part of them, from physical and mental to spiritual. Physically they exude the word *strong* in every capacity imaginable. They work out and exercise daily as a routine part of their life. Only in the military is one encouraged to take an hour during their workday to exercise (and it's not part of their lunch break). They are required to regularly "weigh in" to make sure they are maintaining a healthy weight. During these times they also must take regularly scheduled fitness tests. In the Marine Corps, being physically fit is just as important as being intellectually fit. That is not to say in any way that intelligence is not important.

As a Marine you will almost never stay in one job for more than three years. That means that every few years, you are plucked out of your job and put into a new one. That is practically the opposite of what happens in the civilian world. As a civilian, in order to be successful, we have to be experts in our field and know more than our competition to prevail. In the military, they have to be well versed in a variety of areas to be considered successful. That is in addition to their concentrated occupation. This is called his or her MOS (military occupation specialty), and every Marine has one. The difference is that they are challenged to not only do their MOS in a variety of different settings, but they are also expected from time to time to have a job that has nothing to do with their MOS. The logic behind this is that everybody is replaceable. The institution cannot be reliant on any one single person to operate. Multiple people have to be able to fill the billet. The only way to insure that this can happen properly is to move people around. Despite this concept, regardless of the rank, every Marine is first and foremost a rifleman. Every Marine is capable of serving as an infantryman. Part of the reasoning behind having every Marine trained as a leader, is because they view essential decision making in small maneuvers. This rationale is unique to the Marine Corps, and that philosophy is not shared with the other military branches.

Spirituality is also an important part of the corps. Every battalion has a chaplain who is there to provide spiritual guidance in whatever capacity may be needed for their individual search. A Marine's loyalty is to unit, God and country—in that order.

Working with Marines in a psychological and emotional capacity is truly an exhilarating experience. This was a typical day for me at MCRD (Marine Corps Recruit Depot):

0730: I met with a staff sergeant and his wife. They needed to come in early so his spouse could get to work by nine o'clock. They were having marital problems that had been going on for the past year. This Marine has had two tours to Iraq and one to Afghanistan. He came to the drill field to get a break from being deployed. He had promised his wife that this would be a time that they could spend more quality time together. Unfortunately, the last few cycles had more recruits and fewer drill instructors, and he had to be at work a lot more than expected. In fact, it was not uncommon for him to not get home for a few days at a time.

When he would get home, he was exhausted and just wanted to sleep. His wife was feeling rejected and didn't appreciate that all he wanted to do on his time off was rest. She felt like a single parent and was getting sick of living life alone. Like many situations, the answers were typically found somewhere in the middle. I was working with the staff sergeant on being able to express to his wife that he was tired but that it was not at all a reflection of how he felt about her. We discussed the value of planning out some couple time with his wife, some family time with the kids, and some time for just him. They came to understand that if the time was well organized, then she wouldn't mind when he would "check out." Setting up a schedule for his time off helped everybody manage his "off" time better. They would come back in a couple of weeks to report how things were going.

0830: A sergeant came in for his fourth time. He was referred to me by his first sergeant. I had never had the chance to do a routine one-on-one session with him when he was drill instructor because he worked at the pool, which is where the recruits learn their swimming skills. The first sergeant in the support battalion, where he worked, was like father to all his men under him. He was very comfortable with mental health, having experienced some post-traumatic symptoms himself. He always made it a point to get to know his drill instructors on a personal level. That way, he could tell if things were a little off. There was nothing about this case that required documentation of any sort. This sergeant initially came in with the presenting problem that he felt like he was drinking too much. He didn't think he needed to go to the on-base alcohol program and was confident that he could slow down the drinking on his own with some basic counseling help. As a clinician, it is always a challenge to ascertain how much truth people are sharing with you. It wasn't until this fourth session where he admitted that wasn't having any success in "cutting back on the booze." The night before he drank too much and started texting his ex-girlfriend. They had a tumultuous relationship, and he worked hard to get out of it. He was mortified at the things he had said while intoxicated and was incredibly frustrated about the situation. In his weak moment, he truly opened up to me for the first time. After allowing him to share his situation, I asked just how serious he was about stopping his drinking. Quitting drinking is an incredibly difficult thing to do. It takes a lot of discipline and motivation—both qualities that Marines possess. On the other hand, if he was drinking to numb out the problems he was experiencing, he was going to have to replace that with a deeper understanding of his behaviors and actions. This sergeant appeared ready to take the challenge; he just didn't want to get in trouble with his command. Lucky for the Marines at MCRD, the folks at the substance-abuse center were fantastic and did a wonderful job with guiding Marines through this difficult process. We talked about what a stronger Marine he could be without the effects of the excess drinking. He felt ready but was still apprehensive. He agreed to walk over to the substance-abuse center with me to gather some additional information. When we arrived, John, the alcohol counselor, warmly greeted him. We sat down, and I let the sergeant do all the talking. After a few minutes of dialogue, both men agreed I could leave.

I was now running a few minutes behind and had to rush over to the India Company office, otherwise known as the "head shed," for a 0930 meeting regarding some concerns that the commander had regarding the current training cycle. Luckily, the company commander and the first sergeant were in the office together when I arrived. It was always nice to have the officer and the senior enlisted NCO together when discussing issues regarding the company. They shared with me their underlying concern that the company had not bonded yet this cycle and it was affecting their ability to work as cohesive team. They were not helping each other out and frustrations were mounting. The leaders wanted to see if I could schedule an extra group session with the drill instructors before the scheduled one that was still five weeks away. It was always tricky to find a time when all the drill instructors could attend. We came up with a date for the following week.

From 1000 to 1500 I was scheduled to be in First Battalion doing the Delta Company one-on-ones. As I walked over a few drill instructors stopped to say "hi" to me or waved. I was feeling good and progress was being made. It felt great to have the Marines asking for additional services, and my confidence in my work was growing. I understood the underlying military culture more now than ever.

As I walked in to First Battalion I poked in the CO's (commanding officer) office to say hello. We had a brief chat, and he told me he wanted me to take particular note to the number of new drill instructors that Delta Company had this cycle. He wanted to make sure that there wouldn't be any "hazing" from more senior drill instructors and to pay careful attention to anyone that seems disgruntled. I promised to check in with him again at the end of the day. I walked away, doubting that any of them would complain or present as "disgruntled." Marines don't really do that. They typically take the stoic approach unless something is really bad, but I'd keep my ears perked and look for cues.

In First Battalion I always did my sessions in the chaplain's office. He was kind to offer up the space, and I was very grateful. I picked up the company roster, which told me how many drill instructors were in the company and how many cycles they have had. I used it as a checklist to make sure that I saw everyone. There were twenty-four drill instructors that needed to be seen, and I planned on seeing three or four an hour.

1000: I got up in front of the Delta Company in the classroom where they were being briefed. I stood behind the podium at the front of the classroom. I was now quite comfortable talking in front of a sea of men in uniform, but the thrill never went away. I looked up and smiled. I kept my talk short and stuck to the script: "Hi. For those of you that don't know me, my name is Marjorie Morrison. I am a military life consultant, also known as a MFLC. I am a licensed marriage family therapist and am here to assist you Marines and your families. My role is to help address issues, such as, relationship issues, parent/child communication, job stress, grief and loss, and anything else that is a distraction or impacting your daily life. The MFLC program is confidential with the exception of duty to warn cases. Those exceptions are if you are a danger to yourself or others, or if you report that you are involved in domestic violence, sexual abuse, or child abuse. If your situation is a duty to warn case, I will assist you in getting the help you need. Our meetings are brief and utilize a solutions-focused approach. This basically means that we identify a problem; we target a goal and together formulate a concrete action plan. Does anyone have any questions?" The majority of the men had all met me many times already. This was the third time I was seeing them for the one-on-ones, and I had seen them in groups a couple of times already. They definitely feel more comfortable when rapport had already been built.

1010: The first DI walked in. He was animated and sat right down. He started out by saying, "Good morning, ma'am." The worst part for me about these meetings was not being able to take any notes. I had no way of knowing whom I had seen before or anything specific about them that would help them feel like I genuinely cared. After all, they all wear the same uniform, have closely shaven hair, and to me they looked a little similar. I started out by asking how things have been going for him. He enthusiastically replied that things were going well and that he was excited to start the new training cycle. This company just came off a three-week break, which was enough time to relax a little and get rejuvenated. I asked if he was married. He answered yes and that they had a two-year-old boy and one on the way. His wife was having a tough pregnancy, and he felt bad that he wouldn't be home much over the next three months. I asked him how married life was going. He replied, "Fine. We fight sometimes, but we get along fine." I then asked him what physically or emotionally happened to him when he got stressed out. He didn't know the answer. We talked some more. I explained to him that everyone experiences stress, including myself, and that we all react differently to it. Some people become withdrawn, others drink too much, some become angry and engage in frequent fights; others incessantly worry. He thought about it for a minute and then asked if nightmares could count. I encouraged him to explain. He shared that from time to time he had horrible nightmares. He was deployed in Iraq and was on the front lines. His nightmare was always the same. It was a woman holding a baby in her arms, screaming at the top of her lungs. He described the look in her eyes and how she was blaming him for all the violence that was going on around them. He wanted to tell her that they were there to protect her to bring democracy to her country, but no words would come out. Typically he would be woken up by his wife who would try to calm him down, letting him know he was home and safe now. Interestingly, he continued by telling me that nothing like that had ever happened in Iraq and he had no idea why he kept having the same dream over and over again. I then asked him what he did remember. He replied, "Not much. I can't seem to remember anything from that time in my life." I explained to him how sometimes the brain would do that. It will block out intense experiences as a way of protecting itself. I went over some other possible PTSD symptoms with him. He didn't think he fit the criteria. I asked if he'd like to talk to someone in more detail about these dreams, reminding him that he could schedule a time to see me in the library or I could give him other referral options. He took the referral sheet but let me know he probably wouldn't be calling anyone. The frequency of the nightmares had been reduced tremendously over the months, and he was confident they would eventually go away. He promised to call me should he want to talk further. I had a feeling he was telling the truth and was confident he'd reach out to me if need be.

1030: The next DI came in and eagerly took a seat. He wanted clarification that I wasn't going to take any notes or tell his command anything that he told me. I reassured him that I was not a restricted reporter and that if he told me that he was a danger to himself or others I would need to divulge it. He declared that it wasn't any of those. I encouraged him to share what was going on; it was obvious that he had something that he wanted to get off his chest. He told me that his mom was dying of cancer and was staying at his house. He was nervous that he wouldn't have very much time off to spend with her but didn't want his company to know because he was afraid they would think he was making excuses for not pulling his weight with the recruits. I then asked him what he experiences while under stress and just how stressful the situation with his mother was. He, too, initially did not realize what happened to him when he was under severe pressure. After some probing, he recognized that he became socially withdrawn. He didn't like being around people and wanted to be left alone. He embarrassingly admitted that recently he hadn't even had interest in having sex with his girlfriend. We discussed different ways to help him overcome his situation. We explored the value of talking to his first sergeant about the circumstances with his mother. I also explained to him that he needed to be aware of when he became significantly more socially withdrawn, describing to him that it was his internal cue of when he was under stress and he needed to address the issues before it got worse. I gave him a handout on some relaxation techniques and a handout of mental health referrals.

1045: The next DI was already irritated when he came in. He was frustrated that he had to sit in the same classes every three months when a new cycle started. He felt like it was a huge waste of his time. He then told me that he spent six months in combat in Afghanistan. He was an infantry guy, and he loved to fight. I asked how life had been going since he has been home from deployment. He shared that he had a hard time relaxing and felt a little on edge. When he was busy and with people, he was fine and nothing bothered him; but the second he was alone, his mind would go back to the same image. They were in battle and a rocket-propelled grenade was thrown at them. Blood was everywhere. They waited for help, but it took it awhile to arrive. One of his men died. He knew he couldn't have saved him, but he still felt responsible for what had happened. I gave him the opportunity to talk and share the whole story with me. I was an empathic listener and wanted him to get it off his chest. I was no longer surprised to learn that it was the first time he had ever told anyone the story. I had heard that many times before. I couldn't imagine how someone could keep something like that all bottled up inside. I tried to help him understand how keeping things in could be contributing to his edginess. He didn't realize how easy it was to talk about it and agreed to make an appointment to see a counselor. He at first asked if I could see him, but I explained that as an MFLC I am not allowed to see PTSD. This as one of the places where my contract got sticky. He had built a rapport with me, and I was not going to let him down. I was a little nervous that he might not call one of the referrals, so I encouraged him to call and make an appointment while in the room with me. He decided to call the medical treatment facility on the base and meet with a psychologist. He talked to the intake coordinator on the phone, and they scheduled a first appointment a few days later. I made him promise that he would come by and see me after his first appointment so that I could hear how it went. This was probably the toughest thing about my job. I knew as an MFLC I was not allowed to work with anyone except "short-term, situational counseling" issues. I had to have faith that the referrals where I sent these men were going to take care of them. It's a very precarious position for a clinician to be put in.

The next few drill instructors were fairly simple sessions. One needed suggestions on how to get help for his son who had disabilities; another needed skills to help communication with his spouse. Most were stressed about the job and wanted to make sure that they did a good job. There seemed to be a trend of somatic complaints—either shoulder or back pain to headaches and stomach aches. Drill instructors have to wear the infamous hat that actually is quite tight on their heads and, during the hotter months, can lead to more headaches. My goal was to give these men a forum to talk should they have something they wanted to share and if at the least help them understand what happens to them while they are under stress. It is something very personal and different for everyone. Once they figure it out and learn how to detect stress within themselves, they can employ strategies before things spiral out of control.

At 1200 I left the battalion and went to lunch at the Bayview. This was the only dining restaurant on the depot, and it overlooked the San Diego Bay. I was eating with two of the battalion chaplains who wanted to talk with me about speaking at an upcoming couples retreat workshop they had. I always enjoyed being with the chaplains; they were interesting, kind, and always had a lot of good information to share. Whenever I met with them, I tried to be a sounding board for them to vent to. They hear so much and have a ridiculous amount of personal information that they have to keep inside. I try to give them an opportunity to express any emotions should they have something on their chest that was bothering them. I agreed to speak at their retreat, even though it would be on a Saturday. The workweeks seem to be getting longer every week.

As I headed back to First Battalion to see more Delta Company DIs, I ran into the Second Battalion commander. He asked if I could stop by some time during the next couple of days. He wanted to ask my advice about something. I told him I'd stop by the following morning. I loved when the leadership wanted advice; it was one of the few reinforcers that told me I was doing a good job. I made my way through First Battalion and settled in the office when the next DI came through.

1300: This drill instructor shared that he wanted a divorce. He loved her and didn't want the marriage to end but didn't know how he could save it. He became very quiet when I asked what was happening that he wanted to end it. He seemed kind of embarrassed, and I wondered if it had to do with infidelity. In the Marine Corps, you are not allowed to have an affair. You actually can get kicked out of the corps for such an offense. He finally began to open up some more and elaborated on his story. Turns out that while he was deployed, his wife spent all of their money. He had no idea that when he came home from deployment he would be broke. He always told himself that he would never get a divorce over money, but he couldn't get over his anger. To make things worse, she didn't know what she spent the money on. She bought a lot of new clothes and a puppy, but that didn't account for all of the money that was missing. He found himself no longer trusting her. He felt guilty for being mad at her. We explored his guilt and in doing so, he experienced what in therapy we call a "ah ha" moment. He realized that his parents got divorced over money. His mom was a compulsive spender and his dad finally had enough and divorced her. Prior to our meeting, he never put the uncanny similarities together. We discussed cycles and how sometimes subconsciously we repeat them. Luckily, excessive spending problems had come up with the Marines many times before and I had a handout discussing how to have open communication with your spouse about money without it turning into a fight. As I handed it to him, he asked if I'd be willing to have a couples counseling session with him and his wife. I agreed, and we scheduled a session for the end of the week.

The rest of the DIs were fairly similar. Depending on their age and time on the drill field, I could almost predict what the issues were going to be about. The newer DIs worried about work performance, and the more seasoned DI's worried about the effects the drill filed was having on their relationships and families.

At 1600 the drill instructor I met concerned me. He was on his third cycle, and we had met a few times before, either individual or group. He was having a hard time controlling his temper and came right out sharing that he kept getting into fights with people. Even his brother was mad at him because they got into a physical altercation over the weekend. I asked him if he felt his anger was impacting his daily life, and he quickly answered yes. I then asked him if he was familiar with Family Support Services, the on base counseling center. He vaguely knew what it was but thought of it as the place Marines were sent when they got in trouble at home. I explained to him that they had awesome anger management classes and that I thought he would get a lot out of them. I gave him their number and asked him if he'd like to call now while we were sitting there so that he wouldn't forget. He made the call and scheduled an appointment for later that week.

His whole demeanor changed after that. I think he was ready to get help but just needed the assistance. I knew for anger management he would be in good hands over at Family Support Services.

At 1600 the company commander and first sergeant of Delta Company came in. We scheduled a time in two days for the three of us to meet to go over trends and any concerns they had that I could be of assistance with. I then went into the battalion commander's office to let him know that I was finished and that none of them appeared too disgruntled. They were an incredible group of men under fine leadership.

At 1630 I left First Battalion and headed over to the library to see a Marine that scheduled an individual session with me. He was waiting for me when I arrived. I'd seen him once before, and he came in presenting with issues regarding having a difficult time concentrating and was having a hard time remembering the training schedule. This time he revealed that his difficulties started after his deployment to Rimaldi. I knew that was where a lot of the heavy fighting that took place in Iraq. I was impressed he made the connection. He said he had thought a lot about things after our first session. He noticed that one moment he'd be fine and then the next moment his heart would start pounding, he'd start sweating, and he'd feel nauseous. He said anything could trigger it. The day before he was filling his car up with gas, and the smell of gasoline brought it on. He explained that just getting a whiff of that scent reminded him of the Humvee in Iraq. I asked him what he knew about PTSD and how it presented itself. We went over the symptoms, and he reluctantly agreed that it sounded like he was experiencing the majority of them. He really did not want to let his command know because he was afraid it might hurt his promotion, which was set to happen in the coming months. I expressed to him the importance of getting help. He reluctantly agreed to talk to his first sergeant.

He scheduled an appointment with a counselor over at Balboa Naval Hospital and was able to get an appointment for first thing the following morning.

1730: I spent a half hour doing paperwork for HWM. I returned a few phone calls and called it a day. Another fulfilling day on the depot working with Marines.

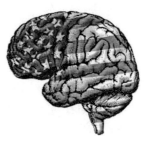

SUCCESS LEADS TO
RISING DEMAND

As time went on, I learned new ways to use my proactive individual sessions more effectively. I had my leading questions, and depending on the answers the DIs would give, I could tell what types of problems they had a propensity toward. For example, by gathering basic information about their coping styles, I could begin to predict what would happened to them when exposed to stressful situations. Some had a tendency toward depression. For others the stress might manifest in different ways, e.g., anger, alcohol abuse, excessive anxiety, suicidal ideation, or even homicidal thoughts. I knew exactly what questions to follow up with to continue to formulate my suspicions. For example, if a drill instructor shared with me that he felt helpless, had difficulty concentrating and remembering details, had a hard time making decisions, experienced excessive fatigue and decreased energy, I would talk with him about the possibility of depression. I would never diagnose him, but I would talk with him about various options he had available to him.

At this point, I familiarized myself with the majority of the military and community programs that the Marines had access to. Our government had done a good job supporting a number of reactive programs that were available to service members. These programs were well needed because so many of the men and women were experiencing invisible wounds. There were almost too many programs, and many were confused as to where to turn. I would try to make sense of what they had available to them. I was able to streamline the referrals to fit their needs. I was also beginning to see major trends in the Marines depending on how much time they had been on the depot. When they first got there, they were anxious mostly because of performance expectations and the fear of the unknown. When they were about halfway through, they felt good because they had started to have mastery over their job and the stress level was lower. Once they had been there for a while, they started to have other symptoms, such as burn-out and marital issues. The majority of these guys had already had multiple deployments and many had issues still lingering from that stress. They had been away from their spouses, families, and kids for extended periods of time. Their relationships had suffered and their coping skills were limited.

I was able to ascertain a lot of information through the groups. I was doing all my weekly scheduled groups and a fair number of "on-demand" groups. When issues would arise in a company, the command would call me in to help build cohesion and help work on the conflict at hand. These groups were very difficult to do. It was really a balancing act between being helpful and not being an excuse for the leaders to not do what they needed to do to solve the problem. It took technique that could be gained only through training or experience. When I got to MCRD, I had very little understanding of what leadership meant in the military. Leadership in the military takes on a different meaning than in the civilian world. Marines rely on their superiors for everything. Their superior is responsible for them and their safety. For the average American, our bosses typically only care about our efforts at the office. They aren't very focused on our safety and do not care very much about our overall well-being.

One Friday when I stopped in to have my weekly visit with my POC, Theresa, she was teary eyed. I had never seen her emotional before and of course I sat down with her to find out what was going on. I learned in far more detail than I had before about her situation on the depot. She had an extremely adversarial relationship with Barbara from Family Support Services. In the past, I had heard gossip that Theresa and Barbara didn't speak, but I never asked her about it, choosing to stay out of the gossip. The stories Theresa shared of the encounters she'd had with Barbara were mind-blowing. They made my little scenarios with her seem like nothing. Theresa showed me a file she had been keeping for twelve years. I couldn't believe my eyes. It was filled with sheets of paper and names of great people that Barbara had fired over the years.

Supposedly, anytime Barbara felt threatened by someone, she'd find a reason to have him or her fired. For Theresa this was an extra-complicated situation because she felt that Lt. Col. Rowe (their superior) always took Barbara's side. Theresa had worked on the depot for almost thirty years, and for her, the last couple of years had been the worst. Barbara, who had been there as long, was making her life miserable. Theresa told me that Barbara would tell Lt. Col. Rowe stories about her that were completely untrue. She then would have to defend herself against things that had never happened. I felt so bad for her. Civilian workers on the depot were beginning to feel like actors on a soap opera. Theresa was such a caring individual. Her father was a Marine, and I always got the sense that she put the Marines first. She was always supportive of me and appreciative of my work. To be honest, I now felt a deeper connection with Theresa. It was nice to know I wasn't the only person Barbara didn't like.

Four and a half months (three six-week rotations) had gone by, and it was time for me to have another rotation out. I knew better than to ask if I could volunteer during the OSD (Office of the Secretary of Defense) required leave. I felt much more reassured this time because I knew Gary (the prior replacement) was coming back. He and I had been in contact throughout the last few months, and he was up to speed on everything that was going on. HWM had also committed to me coming back for four and a half months after the break, so I was a lot less anxious about leaving this time around.

One week before I was scheduled to leave, I had another major disappointment from HWM. John, after one of our worthless conference calls, informed me that Gary wouldn't be coming to replace me. To me, that was devastating news. I had just talked to Gary that morning, and it had been organized for months. What happened? It turned out that John had no control over who filled the open slots. The recruiter from HWM who filled the open positions had scheduled another MFLC named Deidre to come in and replace me. John explained that they were trying to negotiate with Deidre, but she was being difficult and inflexible. She had her heart set on coming to San Diego and was threatening HWM, stating that she had a signed contract for the rotation months ago. He apologized for the inconvenience this may cause me but said he was confident I would have no problem getting Deidre up to speed once she arrived. I hung up the phone, and for the second time in the nine months I had been working at MCRD, I started to cry.

As I was sitting in my office, laying there with my head in hands, Major Collins stopped by to bring me some great news. He had come from a meeting where they were just informed that in the last six months, recruit suicide attempts and drill instructor abuse had dramatically decreased. One of the things the leadership attributed this to was the proactive work that I was doing with the drill instructors. He wanted me to know that although they didn't have a way to prove it, the consensus was unanimous among all the companies; they saw this as a direct correlation with my work. He was so excited to tell me, that at first he didn't notice I was upset. "Are you crying?" he asked. "What's the matter?" I explained to him that Gary, my prior replacement, wasn't coming back and that a new person was taking over. There was no way I could get her up to speed in time. If only they would let me volunteer and stay, just to keep things going at a smooth pace. The number of Marines I was working with was so high, over five hundred, and I had no margin for error on the depot. One wrong move and Family Support Services would have me out of there, and that I was sure of. Major Collins smiled and said that he respected how dedicated I was to my job. He complimented me and said I acted like a true Marine, true commitment to the corps. He reminded me that things went okay with Gary, and I was nervous about that. He was certain things would go fine with the new person.

Colonel Chester was also great and helped me feel better. He repeated that no good program could rely on one person. A strong program was one in which the lead could walk away and things could still flow smoothly. I knew he was right. He also reminded me that, in his words, I went above and beyond what I was hired to do. He suggested that I might want to consider not having the replacement do the groups for the six weeks I was gone. He acknowledged that although it would be a loss for the Marines, if Deidre didn't pick things up quickly, it could cause more harm than good. I felt reassured when he reminded me that these were Marines, and they would help Deidre get along in my absence. He asked me to send e-mails to the battalions, updating them before I left. Of course, I wasn't allowed to do that, because HWM told me not to ever put anything in writing. Up until this point I obeyed their request. This time, I decided to break the "no e-mail" rule and sent four e-mails, one to each battalion addressing their needs while I was gone. I cc'd John at HWM, just to be safe.

This is the e-mail Third Battalion got. The other battalions received similar ones discussing their particular company schedules during the six weeks I'd be gone.

From: Marjorie Morrison
Sent: Wednesday, January 21, 2009 22:16
To: Ketchum Lt. Col. John S.; Smith Maj. Tom M.; Klondike Sgt. Maj. James W.
Cc: john.a.minor@HWM.com
Subject: MFLC rotation - 3 Bn

Hello gentlemen:

I just wanted to give you a "heads up" that next week begins my mandatory 6-week rotation "off" the Depot. A woman named Deidre Levant will replace me. Deidre and I will have a couple of overlap days, so I will make sure and introduce you to her.

As far as pick-up week, this will affect India Co. Deidre is going to shadow me next week during the Golf Co. pick up, so I am optimistic that she will be able to do these on her own.

As far as my groups on Grass Week, it will only affect Mike Co., the week of 2/17. I'm not sure what is the best plan for this. I plan on speaking to Captain Rodgers and getting his opinion. If I had my way, I'd like to come back to do this, but I have a feeling my contract will not allow me to do so.

Unfortunately, I will not be able to attend the Lima graduation next week, but I will be at there at their emblem ceremony tomorrow after the crucible. I will try and attend the India Co. graduation.

Deidre will be carrying the MFLC cell phone that the Drill Instructors all have, hopefully that will make contacting her seamless.

If you have ANY concerns at all, please feel free to let me know or call or e-mail our supervisor: John Minor.

I look forward to returning on March 9th. I'll miss you...

Marjorie

From: Ketchum Lt. Col. John S.
Date: January 23, 2009 3:29:39 PM PST
To: Marjorie Morrison
Cc: <john.a.minor@HWM.com>
Subject: RE: MFLC rotation - 3 Bn

Marjorie,

I know that you will be missed. The impact that you have on the Marines and their families is immeasurable. They trust and respect you and they are comfortable sharing with you information that they would not likely tell anyone else. As well, the advice and guidance you give me has helped me better understand the Marines within my command. We will be looking forward to your return.

John

Lt. Col. John S. Ketchum
Commanding Officer
3d Recruit Training Battalion
Marine Corps Recruit Depot
San Diego, CA

After multiple requests, HWM had finally given me Deidre's phone number. I tried reaching her countless times. She never answered her phone, and we had not made any contact prior to her arrival. Deidre was a woman in her late sixties. She wore a business suit and had a heavy German accent. Before I could even start the conversations regarding the unique work that I was doing with the Marines, she insisted we dealt with her hotel situation. She was not happy because her hotel was fifteen minutes away from the depot and she'd gotten lost trying to get to work. The whole thing was so convoluted, they were paying her airfare from Georgia, they were paying for her hotel suite for six weeks, they were giving her a per diem of over $100 even though her hotel provided daily breakfast and dinner, and she had a rental car with gas and all related expenses covered. I didn't receive any of those perks. I wasn't even allowed to expense my mileage, because I lived less than forty-five miles from the base. HWM saved so much money having me as a local provider, yet they continually sent replacements from out of state. To make matters worse, somehow it was my problem to fix her accommodations.

Deidre was a career MFLC, who traveled around the world through the MFLC program. I had only two days with her to explain the program, and we spent the whole first day dealing with her hotel accommodations. I did everything I could to help prepare her for the six-week job, but she was having a hard time grasping the basic concepts. She had never worked with Marines before but told me a dozen times that she had many more years of experience than I did as an MFLC and assured me that she'd been well received on every base she'd been to. She said she would be fine. I gave her a specific schedule to follow and told her all she needed to do was keep things "status quo" until I returned. She was not happy about the heavy workload and the long hours (I even cut a lot out for her). She informed me that in all her years of MFLC experience, she had never had to put in the type of hours I was requesting. She had some physical ailments and wasn't an early riser. She also did not want to work on the weekends because she had some trips planned. I tried to lighten her load and eliminated all of the groups and some of the other events from her schedule. I urged her to stay away from Family Support Services and explained that there was a lot of history and tension there. I found myself leaving the depot feeling very distressed again. Perhaps I had learned to take my job too seriously. I really didn't want to leave.

Ultimately, I enjoyed the break and spent a lot of time with my kids and family. I didn't hear from Deidre once. HWM reminded me again, that in keeping with the OSD (Office of Secretary of Defense) guidelines, I must maintain my distance. I did, however, hear from a lot of the Marines. They had become accustomed to communicating with me via text message. Texting was most definitely the common way Marines conversed. I was never able to text with the MFLC phone, so I mostly used my personal cell phone when communicating with the officers and senior enlisted. Every few days a Marine would call or text and share a situation he was experiencing. Sometimes they wanted guidance and other times they just wanted to vent to someone they knew would understand. Unfortunately, I was not hearing good things about Deidre. I felt really bad about the situation but always tried to remain positive with them. The upside was the experience seemed to make the Marines miss me more. It appeared that my absence was felt more this time around.

Unlike the last six-week break, during which I delved into the history and Marine Corps information, this time around I focused on formulating the proactive counseling program I was running. I began by researching the available counseling programs that were already in existence. I couldn't find any proactive ones. Everything out there was based on what I considered "the outdated reactive model." A person has a problem and goes to get help. Half the time, the problem is so far gone that it takes extreme interventions to repair. In other instances, the fear of the unknown, coupled with a determination not to succumb to feeling weak, prevents service members from seeking help. It was so obvious to me that talking to these guys ahead of time was a really good way to help prevent mental health issues. Why wouldn't our system want that for them? This wasn't *my* program; it originated from the Marines themselves. They wrote it; I was just implementing it. They deserved to have it more formalized.

I organized a giant binder and made dividers for each company and each battalion. It wasn't for keeping notes. I put in the companies' rosters so that I could put a check mark after a Marine had been seen. I'm a compulsive person, and if there were a drill instructor that I missed, I would make a point to see him at some point later in the cycle. In front of each roster, I put a checklist. It had all the important dates for that company: when they were picking up, dates for the drill instructor one-on-ones, series commanders and chief groups, meeting with the first sergeant and company commander, initial drill, grass week groups, final drill, end of cycle groups. There was a slot to put the date each was scheduled and the date it was completed. I wanted accountability for the program so that the next time a new MFLC rotated in, everything would be spelled out. I made sections for trends to be aware of and created a second binder of materials to hand out. By the time my six weeks were up, I had formally written up what looked like the beginnings of a complete and comprehensive proactive counseling program.

I had learned not to let anything surprise me anymore. As I headed back to MCRD, I had no idea what I was going to come back to this time. I knew it was not a good sign that the first words out of Deidre's mouth were, "I don't understand why you told me not to go to Family Support Services. Barbara and Gretchen don't have a problem with the MFLC program; they have a problem with you. They think you bad-mouth them so all the Marines will see you and not them." I couldn't believe what I was hearing. Weren't we all supposed to be there to support the Marines? One of the many things that I had learned to love about the Marine Corps was how they always worked together as a strong team. I couldn't imagine that while they were out fighting the war in Afghanistan two infantrymen would get into a fight about who should hit the enemy. Wouldn't that just give the enemy time to get away? The way I viewed it, if Family Support Services was going to expend its energy competing with me, the innocent Marine who needed help could slip away. Why couldn't we all be on the same team? I honestly just didn't get it. My frustration was amplified due to the fact if only HWM would get involved and help mitigate things between the two programs, I knew we could make it work.

On a good note, Deidre had an easy experience slipping into the role of doing the individual sessions. She was amazed at how much the Marines liked to talk. She said the job had been easy because it was her first MFLC assignment where there was a schedule to follow. She had support from the Marines everywhere she went. It was practically a foolproof program, plus she only had to do about half of what I was doing. Deidre was a typical HWM MFLC. She was used to sitting around an office, doing minimal work and collecting a paycheck. She worked hard this cycle, but I think like me, she found it rewarding.

Things with Family Support Services went from bad to worse over the next six weeks. I always made sure to schedule things around Gretchen's class time to avoid taking DIs out of her class time (a complaint that she once lodged against me). It was a major hassle for me because I had only two days to see more than thirty Marines, but avoiding conflict with her was worth the effort. It proved to only be a short-term solution. Now, Gretchen was changing her class times last minute. I would check the company schedule at the beginning of the week and arrange my days around her time. It seemed like every week she would change it. That meant that I couldn't see the DIs for the ninety minutes she originally scheduled and then again for the other ninety minutes of her time. I was becoming increasingly frustrated with her but still always made a habit of smiling at her when passing her in the hall. I resorted to the notion of "kill them with kindness." Of course, she never smiled back. She would always give me a nasty look. When she would see me, she'd sneer at me and say, "Don't even think of taking them during my time." Although I considered myself a master at time management, the windows of time to do my sessions were shrinking.

The chaplains had started referring to me on a regular basis now. I really enjoyed working with them. I was seeing couples, individuals, groups, more individuals, more groups, and more couples. The days were getting longer and longer. The phone never stopped ringing. One night I got a call at midnight from a drill instructor that had come home unexpectedly and found his wife in their bed having sex with his cousin. He was feeling like he was going to explode, but decided instead of hurting someone he would call me and try to calm down. I hung up the phone at 0100, only to be woken again at 0400 by a BMP who called because his roommate was curled in a ball and wouldn't stop crying. He tried to talk to him, but he seemed inconsolable. He'd tried calling the Marine "on duty" line, but they weren't answering. It took about thirty minutes for me to get him the help he needed to take care of his fellow Marine. At 0600 the phone rang again. This time it was the depot priest calling to see what time I was coming in because he had a distressed conscientious objector Marine that he wanted me to see.

On that day I was supposed to start at 0730 at the on-base Starbucks with a new company commander who wanted to talk to me to get advice and feedback on how best to lead this new company. He had heard that the drill instructors were not pleased with the past commander and wanted insight from me on how to approach them. That was one of the things about Marines that I loved: they were always striving to learn new ways to do things better. At 0830 I had a couple coming in. She was a Marine stationed at Miramar, and he was a drill instructor at MCRD. She'd just come home from being in Iraq for a year, and they were having marital issues. They had been married only two months before she was deployed. Being a drill instructor, he was hardly ever home, and they were fighting over typical issues such as domestic chores, lack of sex, jealousy, and insecurity about their future. That session couldn't last more than forty-five minutes, because at 930 I had to be on the other end of the depot for my BMP group. At 1030 I was starting my individual sessions with Golf Company, which was picking up that week. Gretchen was scheduled to come in from 1130 to 1230, so I had committed to go to the Lima Company final drill during that time.

At 1230, I had to be back at Second Battalion to do more one-on-ones. The size of companies depot-wide had been growing, which meant there was more DIs each week who needed to be seen. At 1630 I was seeing a Marine who was on quota. That is what it is called when a drill instructor goes over to Support Battalion to work. Typically the hours there are much better, and it's seen as either a reward for a good tour on the drill field or as a punishment because the DI had gotten in trouble and needed to get pulled out for a while. This Marine was on the good behavior side. He was a gunnery sergeant who had been referred by his company commander to see me. It was made very clear that this was not a mandatory, documented session. It was more a "Hey, I care about my Marine, and I'd like to see him get the help I feel like he deserves." This was going to be his third session with me. The last time he'd come in he'd broken down in tears after admitting that he wasn't able to shake the image of the faces of the people he had killed in Iraq. He had so much guilt over the Purple Heart that he received. He didn't feel like a hero; he felt like a murderer. I had heard this type of story dozens of times from Marines. Regardless, it was still hard to hear. They held so much guilt for their actions at war. This gunny was compensating by excessively drinking. He was tired of it and wanted to change but didn't know whom he could trust to talk to. He was afraid that getting more intensive help would hurt him professionally. Thankfully after that session, he agreed to go see someone at Navy Balboa Hospital. I knew they had a great PTSD program and felt good that he would be in good hands.

I had a half-hour hole in my late afternoon from 1730 to 1800, which undoubtedly would be filled with returning phone calls. At 1800 there was the First Battalion's new hat dinner. That is where the families of the new drill instructors come and meet everyone. The battalion commanders liked me to go to these so I could introduce myself to the spouses should they ever need anything.

I thoroughly loved every second of my job. My heart went out to the Marines, in an empathic way, not a sympathetic way. They had some tough issues to work through. But they had the ability to do the work and knew they could get through it. They knew better than anyone about hard work. They understood that if you put the effort in, the hard work would yield results. In fact, their ability to utilize techniques and implement change was better than any civilian's I had ever worked with. They were having positive results from the mandatory counseling, and the better results they were achieving, the more they would tell their fellow Marines, and the more people were coming in to get help. I was happy to be the catalyst in the process. What I really learned was how early detection directed these men to the right place to get help tailored to their individual needs. Everything made sense and we seemed to figure out a solution to the growing military mental health crisis.

The downside was that things had reached a point to which there was no way I could maintain this pace all by myself. The tough part again was that no single person knew everything I was doing. I had been thinking that the depot could really use another MFLC. At the rate things were going, there was most definitely enough work for two of us. Plus, I was only working with the RTR (the recruit training regiment). I wasn't providing any services for the rest of the depot. By the sound of the HWM conference calls, I was doing about ten times as much work as the average MFLC. It didn't make me envious. I'd much rather be busy than not. I hated those early days when all I could do was take inventory of materials in the supply cabinet in Family Support Services. It just made me frustrated that the resources weren't being used to what seemed like their greatest potential.

The next day I had a meeting with the Depot Sergeant Major, the highest-ranking enlisted Marine on the depot. The Depot Sergeant Major is, for all intents and purposes, the same rank as the general. Sgt. Maj. O'Conner was an incredibly personable Marine whom I would run into around the depot frequently. He liked the program I was doing and thought it would be a good idea to do the same type of thing over at recruiters school. Recruiters have a different set of issues from drill instructors. They are often placed in remote locations and can become very isolated. To me it was a huge compliment that he liked the program so much that he wanted to see it expanded. I explained to him that although I agreed with him wholeheartedly, there was no way I could tackle that at the current time. I could barely keep up with the five hundred drill instructors I was working with. But I was confident that with some additional help, we could make it happen. I had the RTR (Recruit Training Regiment) program so well structured that almost anyone could come in and take over. I was optimistic that I could start a similar program over at recruiter school. He asked if there were anything he could do to help get another MFLC. I told him it'd probably be best to touch base with Theresa (my POC) because she knew the right contact person at HWM. He told me he would e-mail her, and thanked me for all my hard work. I went to shake his hand, but instead he gave me a hug. "Marjorie." He smiled. "You are one of us. If you ever need anything, you let me know." Those words meant so much to me. I felt such honor. I was so proud to be considered one of them. That was most definitely one of the greatest compliments I had ever received.

Later that week I saw Colonel Chester at the Company Commanders Symposium. That is where all the company commanders in RTR (Recruit Training Regiment) come and discuss pertinent and current issues. It was a highly confidential course, but they always encouraged me to come. I could never stay the whole time because of my schedule, but I loved to hear the great camaraderie that would come out of those meetings. The conversations were always deep, and the discussions revolved around issues that felt so important—making and maintaining outstanding Marines. I enjoyed listening to the respect they gave each other as they spoke. The first sergeant symposiums were equally uplifting for me. It's always impressive to see and hear how leaders handle themselves in a large room. Of course there is ego, but it was always "in check" and it didn't ever appear to get in the way of the mission at hand.

Colonel Chester commented to me that he hadn't received much feedback from me lately. He knew that I had been busy;

after all he'd seen me practically every day at some event or another. He was curious if I had any feedback that he could benefit from. I apologized that I hadn't had an opportunity to stop by but explained how occupied my days had become. It was funny to think about how far I had come. The colonel wanted me to stop by and wanted my feedback. Knowing how busy we both were, he asked if I "wouldn't mind just shooting him an e-mail." I regrettably had to explain to him that I was not allowed to send e-mails anymore because Family Support Services had called my contractor complaining, which resulted in a stern warning against any future e-mails. That was the first time I had ever suggested to him that there was any sort of animosity with Family Support Services. He was visibly agitated and stated, "You don't work for Family Support Services; you work for me. I'm in charge here, and I benefited greatly from your e-mails."

There was the familiar pull again between walking on eggshells and just being able to do my job. It was my fault that Colonel Chester didn't know and understand the tensions between Family Support Services and myself. I'd never told him. I never gossiped about it to anyone. It would be completely unprofessional, and I felt that it would just make me look bad. I never wanted to be seen as a gossip. As a counselor, I needed to be seen as a trusting person that could keep things confidential. That next day I decided to send Colonel Chester an e-mail:

From: Marjorie Morrison
Sent: Friday, March 27, 2009 13:22
To: Chester Col. Craig T.
Subject: MFLC

Hi,

As promised, I wanted to keep you abreast on trends that seem to be consistent across all battalions.

First off, the new company offices at WFTBn are outstanding. I think it is going to inadvertently help the companies that are following and leading each other keep in touch. I know they are having some growing pains, but with all the companies in the same hall, the communication should greatly improve.

The current big issue right now is medications. DIs feel tremendous stress trying get the recruits their meds and keep the logs up to date. I understand that it is a very serious part of their job, but there do seem to be some discrepancies across the companies and battalions as to how this is handled. It appears to me that it may be a training issue and perhaps more time needs to go into instruction during p/u week. Another option could be to have corpsmen dispense or have a medication station at the "chow hall" during meals. Clearly, the majority of the issues seem to be present during first phase when the restrictions are more tightly mandated. The interesting thing to me is that each company seems to have issues with it and all have slightly different ways of handling it.

Another topic that comes up a lot is that TIMS isn't used to its greatest potential. I know that Capt. Cooley is trying out a test database this cycle in Bravo Co, so perhaps this will streamline some of the duplicate work DIs do. I hear all of the time how they have to hand write things multiple times that they should be able to pull off a database.

That brings me to the next big issue. The DIs always need to make copies and the S4 closes at 4:00 and isn't open on Saturdays and Sundays. This means they have to buy their own printers and ink cartridges. They become increasingly frustrated because they end up spending extra money out of their pockets.

Boy....do I sound like a complainer?! I'm sure you have heard this all before, but just wanted to let you know the same issues I hear over and over again!

Have a great weekend,
Marjorie

From: Chester Col. Craig T.
Date: March 27, 2009 3:38:48 PM PDT
To: Marjorie Morrison
Subject: RE: MFLC

Marjorie - thank-you. This is a good way to communicate. The issues you raise are continuing problems, but we can make them somewhat better, particularly the copier issue - the ROOD always has access to that S-4 copier. Thanks again for all your outstanding work.

Col Chester

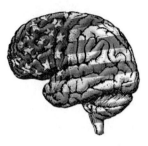

NEVER-ENDING TURMOIL

A few days later, a very distressing thing happened. I was at Camp Pendleton for the day and I received a call from Theresa (my POC), which almost never happened. She told me that Lt. Col. Rowe (her supervisor) had forwarded to her an e-mail that Barbara had sent to him regarding me and the MFLC program. She needed to talk with me about the e-mail and wanted to do it in person; she felt that the matter was urgent. I had an absolutely packed day up at Camp Pendleton, which was about forty-five minutes north of MCRD (Marine Corps Recruit Depot). She suggested that I cancel my appointments and come down so that she could show me the e-mail and we could discuss it. I was so frustrated; I barely remembered the forty-five-minute drive. I had to cancel a full day of counseling sessions with Marines to deal with yet another Family Support Services complaint about me. I couldn't imagine what their complaint was now. It seemed like every day in the past few weeks someone had told me something derogatory Gretchen had said about me. Although it was annoying, I continued to not engage in the conversation about it. My response was almost always the same, "Sounds like she doesn't like me."

When I arrived at Theresa's office, she asked me to have a seat. She was very sweet and said, "I know this is going to be hard for you to read. Please keep in mind the source it is coming from." I sat down and took a deep breath. The first two-thirds of the e-mail I had heard many times before. Barbara went on about the domestic violence case that had happened at Family Support Services the year prior, repeating that I didn't know what a domestic violence case was, and therefore my clinical skills couldn't be trusted. She then went on her usual rant about me, saying that I say negative things about Family Support Services and, of course, her frustrations with the MFLC program. I was almost certain that part of the e-mail was a cut and paste from the e-mail she had sent to HWM about me the previous year, before I was moved out of the Family Support Services office.

It was the last part of the e-mail that literally stunned me. It said that Chaplain Stone had come to her because one of his Marines had told him that I was bad-mouthing Family Support Services. She actually quoted the derogatory things I had supposedly said. I knew for a fact that I had never said anything even close to that. The gist of her complaint was that I had said the Marines should see me for counseling instead of them, because the Family Support Services reports everything back to the command and that I don't. Her other issue was that I was "splitting" and trying to turn the Marines against Family Support Services. All I could think of was the expression "look at the pot calling the kettle black." Could she be serious? I had never turned anyone against her; on the contrary, it always felt like they were trying to turn people against me.

The whole thing was so irritating. I knew I had never said anything even close to that, although it was true that I could keep conversations confidential. That was just the nature of the MFLC program. My big question was why would this Chaplain Stone say these things? I didn't even know him; I had only met him once, and it was a brief introduction. He was the chaplain in the Support Battalion, so he wasn't really among my direct contacts.

Theresa came around the desk and put her arm around me. She consoled me and told me that Barbara was probably really pissed off because the depot sergeant major wanted another MFLC. She suggested I go talk to the chaplain and get things sorted out. While I was in Theresa's office, my cell phone rang three times. I didn't pick it up for obvious reasons, but the fourth time it rang, I answered it. It was a first sergeant from one of the training companies. One of his drill instructors had just shared with him that the night before his wife had left him, packed up her things and the kids, and disappeared. He was irate with his wife but was blaming the whole event on the fact that since he was a drill instructor he was never home and couldn't tend to her needs. He wanted to know if I could find any time in the day to see that Marine. Like always, I said of course and scheduled a time to go over. I wondered if the Marines could ever fathom the stupid drama that kept popping up and getting in the way of my helping them. Of course I would never say a word.

Before heading over to the anguished Marine, I stopped by the Support Battalion to talk to the chaplain. Unfortunately, he wasn't in his office that day. I called him and left a distressed message, asking him to call me as soon as possible. I truly was perplexed. I had no idea what this was about and where it came from. I went to the Support Battalion CO and shared with her what I had learned through the e-mail. She was one of those very wise women who always says profound things at just the right time. Her response was, "Let the XO investigate this. Let him peel back the layers of the onion. I know the truth will rise and everything else will sink." I knew I had never bad-mouthed Family Support Services, so I was happy to have some intervention and held credence to her words.

The next day the Support Battalion XO, Major Trimm, called me into his office. He asked me to tell my side of the story. Honestly, I didn't have a side. I had no idea what the heck was going on. He let me know that he had spoken with the chaplain and he relayed his supposed story. One of their Marines was going through a difficult time because of a bitter divorce. The chaplain reported that when he suggested to the Marine, gunny (Gunnery Sergeant) Romero, that he should go talk to someone in Family Support Services, he replied that he didn't want to go there because I had said negative things about them. Listening to this brief story refreshed my memory to an event that had happened a couple of weeks prior.

This is what I recalled: I was walking by the Marine's office when the man inside stopped me. He asked if he could set up an appointment to see me. In brief dialogue, I asked him if he had talked to anyone about his situation. I made it a point to always do that, because if someone had an open case at Family Support Services, I couldn't see him or her. This Marine had said that he had gone to the chaplain for help and that he'd sent him over to Family Support Services. He went voluntarily but had no connection and didn't feel comfortable with the person he saw there, who happened to be Gretchen. He felt like the session was punitive, and he didn't want to go back. He was also upset because Family Support Services reported everything about his case back to his command. I apologized to him for his experience but explained that once he was in the Family Support Services system I wasn't allowed to see him. I did say he could look into it with his command, and since he wasn't required to go to Family Support Services, he may have other referral options. I assured him that if he could go elsewhere I could give him some options. The crazy thing was, I even remember telling him that he really should give Family Support Services another try. I always wanted what was best for the Marines first, and knowing how the system worked, I was afraid that he actually may not have another option. I also remembered that there was another Marine in the room, so I didn't want to delve too much into his personal situation because I didn't want to make him feel uncomfortable. I couldn't figure out how the story got so twisted. Where did the chaplains version come from?

After I finished explaining my side to Major Trimm, he called a Marine in the room that I had never seen in my life. He stated his name, Lance Corporal Desmond, and upon entering the room, explained that he was in the office next door (not in the room with us) and had overheard the conversation between Gunny Romero and me. He reported that he had heard me say that the counselors at Family Support Services were mean and that they didn't try to make connections with the Marines. He then added that I told Gunny Romero that he shouldn't go there for help. It was one of the strangest experiences I have ever had in my life. This young Marine was sitting right in front of me, telling me that I said things that I knew for a fact I'd never said! There are no words to describe how bizarre the experience was. Major Trimm excused the Marine and then called the chaplain in the room. As soon as he walked in the door, he accused me of splitting services between Family Support Services and myself. I don't remember half the things he said because I was in such a state of shock and disbelief that I think my mind shut itself off in protection, and I stopped listening. I remember his very condescending tone and how he looked at me with true disdain. Why was he so mad at me? Where was all this anger coming from?

Major Trimm asked me to come back in the morning because he wanted to hear from Gunny Romero himself and the other Marine who was in the room when our conversation transpired. I agreed. What choice did I have? This had already sucked up my entire day and now it was going to linger into the next day. What a waste! Something felt very screwy with this story, but I had no idea what was happening.

I got in my car and left the depot. I took a drive down to the beach. I didn't want the Marines to see me so distressed, and I needed some time to collect my thoughts and pull myself together. I was getting tired. The long hours away from home and the constant drama with the folks in Family Support Services were really starting to get to me. Maybe it was time for me to give this all up. I reminded myself that before all of this, I had a flourishing practice and a beautiful office close to home. I used to have control over my schedule, and it was easy to clear some time to go to a school show or my kids dance recital. Now I was so busy, and I spent every waking moment at MCRD. I knew I had many people and physicians that would refer to me in my private practice, and I'd be right back to a full-time caseload in no time. As good as that sounded at that moment, I knew deep down I could never abandon the Marines. It wasn't their fault that Family Support Services didn't like me. It wasn't their fault that HWM never had time to help mediate things between us. The Marines had grown to rely on me, and I wasn't ready to walk away just yet. Besides, every day I learned more about life just being in their presence. My existence felt like it had meaning when I was working with them, and for that I could find the strength to put up with the latest commotion. I took a few deep breaths and headed back to the depot. I had eight more drill instructors that were scheduled for their one-on-ones that day, and I intended to give them my best.

The next morning I walked into Major Trimm's office feeling numb and discouraged. Today was round two when I would hear from Gunny Romero. When I sat down, Major Trimm smiled and asked if I was ready. Despite being a person who always smiles, I couldn't find my facial muscles to even fake an attempt. First he called in Staff Sergeant Lamont. He was the Marine who shared an office with Gunny Romero. Major Trimm started out by asking him if anyone had talked to him about why he was there. The staff sergeant replied no and that he had no idea what this was about. Major Trimm's next question was whether he knew who I was and how he knew me. He replied, "She had walked past my office, which I share with Gunny Romero. He had asked her to come in." He continued by recounting the conversation that transpired with me. Amazingly and thankfully, his recollection was exactly the same as mine. Major Trimm probed him, asking if I had said anything derogatory about Family Support Services. He exclaimed, "On the contrary, sir. She encouraged him to go back to them and give it another try." Now my smile was starting to come back.

Major Trimm thanked the staff sergeant and excused him. He then called in Gunny Romero. He asked him the same questions he had asked the other Marine. Gunny Romero had the exact same remembrance of the scenario as his office mate and me. Gunny, who claimed to have no idea that there was any drama about this, went on to compliment and say nice things about me. He said he was having a really hard time and would really like to see me for some counseling. Both men added that, Gunny Romero and Staff Sgt. Lamont, reported never having talked to the chaplain about their conversation with me. I was so happy to hear that we all remembered the same conversation. I now knew I wasn't going crazy, but I was also still very confused as to how it got all turned around.

Here is how I learned the truth revealed itself. Lance Corporal Desmond (the Marine from the other room whom I had never seen before) overheard the conversation I had with Gunny Romero. For some reason he told the chaplain what he thought he heard me say. I still have no idea why. It is my understanding that one day while the chaplain was at Family Support Services, and at the prompt of Barbara's probing questions, he had told her some version of what had transpired. He never asked the two men who had the conversation with me for facts. Somehow he got caught in Barbara's web, and the story got spun completely out of control. I was torn between feeling pissed off that this had happened in the first place and being happy that I had been vindicated.

I left the office and placed an emergency call to John at HWM. I felt it was imperative to fill him in on what had happened. John reinforced that I did the right thing by not seeing Gunny Romero initially because he had been seen at Family Support Services. Although it was nice to have him validate me, I desperately needed intervention with Family Support Services, and I needed it from HWM. It was only a matter of time before something like this happened again. I pleaded with John for HWM to help me and get involved. I was willing to do anything to make peace with Barbara and Gretchen. I explained to John that things were escalating and I urgently needed help mediating the situation. I expressed that I had hoped if I'd stayed off their radar things would quiet down, but it had been the contrary. Unfortunately, John held firm and told me that any intervention at this point would just make things worse and I just needed to continue and keep my distance from them. It was so frustrating! I had been hearing the same thing from HWM for months. It was crystal clear to me that there was not going to be any support from them. They truly did not care!

The next day I received a phone call from Chaplain Stone. He asked if he could schedule some time to see me. I was a little ambivalent because he had said some pretty horrible things to me, and to make it worse, he hadn't done his homework before he condemned me. On the other hand, I'm human, I believe in forgiveness and was always willing to give a situation a chance for reconciliation. We scheduled a time to meet later that day in his office. He was very endearing and quietly cried as we sat down. He handed me a bouquet of flowers and apologized for what he did and said there was no excuse for his behavior. He went on to say that the whole thing was out of character for him. Apparently when he saw Barbara, she started inundating him with questions about me, and then she flooded him with talk about what a terrible person I was. He didn't know me, so he figured she must be right. He admitted that he got caught up in a trap and falsely accused me. He asked if I could ever forgive him. Of course, I accepted his apology and chalked it up to a big misunderstanding. I tried to make him feel better by telling him that it could happen to anyone.

I did feel bad for him. I'm sure Barbara was pretty convincing. I've seen her scathing e-mails about me. In fact, I've seen many of her ranting e-mails about others as well. I had heard that Chaplin Stone got in big trouble with the command for what had happened with me. I certainly didn't wish him ill, and I felt bad about his reprimand. I was working here for one purpose and that was to bring mental health services to these Marines. This was the mantra that I would tell myself on a regular basis when stuff like this would happen. The Support Battalion XO Major Trimm promised to talk to Lt. Col Rowe (the POC over Family Support Services) and tell him the whole story. I trusted that he would do so.

My consolation prize from the whole experience was that the chaplain asked me if I could see one of his Marines who needed some counseling. I think this was his sort of a peace offering. I thanked him for entrusting me to work with his Marines. Truthfully, I had no idea how and when I was going to squeeze his referral in. At this point, I was two days behind, thanks to this fiasco. I stayed a little longer that night to see his depressed Marine. He was a good guy who needed the help, so I was glad I did.

Putting this behind me, I went back to focus on the drill instructors. I had some new ideas that I wanted to implement, and I was anxious to talk with the battalion commanders regarding them. The main addition was working on team and group cohesion. I wanted to delve into this a little deeper and had suggested making some minor changes. The feedback on this suggestion at the company level was phenomenal. Since I wasn't supposed to send e-mails, I had gotten into the habit of stopping by the battalions every Friday to fill them in on the week. This week, I was so far behind I wasn't able to stop in. I decided to send the three training battalions one mass e-mail. If the e-mail got in Family Support Service's hands and they reported me, then so be it. I had a job to do, and I was starting to get really tired of these people getting in my way.

From: Marjorie Morrison
Sent: Friday, April 10, 2009 16:20
Subject: MFLC WFTBn Update

Good afternoon Gentlemen:

I wanted to let you know that my green belt groups up north have been going very well. I've received very positive feedback and Tuesday mornings at 9:30 during Grass Week seems to be a perfect time. The drill instructors at WFTBn are getting used to the schedule and the majority of the green belts have been able to attend.

My difficulty has been finding a time to get all of the seniors together. A couple of months ago a chief (India Co) asked if he could join in the group with his 3 seniors. I met with the four of them and then did the same for Follow Series. This week, I've had the opportunity to meet with the India seniors during pick-up week and they have reported back to me that they found those "smaller, senior/ chief groups" very beneficial. I'd like to be able to incorporate this into my rotation with the DIs. I'm not sure when in the training schedule this would work, but I'm confident with a little trial and error, I'll find a slot (most likely during second phase).

I am going to start this upcoming Tuesday afternoon with Lima Co, who was very supportive of the idea. I don't expect any resistance from any of the 12 companies, but wanted to open the forum to you for any feedback before I get started.

Thank you so much for your continued support and please let me know if you have any thoughts and/or opinions. I will keep you posted on how things go.

Have a nice weekend,
Marjorie

From: Smith Maj. Tom M.
Date: April 10, 2009 5:12:50 PM PDT
To: Marjorie Morrison
Subject: RE: MFLC WFTBn Update

Marjorie,
Thanks for the feedback. We highly appreciate the support that we receive from you. Happy Passover!

Maj. Tom Smith
Executive Officer
3rd Recruit Training Battalion
Recruit Training Regiment, MCRD, San Diego

That day I sent a separate e-mail to Colonel Chester:

From: Marjorie Morrison
Sent: Monday, May 11, 2009 22:10
To: Chester Col. Craig T
Cc: Brogan Lt. Col. Bruce A
Subject: MFLC update

Dear Col. Chester,

I hope you are doing well. Per your request, I wanted to give you a brief update on my work.

I have been kept very busy here at MCRD and my "set" schedule seems to be working out quite well. I have successfully been meeting with every drill instructor one at a time during pick-up week, followed by a group with the 2 chiefs and 2 series commanders, and a meeting the following week with the 1st Sgt. and CO. I do green belt groups during Grass Week, senior belt and chief groups during Firing Week. I attempt to attend as many of their events as possible, including: initial drill, final drill, graduation, etc. Needless to say, the 12 companies see me multiple times throughout the cycle!

Interestingly, I think that DIs quality of life has improved over this past year. They are, overall, getting more time off, which directly affects their family life, which continues to improve over time. For example, when I do my pick-ups, I keep tally marks of how many marital issues are occurring in a given company. With each subsequent cycle (with the exception of 2 companies), these numbers continue to decrease. When I probe as to why things are better, it's almost always because they are home more (at least one day a week). They are able to relax a little and spend time with the family before heading back. In contrast, there have been two companies that have an increased number of marital conflicts. In both situations they have very senior chiefs, and seniors that have been on the Depot for a few years (I call these "pre Glass Case DIs"). My conclusion is that although there has been significant change, the "old ways" still exist and I am optimistic that time will solve that dilemma.

On the same note, it is not uncommon to find green belt drill instructors that are conflicted between what they are being "told" to do and what they are "expected" to do. I also recognize that change is going to be slow because each company has a 1st Sgt. that was previously on the Drill Field, during very different circumstances. So although they understand the intent, they may fall back by default into past behaviors, again reinforcing these conflicting orders. This is not to say that every 1st Sgt. is this way; it's merely a trend I've noticed.

Overall, I do believe things are moving in a very positive direction.

The winter months have brought about a series of new challenges. The companies are "stacked" with many "hats" and the number of platoons is small. Although the level of training should be high (compared to summer months), it seems to be creating new issues. In some companies, the issues manifest in the recruits (i.e., multiple injuries, illnesses, and of course the "huffers"). In other companies, the repercussions have been more apparent in the DIs behaviors and actions. In essence, too many people trying to train too few recruits seems to put extra stress in the system. Hopefully once the platoon sizes increase, the issues will decrease. A good thing that has come of this is that the companies are communicating with each other to help prevent similar mistakes. For example, Kilo has spent time going over their experiences with Mike Co (which has all 5-hat and one 6-hat teams for 335 recruits) helping them avoid some of the issues they've had. Charlie has done the same with Delta, and Golf has with Hotel. I love that level of synergy and hope it will help prevent problems from reoccurring.

Things seem to be getting a little better with having access to the copiers. Issues with dispensing medication seem to be improved. There was a lot of grumbling about the Thursday out post briefs because seniors wanted to spend time with the recruits' families at the Bayview, but since you have moved the time up an hour, I've heard fewer complaints. Some new issues with the "new marines" having moved upstairs, but change is often followed by resistance and I'm sure once they get used to it, things will settle down.

I have been flooded with referrals. Both for individual and couples work and company "team building" work. All the DIs have the MFLC phone number stored in their phones and I've been averaging 20 plus calls a week from them. In addition, co commanders and 1st sgts call me very frequently for assistance with their companies. This can be anything from doing extra groups to meeting with teams, etc. I feel very grateful that I have a very nice working relationship with all 12 companies and have really enjoyed getting to know them and their different personalities. In addition, I help out in Support Bn and do a weekly group with the BMPs. You wouldn't believe how much insight I get from them, having just completed training. They provide me with a completely different perspective. I also spend one day a week at WFTBn and support their marines as well. Although I often put in

12-hour days, it pales in comparison to what the DIs put in. I would love to see another MFLC here on the Depot to provide the same support to H&S and the Recruiters. (I can barely keep up with RTR.)

I spoke with Sgt. Major Calvin a couple of weeks ago about writing a class for DI school. I think it would be very beneficial for the DIs to learn how to work with and motivate people with different personality types. My idea is to break the average personalities into four categories (i.e., the bully, the jokester, the intellect, etc.). The class would be broken up into triads. Each group would get a vignette of different probable recruit situations (i.e., a recruit who refuses to train). One student acts as the DI, one as the recruit, and one as an observer who will give the feedback. The students rotate, playing different roles. On the drill field, the experienced DIs have learned how to change their behaviors depending on the personality of the recruit, but the new hats have such a hard time grasping this concept. I really believe an experiential class would be helpful and expedite their learning curve. Sgt. Major was very supportive and I told him that I would write the curriculum and let him know how much class time it would take. Please let me know if you have any thoughts.

On a personal note, I'm thoroughly enjoying my job and continually learn from these outstanding marines every day. This morning I went to a 6 am boxing class at the "Throwdown" with Sgt. Maj. Simpson and Lt. Col. Becker. It was a pretty pathetic site, and I'm very grateful for Ibuprofen!

I imagine that things are getting hectic for you as your move gets closer. I hope as your tour here comes close to its end, you can reflect on all of the positive changes you have brought to this depot. Although you have been the only RTR commander I have ever known, I know that you have made significant contributions. I especially respect the work you have done in the area of core values and incorporating them into values-based training. You will be missed.

Take care,
Marjorie

From: Chester Col. Craig T.
Date: May 13, 2009 1:26:54 PM PDT
To: Marjorie Morrison
Cc: Brogan Lt. Col. Bruce A.
Subject: RE: MFLC update

Marjorie,

Very good report - thank-you. Some of your observations are cyclic occurrences. For example, getting used to 5 hat teams only occurs during this time of year and will adjust back this summer. Interestingly, that also accounts for the additional "family time" you note. Unfortunately, that will go away also this summer when the companies return to doing back-to-back cycles.

Your words on the 1st Sgts are to be expected to some degree - I will tackle that issue head on during the upcoming 1st Sgt symposium.

Keep up the good work and thanks for all the "above and beyond" work you do.

Col. Chester

From: Brogan Lt. Col. Bruce A.
Date: May 12, 2009 9:36:31 AM PDT
To: Marjorie Morrison
Subject: RE: MFLC update

Marjorie,

Thanks for all this good info. You do awesome work. I have sent Lt. Col. Rowe a message asking him about adding another MFLC to the Depot. I'll keep you posted.

Bruce

Lt. Col. Bruce Brogan
XO, RTR
MCRD San Diego

The following week Lt. Col. Malone from Second Battalion (CO) called me. He had just gotten back from a trip to Parris Island (that is the other Marine Corps Recruit Depot for Marines east of the Mississippi River). While he was there, he talked to them about how great the MFLC program was in San Diego. He was stunned to find out that their MFLC didn't do the same thing there. I briefly knew the Parris Island MFLCs (they had two) because of my weekly conference calls. I also knew that they had a hard time getting any work on that base because they were held on a very tight leash and not allowed to make too many connections there on their own. Lt. Col. Malone wanted to help facilitate a connection between the Parris Island MFLCs and their battalion commanders, so I gave him the contact phone number. I was hopefully optimistic that they would be able to start a similar proactive counseling there as well.

The next day I received a call from the FRO (family readiness officer) who worked for one of the generals at Marine Corp headquarters. Somehow the general had heard about the proactive counseling work I was doing with the MCRD Marines and wanted to inquire about doing the same type of program for the recruiters. Wow! From an outsider's perspective, one could say that things were going great. Marines were seeing the benefits of proactive counseling, and the program was receiving very positive feedback. I was content.

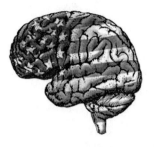

DISMISSED

The following Thursday everything changed. This particular Thursday I had a typical super-busy day. I had fourteen more drill instructors that needed to be seen individually. I also had two groups scheduled that day, plus three individual sessions and two couples. Golf Company was graduating the next day and the first sergeant was giving a speech to the parents that afternoon that he wanted me to hear it. We had worked together on his anxiety of public speaking, and he was really proud of the success he had made. Of course I wanted to be there to support him. Lastly, I had the weekly useless hour conference call with HWM at 1300.

At the end of the conference call, John asked me to stay on the line. He'd done that only once before, the time Gretchen had called to complain about my e-mailing command. This is what he said to me, "Donna (his supervisor) is trying to get a hold of you and you need to call her right away." I asked him what it was about, and he coldly replied that he was not at liberty to discuss it with me.

I hung up and called Donna right away. She answered her phone, which was a first. She started out by saying that she had been trying to reach me all morning and hadn't been able to get through. I immediately responded to her explaining that I had both my personal cell and the MFLC cell with me all morning and I'd never received a call from her. I checked both phones while we were talking, and there was no record of a call from her. She then very casually said, "Hey, I've got some bad news. I've received word from Marine Corps headquarters to have you removed from the base. You have thirty minutes to collect your belongings and get off the base."

I was dumbfounded! That was it? Was that seriously all she was going to tell me? After I could catch my breath, I asked, "Why?"

Her response was even more remarkable, "I can't tell you, but it came through a high chain of command. These things just happen from time to time." She went on to say that I could not, under any circumstances, talk to anyone. My instructions were to take all my belongings because I wouldn't be coming back. She had to go because she had another call coming in. It was as though the whole thing meant nothing to her.

I hung up the phone and sat frozen in my chair. I had no idea what to do. Was someone going to tell me what happened? Was I supposed to just not show up to my scheduled appointments? How could I do that to these Marines? In a trance, I walked over to my office and packed up all of my things. It was like a bad dream, but somehow I knew it was real. I should have seen it coming. It was only a matter a time that something like would happen. Somehow I believed that if I stayed out of Family Support Service's way and provided quality work, they would eventually leave me alone, I was wrong! I took about ten trips to the car, carrying boxes filled with books and papers. I had accumulated a lot in that office over the year I was there. I had no idea what I was supposed to say to the people in the library where my office was located. How was I supposed to explain the mass exodus of my stuff? HWM told me I wasn't allowed to talk to anyone. Why did I feel compelled to still follow their orders and listen to them? After all, they never listened to me.

On my last trip to the car, I saw Gretchen standing in front of the Family Support Servicesdoor. She had a huge smile on her face as she watched me load my car. I'd say that was my lowest point, right there.

I went back in the library to say good-bye to the librarians; now I was mad. "Guys, I was just fired for an unknown reason, and I won't be back." It felt like those words were coming out of somebody else's mouth. They clearly were as shocked as I was. They hugged me and made me promise not to be a stranger. A stranger? Clearly that was what I was to HWM; they knew nothing about me and very little about the work I was doing.

I started to make my way off the depot. As the exit approached, I turned around. I had to at least say good-bye to Theresa. She was my POC, and surely she had to know something about what went down. Would it be so bad for me to talk to her? When I entered her office, she had a huge smile; she addressed me the way she always did: "What's up, girl?" At that moment it became obvious to me that she didn't have a clue.

I looked her dead in the eye and quietly replied, "I was just fired." She looked like she had just seen a ghost.

"How could you be fired? You work for me. I am your supervisor. I'm the only one that can fire you."

I told her what Donna from HWM had said. Theresa was pissed! I could almost see the steam coming off her head. She immediately picked up the phone and called Donna. Unfortunately she got her voicemail. She left her a message explaining that she was my POC and that no one had the right to fire me or go above her head without her knowing about it. She demanded a call back and wanted someone to explain to her what had transpired. She gave me a hug and told me how sorry she was. She hated to add my name to her list of good people that

Barbara had gotten rid of over the years. She promised to call me as soon as she knew something.

I drove toward the exit of the depot in a complete daze. Just as I approached the gate, I got pulled over by the military police. What were they going to do, handcuff me? Put me in jail? I had no idea what was going on? Was I in the middle of a dream? Wasn't there somebody who could tell me what was happening? I pulled off to the side of the road. The officer came up and asked me for my ID. My hands were shaking as I fumbled through my purse to get it. He looked at the ID and then at me.

"Ma'am, did you realize that you did not make a complete stop at that stop sign? I'm going to need to give you a moving violation."

I guess that was the thing that made me snap because it was at that point that I started sobbing. The officer, concerned that I was overreacting, explained to me that it was simply a military violation and that it wouldn't go on my driving record. I finally pulled it together enough to mutter to him that I had just been fired. I pointed to the back of my car, which was filled with moving boxes. Under the circumstances, he let me off with just a warning. That was about the only positive thing that happened that day.

As I drove off the depot, I decided to call Donna again on my way home. How could she just zing me with that news and not give me any information? What if it was a situation similar to what happened with the chaplain and I was accused of something I didn't do? Even worse, what if it was because of the situation with the chaplain? What if Barbara sent her original e-mail that Theresa had shown me to Marine Corps headquarters before the real truth came out?

At this point it was all speculation on my part. Luckily she answered her phone. She still wouldn't give me any information. The only comments she made was, "I know this is easier said than done, but don't take it personally. This kind of stuff happens from time to time." She also said, "Look, I can tell you that technically you are not to contact anyone, but I can't make you do that." The last thing she said was that she was going to be out of the country the following week and that we would touch base the week after that. This whole thing was no big deal for her. It was as though this was just one of the many things she had to do in her busy day. In my mind, she clearly couldn't have cared less about me and certainly didn't care about the Marines I was working with. All she seemed to care about was her liability and saying and doing the right thing for her contract. There was absolutely no human compassion.

The last thing I said was, "Are you serious? You told me to collect my stuff and leave the depot. I did exactly what you told me to do. The only person I contacted was my POC who knew nothing about this, and you are not going to give me any indication of what happened. To make it worse, now you are telling me that you won't have time to talk to me about it for two weeks?"

Her reply: "Yes."

I pulled into my house. How would I explain this to my family? How was I to make any sense of this? They all knew how much I loved my job and how much passion I put in it. Every night I told them stories about how incredible the Marines were. In most cases if you get fired, you know what you did. I had never been fired from anything in my life.

My husband was, of course, supportive and spared himself from saying, "I told you so." He had warned me something like this could happen repeatedly. He did say, "If I were you, I'd call someone." Perhaps he was right, but I couldn't decide whom to call. I couldn't even think straight.

I decided to call Colonel Chester, after all he was the head of the whole recruit training regiment. First I called his office. There was no answer. I had his personal cell phone number for emergencies, but I had never used it. This felt as close to an emergency as ever. My fingers were trembling as I dialed the phone. I almost hoped he wouldn't answer because I was so humiliated to say the words "I was fired." He did answer the phone. I calmly said, "Sir, I'm sorry to bother you, but I wanted to let you know that I was fired this afternoon."

His response was almost exactly like Theresa's—sheer shock! "How can someone fire you? You work for me." He went on to say, "I'm in charge here, and no one is getting rid of you without my consent." He told me not to worry and that he would get it straightened out. A couple of hours later he called back to tell me that he was trying to reach his chief of staff but that he was already gone for the day. I thanked him for his efforts and asked him to please keep me informed when he heard something.

Within a half hour of hanging up with Colonel Chester, Captain Lewis from Fox Company called me. Apparently his first sergeant had been in the RTR (Recruit Training Regiment) where Col. Chester works and was in the RTR Sgt. Major Calvin's office when Col. Chester walked in asking to speak to the sergeant major in private. First Sgt. Ryan was not positive that what he'd overheard was correct, but he was pretty sure that he'd heard Col. Chester say that I had been fired. The first sergeant immediately went back to the office and told his company commander what he thought he had heard. Captain Lewis was calling to find out if that rumor could possibly be true.

I had no insights to share with him; I could only to confirm that yes, it was true that I had been fired. He fell silent. I would have broken the silence, but I didn't want to cry. He finally spoke again and said, "Marjorie, you have been the greatest support that I have ever had in my nine years as a Marine. Just today, I was with two other company commanders, and we were saying how much you have helped us be better commanders. I don't understand why the corps does things like this. They say they want what is best, but then they take away the things that help us.

I knew Captain Lewis felt bad, but I also knew it was not the corps' fault. I believed that they did want what was best for the Marines, but unfortunately, they were listening to the wrong people. He asked if there was anything he could do to help. Maybe the right answer would have been to tell him to talk to everybody and let's fight this, but I didn't. I asked him not to tell anyone. I had no idea what they fired me for, and I didn't have the energy to wage a war when I didn't even know the facts. The only thing I did know was that I had never intentionally done anything wrong. I had always tried to stick to my work and avoid the drama. Clearly, that strategy did not work for me.

As I hung up the phone, I felt so bad. I had let them down and there was nothing I could do about it. There were three messages on my phone. All three were from sessions that I didn't show up to earlier in the day. What was I supposed to do about tomorrow's appointments? This just felt so terribly wrong on all accounts and there wasn't one thing I could think of to fix it.

My husband knew I was distressed (to say the least). In the midst of my comatose state, had arranged an impromptu vacation for us. I most definitely needed the time away. Lt. Col. Becker's call was the only call I took while I was gone. She wanted to check in on me. She had nothing to report but wanted me to know that word had gotten out and everyone was up in arms at the depot. Colonel Chester and the other battalion commanders were all very upset about it. I knew she felt so bad for me. I hated the pity and felt so humiliated.

I couldn't help but go over things again and again in my head. I kept asking myself what I could have done. How can they just say, "Leave," and not even tell you what you did wrong? Shouldn't there be some sort of investigation or an opportunity for me to defend myself? Then I would remember whom I was dealing with.

Barbara had threatened multiple times that she knew someone at the OSD (Office of the Secretary of Defense) who knew the person that oversaw the MFLC program, and she could make it go away whenever she wanted. Why shouldn't I have known that she would do this? Why shouldn't I have known that HWM would of course take her side? They never cared about providing quality services. I didn't believe they cared about the Marines, and I knew they certainly didn't care about me, or the work I was doing. The only thing they cared about was maintaining their contract so they could benefit from their fat profits. The whole thing was so sad.

Every once in a while, I could move out of obsessive thinking; vacationing for a long weekend really hit the spot. The beach and sun were helpful. I slowly started feeling better. I knew I would be okay. I'd miss the work, but I would prevail. It was the Marines I felt so bad for. Those committed men and women got so shafted by the very programs that exist to help them. Our society has been going about treating mental illness all wrong. We need to reach these young men and women from the beginning. Build rapport with them. Help them learn about themselves and provide them with the necessary resources to be the best people they can be. On the other hand, I knew I couldn't tackle the military mental health system myself. Maybe there was something I could do, but I couldn't think of a thing. All I could think about was the drill instructor that was supposed to come in that day that had finally stopped drinking. He always said that our weekly sessions were what got him through the next week staying sober. And the Marine and his wife that just had three young nephews descended upon them because their dad was deployed in Afghanistan and their mom was battling cancer. They were stressed and really benefited from the strategies and parenting tools they received in our sessions. I had to stop thinking about the Marines that I essentially abandoned. There was no point.

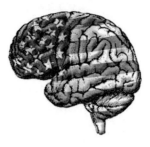

ACCEPTING THE
UNACCEPTABLE

While I was on vacation, I made a decision that regardless of what came out of the depot's efforts to keep me, I wasn't going back. I just couldn't do the work I was doing under the convoluted contract anymore. I returned to countless messages on my answering machine. Some of them were so beautiful that I had to hit delete before they were even over, because listening to them made me tearful. A few of the messages were really gut-wrenching. In one, a Marine started out by apologizing for calling me on my personal cell phone and said his chief had given him my number, which he had from a text I had sent him last cycle. He then started inconsolably crying. He told me that I had saved his life. He had been contemplating killing himself but never told anyone. After he'd met me for a one-on-one session, he had realized how easy it was to get help and started seeing a therapist outside the base. I had sat with him while he called and made the appointment. He felt guilty that he had never thanked me in person. He wanted to let me know that his wife was pregnant, and they were going to name the baby, if it was a girl, Marjorie. I remembered him well and plan on saving that message on my phone forever—It was quite possible the nicest thing I have ever heard.

Another emotional message was from a Marine I also remembered well but had no idea how he'd gotten my phone number. At the end of my first mandatory one-on-one session with him, this drill instructor had lingered. He didn't want to leave the office. I could tell he had something on his mind that he wanted to share. I had gotten pretty skilled at figuring out how to get these guys to talk, but I had to take my time with him; he was quite reluctant. Finally, after some gentle probing, I said, "I have a feeling there is something that you want to talk about, but you are holding back."

He looked surprised and replied, "How do you know?" I laughed.

"That's why I have the job I do."

After some hemming and hawing, he told me he had a lump on his lower abdomen. He made it really clear that he didn't want to tell anyone because he didn't want to be seen as weak. He was a new drill instructor and didn't want to let his team down. He was pretty sure it was nothing, but he was still a little nervous about it. I talked to him about options, but he was pretty adamant that he didn't want anyone to know. I reminded him that I could keep things confidential as long as he was not a danger to himself or others. Having a lump fell into the category of a danger to him. I also knew his company command very well, and both the first sergeant and company commander were extremely understanding and caring men. The drill instructor finally agreed to tell the first sergeant but asked if I could be there and do the talking for him. I had witnessed many Marines that were stoic like this; they would avoid showing weakness at all costs. Of course I agreed to be there and to help facilitate. To make a long story short, it turned out he had cancer. He was another who had called to thank me for saving his life.

During that first week I was gone, I had tons of messages. Every day more and more people would call or text me after hearing the news. Colonel Chester had asked me not to contact anyone until he was able to sort the mess out. I heeded his request and didn't return any calls. A week had gone by before Colonel Chester and I communicated again. He said he hadn't gotten anywhere yet. He let me know he was working on it and that it had been taken to a high level, but the progress was slow. He was optimistic that he was going to get me back and wanted me to work directly for the regiment at the RTR (recruit training regiment) for my next contract. He said that Family Support Services had issues with me and they were the culprits behind this, but he still had no idea what they fired me over. Suffice it to say, I hadn't learned anything I didn't already know. The only thing he was able to add was that they were being very secretive with him, as though they were trying to hush or hide something. I thanked him for all his efforts in trying to sort this out.

I recognized that this man was in charge of the entire recruit training, from the drill instructors to the recruits. He probably had well over a thousand people that he was responsible for, and I could tell he was expending a good amount of time trying to help me. I hated telling him that no matter what the outcome was, I wasn't coming back. It wasn't that I had a lack of commitment to the Marines; it was that it wasn't a conducive contract for me to work under–anymore. He understood and shared my frustration. I told him that I had the proactive program almost completely formalized. I wanted him to know that I would be willing to come and teach it to Family Support Services, so that they could run it themselves. He liked that idea and asked me how long I thought it would take to train them, and how much money would it cost. I figured it would take about two days and replied that I would do it free of charge. As much as the thought of training Family Support Services pained me, I knew that the Marines were the ones that would lose if I didn't share my knowledge and that was more important than my ego. He said he had been talking a lot with MCRD at Parris Island and had shared a lot with them about the program and me. Apparently, they also would like to implement the same approach for their drill instructors. He wanted to look into having them fly out so that I could train both depots at the same time. We agreed to touch base the following week.

I had one dilemma that put me in a precarious position. I had received a couple of e-mails and a text from Gunny Romero. He was the Marine who had gone to Family Support Services, had a bad experience, and touched off the situation in which the chaplain who accused me of bad-mouthing Family Support Services. In his messages he sounded really depressed, and the messages were getting more distressful. I think he was blaming himself for what happened to me. I wasn't sure what to do, but I didn't want to just leave him hanging. I didn't want to contact him directly; in fact, I hadn't contacted anyone at MCRD (Marine Corps Recruit Depot) except Col. Chester. After deliberating, I decided the best thing to do was to send an e-mail to his battalion commander. I knew she was familiar with the situation, so I wasn't breaking confidentiality. I cc'd Donna at HWM—I don't know why; I guess just to cover myself since they told me not to contact anyone.

From: Marjorie Morrison
Sent: Thursday, May 21, 2009 10:43
To: Becker Lt. Col. Linda A
Cc: Donna.J.White@healthnet.com
Subject: MFLC

Hello Lt. Col. Becker,
I was asked to not contact anyone, however I wanted to let you know that the BMP office has contacted my

cell phone in regards to the BMP groups that I do on Mondays. They were letting me know that they will not be there on Monday due to the holiday. They wanted me to respond to the message to insure that I received it. Would you mind telling them that I will not be returning?

Also, I wanted to let you know that Gunny Romero has been trying to contact me (via text, e-mail, and VM on my personal cell). He wants to talk to someone and says that the MFLC phone refers him to Family Support Services. I feel comfortable sharing this with you, because I know you are aware of his situation. I am concerned about him; he seems quite desperate/ upset. It might be a good idea for you, or someone, to touch base with him and go over some options.

I greatly apologize if this e-mail puts you in an uncomfortable situation, but I'd hate to think of the consequences if something were to happen and I didn't say anything.

Sincerely,

Marjorie Morrison

From: Becker Lt. Col. Linda A.
Date: May 21, 2009 11:39:05 AM PDT
To: Marjorie Morrison
Cc: Donna.J.White@healthnet.com
Subject: RE: MFLC

Marjorie,

Thank you for letting me know that my marines have contacted you.

Nothing uncomfortable for me, it would be worse if my marines were left hanging and something bad happened. I will let them know that you are unavailable and get them referred elsewhere.

Take care, and thanks again for letting me know.

Lt. Col. Becker

Lt. Col. Linda A. Becker, USMC
Commanding Officer, Support Battalion
Recruit Training Regiment
Marine Corps Recruit Depot
San Diego, CA

The following week I left Donna at HWM a number of messages, she should have been back from her trip at this point. I got no response. I decided to call Lt. Col. Rowe. He was the commander presiding over Marine Corps Community Services, and was the POC over both Barbara and Faye. He was set to retire in a few months and I could imagine he was pretty upset that my situation popped up at the end of his career. In the military, once you put in over 20 years, you get retirement benefits for the rest of your life. The last thing a Marine wants is something that could interfere with an honorable discharge. I had no idea where he stood on my being fired. I assumed that he cleared the decision, but I wasn't sure. I remember the time Faye told me how Barbara had him wrapped around her finger and how he always took her side. I figured if he had anything to share with me, I'd have heard it by now. On the other hand, if someone could give me any insight it would probably be him.

When he answered his phone, I said, "Hello, sir, this is Marjorie Morrison."

Before I could say any more, he said, "You aren't supposed to be calling me or anyone. I'm reporting you!" He then hung up on me.

All I could think of was, *Could somebody please tell me what I did?* There must have been some giant misunderstanding.

After that, I called Donna again. This time I was crying. I got her voicemail and left her a sobbing message. I asked her to please call me and tell me something; I was feeling desperate for information. That time she called me back. I'd like to think it was because I was crying, but I was pretty sure it was because Lt. Col. Rowe had called her to report me. She was brief. Pretty much all she said was that she was really disappointed at how unprofessional I had been in how I handled this and I shouldn't have contacted anyone. She let me know that in a few weeks I would have a conference call with her and a grievance person from HWM. I asked her a few questions, but she wouldn't answer any of them. She was very rude, and hung up.

How was I unprofessional? I made one phone call to Col. Chester and then a week later made a second phone call to Lt. Col. Rowe. That was about as professional as I knew how to be. The only unprofessional thing I did was not show up to see the Marines that I was scheduled to see when they fired me. And where was her accountability? She certainly hadn't handled this with professionalism. Now that I was getting my hand slapped for being "unprofessional," I had wished I had spoken up more before I left.

I left numerous messages for Donna over the following weeks. I never heard back from her or anyone at HWM. I never had a conference call with a grievance counselor. The only contact I ever had with HWM after that was a generic e-mail I received a couple of months later thanking me for my services and letting me know that my MFLC contract had been terminated.

Weeks had gone by. The e-mails from Marines that I had worked with continued to roll in. Although reading them made me feel good, it left a bittersweet sentiment. I didn't respond to any of them. Perhaps I should have, but I didn't know what to say. How was I to explain?

Despite a few more conversations with Col. Chester, I upheld my end of the bargain to keep silent. I had learned that Family Support Services didn't want me to teach them about the program I was running there. That wasn't much of a surprise. However, after a month went by and I still knew nothing, I decided it was time to speak out. The downside was that I barely had anyone's e-mail address because I was always forbidden to e-mail. I sent this e-mail out to a few of the addresses I had.

From: Marjorie Morrison
Sent: Tuesday, June 16, 2009 10:51
Subject: MFLC

Hello Everyone,

It's been over a month since my departure from the Marine Corps Recruit Depot and I thought it was time to send a note. Unfortunately, I have no more clarity on my situation and reason for my termination than I did the day I left. After leaving multiple phone messages with my contractor and not receiving any in return… I finally gave up!

First and foremost, I want to thank you so very much for the beautiful e-mails, phone and text messages I have received. I cannot tell you how much I appreciate the kind words. Please know your gratitude, support and encouragement have carried me through these past few weeks. I also want to send an extra thanks to Colonel Chester who has been an incredible advocate for me and my work. I am eternally grateful for his tenacity and passion in trying to help me and the Marines in every way he can.

I'd like to tell you what a truly amazing and rewarding experience it has been working with all of you. I am so grateful that I have had this past year to learn and grow from each of you. Your morals and values and how you exemplify honor, courage, and commitment are tremendous. You are wonderful role models for all of society to emulate. I will always be your biggest trumpeter! I love what you stand for and your unsurpassed dedication and enthusiasm is something I will always try to replicate.

Currently, I am back in private practice and am diligently working on formalizing the counseling program that evolved while I was at the depot. I am hopeful that I will have the ability to train counselors on how to do the one-on-ones and the groups. I believe collectively we have found that taking a "proactive" approach to mental health was very effective and I would love to see that continued in my absence. In addition, I am becoming a Military OneSource provider and hope to continue working with military members, families, etc.

Lastly, please don't be a stranger. I would love for you to continue communicating with me via e-mail, my personal phone, or text. I'd like to continue hearing about the exciting things you are all doing. I hope you can find a little time to enjoy summer and appreciate our beautiful San Diego weather (as soon as the "June gloom" goes away).

Thank you for everything, take care, be safe, and of course....

Semper Fidelis,
Marjorie

I received many responses via texts on my phone. Marines were glad to hear from me and appreciative that I broke the silence. Many of them had no idea where I had gone and were genuinely happy to hear I was alive and well.

Here are just a few e-mailed responses I received:

From: Kurtin 1st Sgt. Samuel S.
Date: June 16, 2009 1:11:56 PM PDT
To: Marjorie Morrison
Subject: RE: MFLC

Marjorie,

First of all I cannot say how much I miss having you around.

I can say personally that I have never met anyone like you. Had it not been for you one of my men would have been running around here with testicular cancer. I still am and always will be indebted to you for the awesome climate you have helped create in Charlie company:

Men of integrity and they are open and honest with their feelings.....Can't beat that!

I am sorry things happened the way they did, but in the end we are all better off for what you have done. I know you have a better understanding as to what it means to be a United States Marine as I have a better understanding of what it is to be a good listener.

Thanks for everything and keep in touch.

1st Sgt. Kurtin

From: Becker Lt. Col. Linda A.
Date: June 16, 2009 2:49:19 PM PDT
To: Marjorie Morrison
Subject: RE: MFLC

Marjorie,

Enjoy your trip.

Put all of this behind you, time truly does heal. That which does not kill you will make you stronger.

Take away the good that you did for so many. You did so well that the establishment lashed out for the intimidation you were to them.

We are Marines, we know all good things must come to an end, and many times a good program that works wonders (like you started) slips by the wayside for the wrong reasons. Add on top of it that you are a smart, attractive, ambitious woman of courage, and some folks will just seethe with envy and jealousy. It will one day be their undoing. It is comforting to know you haven't forgotten about us.

I have been meaning to call, but have had a very busy last three weeks, just know that I hope you are OK.

Did I mention enjoy your trip? For you are going to Israel - how cool is that??????

Maybe we can get together when you get back,

Linda

Lt. Col. Linda A. Becker, USMC
Commanding Officer, Support Battalion
Recruit Training Regiment
Marine Corps Recruit Depot
San Diego, CA

From: Smith Maj. Tom M.
Date: June 16, 2009 7:27:49 PM PDT
To: Marjorie Morrison
Subject: RE: MFLC

Marjorie,

You are missed and many of us are just as bewildered as you. I do know that efforts have been made on your behalf, however I am not sure of their results. Your work here was appreciated by many and you are missed. If this is the end of your reign on MCRD, I hope to bump into you some time. Take care and Semper Fi.

Maj. Tom Smith

Executive Officer

3rd Recruit Training Battalion

Recruit Training Regiment, MCRD, San Diego

From: Brogan Lt. Col. Bruce A.
Date: June 16, 2009 4:18:16 PM PDT
To: Marjorie Morrison
Subject: RE: MFLC

We miss you Marjorie. I am so sorry the Marine Corps and MCCS let you down. RTR lost a great resource when you were let go. We are our worst enemy some-times. I wish you all the best. I know that whatever you do, you'll be successful. I hope Col. Chester invites you to his Change of Command so we can all thank you in person.

Take care,

Bruce

Lt. Col. Bruce Brogan

XO, RTR

MCRD San Diego

From: Granger Sgt. Maj. Mitch J.
Date: Jun 16, 2009, at 10:51:23 AM PDT
To: Marjorie Morrison
Subject: RE: MFLC

There is only one reason this happened to you—You were so awesome and set the bar so high, no one could keep up! You are one of the most incredible ladies I have ever met. You are smart, talented, funny and get along with everyone. My men are all much better off having had the opportunity to know you.

I know you will take what you have learned here and help all of us with your knowledge. If anyone can change the system, it is you.

Let's get coffee.

Semper Fi,

Mitch

From: Barry Thompson
Date: June 16, 2009 8:03:00 PM PDT
To: Margie

Marjorie,

I read your e-mail today, and I am very sorry to hear that you are gone from the depot. The drill instructors and officers all speak very highly of you and appreciate all the help that you have provided. Earlier today, before receiving your e-mail, I was actually talking to the Delta Commander about contacting you in hopes of getting some insight into the climate of Mike Co before I take over as company commander on 2 July.

I can't tell you how disappointed I am that you no longer work at MCRD! I hope that you are doing well, and that I'll see you again sometime.

Barry

From: "Malone LtCol Brian G" <brian.malone@usmc.mil>
Date: June 3, 2009 2:43:31 PM PDT
To: Marjorie Morrison

Marjorie,

Don't know what to say except we are all a bit in shock and disappointed in the turn of events. I know you did fantastic things for the DI's and all the Bn's, and they definitely miss you. Not sure how this whole thing turns out in the end, but we are definitely better off due to the support you provided. You are always welcome to come by and visit us.

Brian

From: "Gumps Capt Larry G"
Date: June 17, 2009 6:49:19 AM PDT
To: Marjorie Morrison
Subject: RE: MFLC

Thanks for showing a great deal of class through all this. Keep your honor clean. You are a super star!

Semper Fidelis,
Capt Gumps

From: Paul Ryan
Date: June 17, 2009 9:34 AM PDT
To: Marjorie Morrison
Subject: RE: MFLC

You are amazing. We use words like Honor Courage Commitment. Ms. Marjorie you have done more for the Company then anyone out there. From me to you I want you to know as I approach my twenty-year mark and possible retirement people like you are the reason why I love what I do. You will have a friend for life with me. Office is still in the same spot, stop by, I'd love to see you again.

1stSgt

From: "Wilders LT Robert" <robert.wilders@usmc.mil>
Date: June 17, 2009 8:22:59 AM PDT
To: Marjorie Morrison
Subject: RE: MFLC

Marjorie,

It seems that I have been in the dark concerning this. I was on leave quite some time over the last month and didn't realize what had transpired.

Please keep in touch, it has been a pleasure getting to know you and your impact here will be felt in generations to come.

Thank you for this e-mail and blessings on you and your family. My contact information is on the bottom of the e-mail please save it, I believe we have future projects to work on collectively.

God Bless you!

Chaplain Wilders

LT Robert W. Wilders CHC, USN
Battalion Chaplain
3rd Recruit Training Battalion
San Diego, CA

From: Simon Maj Steve X
Date: June 17, 2009 12:14:45 PM PDT
To: Marjorie Morrison
Subject: RE: MFLC

Marjorie,

Take this experience and share it. Don't stay silent. If you do, they win. We will always be there to support you.

You are the best! Never lose your passion!

Steve

I received over thirty emails, all sharing a similar sentiment. There still was no word on what transpired and what grounds they fired me on. One credible source said it was because I had worked a few times with the domestic violence case at Family Support Services the year prior. Another source said it was because after I was warned to not send e-mails, I sent them to command anyway. My speculation is that Barbara had sent an e-mail to Marine Corps headquarters in the situation regarding the chaplain with the Marine overhearing something I never said. She probably sent it well before I was vindicated. I was beginning to realize that I might never know the truth; to this day, I can only guess. When you're a contracted employee, they don't have to give you a reason.

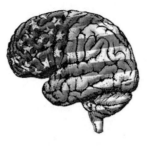

STILL CONNECTED, STILL CARING

That summer came and went. I was fortunate to travel to Israel twice, once in June with my family and friends to celebrate my daughter's Bat Mitzvah, and then again in August when I was invited to travel with a group of elected San Diego elected officials and community leaders. We heard from many speakers that trip, but my favorite was a retired general in the Israeli army. After her lecture I went up and introduced myself to her. I asked her how mental health counseling was handled in the Israeli defense force. She enthusiastically answered that mental health was seen quite differently in Israel than in the United States. In Israel, all of the soldiers met with counselors before they were sent to the fleet (the front lines). Mental health counseling was part of their on-going training.

I couldn't stop thinking about that. How could it be that a nation as great as our own potentially could be getting it all wrong? Why was it that we weren't preparing our soldiers to be mentally fit the same way we helped them be physically fit? The answer was unfortunately too simple; deep down, we still viewed mental health counseling as something for the weak. We are a reactive society, dealing with issues only once they have become a full-blown problem.

There was a part of me that wanted to try to formalize my program and pitch it to the Department of Defense. But who was I? I was just one person. Not a university, not a corporation, let alone an institution. How could I possibly change things on my own? Institutions have received millions of dollars to do research on the field of military mental health. How could I compete with that? How could it even be possible that I might know more than they do? If I did, it was only because I listened. I had no idea when I arrived at the MCRD what was needed. I had the greatest teachers. I simply complied and did what they asked me to.

Later that month I received a call from one of the company commanders. He asked me if I would attend his change of command. This was the fourth change of command invitation I had received since I left. I had graciously declined the previous three, including Colonel Chester's. As much as a part of me wanted to go, I couldn't bring myself to go back there. What if I ran into Barbara or Gretchen? What would I say to people when they asked me what had happened? I thanked him for the invite and explained that I was really busy. I also told him that I had been asked not to return to the depot the day I was fired. He laughed and said, "I am inviting you as my guest and, therefore, you have every right to be here. I wouldn't have been nearly as successful as a company commander had it not been for your support, insight, and intervention. It would mean the world to me if you would come." How could I say no to that? Reluctantly, I agreed to go.

I was a nervous wreck that hot August day. MCRD was the last place on earth I wanted to go. With my luck, Gretchen and Barbara would be the first people I'd see and they'd have me escorted off the base. Or worse, what if they had my car on some type of heightened alert and the guards wouldn't let me in the gates? I was starting to feel paranoid.

I was relieved when they let me through the gate with no questions asked. I didn't want to get there early, but I didn't want to get there late. I sat in my car for about two minutes and took a few deep breaths before heading to the crowd. I felt much worse than I ever did before going into the battalions for the first time.

It was an unusually large crowd for a change of command. I attributed this to the fact that everyone loved Captain Lewis. He was an all-around amazing guy, a great leader who really, genuinely cared about his Marines. I quietly slipped into a seat. A different company commander was the first to see me. He came up to give me a hug. A couple of other Marines spotted me and also came up to me to give me hugs. I was relieved to hear the announcer say that they were about to begin. I desperately wanted to sit down and avoid the spotlight. I'm sure it was my imagination, but it felt like a couple of hundred eyes were staring at me. I had attended change of commands dozens of times before I was terminated. This one was different. I was uncomfortable, nervous, and sad. How depressing this whole situation was. I couldn't help but feel horribly pathetic. Marine after Marine after Marine had called me over the past months, asking me to get my own contract, begging and encouraging me to write my own program and come back to provide services for them. I hadn't done one thing.

I was a coward and didn't have the strength to fight back. I had slipped back into my old life, with my old practice. Things were so much easier for me now. I was scared of MCRD, genuinely scared. I didn't trust the institution anymore, and I didn't know who had my back and who didn't. Maybe I should have been more open with the Marines about the conflict with Family Support Services. Maybe I should have tried harder to fix things with them, even without the support of HWM. The whole time I was there, I never said a bad word about anyone. Why did I always have to act so dignified? In the end, it certainly did not help me.

I was deep in thought when the ceremonial part of the change of command ended. The next part was when the company commander got up and gave a speech. I don't remember exactly what he said, but it went something like this: "Ladies and gentleman, there are many people here that I would like to acknowledge, but before I start, there is a very special person here that I want to recognize. That is Marjorie Morrison. Marjorie has been our gem. She is truly an example of a diamond in the rough. She has helped me grow and learn how to be the best commander possible. Thanks to her tireless and ongoing support, this company was able to have four incredibly successful cycles. There are very few people that I can honestly say have changed the course of my and our Marines; Marjorie is one of those people. For those of you here that have had the chance to work with her, I know you understand and agree with what I am saying. She has this way of making everyone feel respected and important. She really cares, and I cannot thank her enough for being here today."

I couldn't believe that he just said all that! In front of all those people, he publicly recognized me. It was so nice, it made my heart melt. I couldn't cry; I had to stay strong. When the ceremony ended, a crowd formed around me. Everyone seemed so genuinely happy to see me. It was an amazing feeling. Marines were telling me how much they missed me, how much they valued the support I gave them. Drill instructors approached me and said they didn't realized how much they had gotten out of the sessions until they didn't have them anymore, and many told me that not having me as a resource anymore was a big loss for them. If I could have scripted the afternoon, I don't think I could have possibly written it any better.

As I was leaving the depot, a drill instructor across the parade deck recognized me. He came rushing over to where I was walking. He looked at me with wide eyes and exclaimed, "Marjorie, I can't believe it. I thought I'd never see you again. Remember how my wife couldn't get pregnant and she was really depressed? You helped her with all your relaxation techniques. Well, now she is pregnant. You helped us so much with our marriage and communication. She always says that she owes it all to you. We tried calling you, but the MFLC number said you don't work here anymore. I just wanted to say thank you, for everything." I gave him my sincere congratulations and got in my car.

Hands down, it was a great afternoon!

My private practice had picked up right where I had left off. I was booked back-to-back four days a week and took a day off, just for myself, to exercise and meet friends for lunch. My income had gone up since I left the depot. Suffice it to say, I was making more money, working less, and didn't have anyone trying to sabotage me.

I never lost contact with the Marines. Somehow they would find me. Every week I'd hear from one of them, sometimes because there was good news to share, like a promotion. Sometimes they needed guidance on a particular issue. I never minded talking with them. I'd meet them for coffee and if they had issues that needed therapeutic intervention, I'd help them with referrals.

They would always leave the conversation with "You were one of the best thing we ever had; can't you get some funding and do your program? It was so much better than anything we ever had."

I always gave the same response, which was, "You never know, maybe one day."

The truth was, I thought about it every day. But I was only certain of one thing: I didn't have the courage to take on a mission like that. I learned the honor and the commitment from the Marines, but I hadn't grasped the courage. The Marines have it all: honor, courage, and commitment. I was afraid of those people in the Family Support Services. They had me fired me, for all intents and purposes, for no reason at all. If they had a reason, no one shared it with me. A stronger person may have stood up to them, or at least made some sort of waves. Not me. I crawled back into the familiar and easier way of life. Every time I talked to a Marine I felt guilty. I knew what they needed, and yet I wasn't willing to put myself out there to try to get it for them. I had been burned, my pride was hurt, and I wasn't gong to put myself out there again.

I received a phone call early one October morning, five months after leaving the depot. It was from a Marine I hadn't talked to in many months. He started out by apologizing for calling and told me that he'd gotten my number from someone who'd gotten it from someone else. I could tell he was upset, so I reassured him that it was no problem that he had my number and asked if he was okay. He started hysterically crying. He told me that his brother had just been killed in a car accident and he didn't know what to do. We talked for an hour, and at the end of the call, I made sure he had someone with him and I talked to that person about supporting him and assisting him to get services.

This was hardly the first time I had spoken to a crying Marine—that had happened dozens of times before. What was so powerful about this particular phone call was that it proved a point. Reach these guys proactively, before they have a problem. You never know when they might need help, but when they do, they will remember meeting you and reach out. I was glad he called me.

Later that same day something very tragic happened. Driving home from work I heard on the radio what had transpired at Fort Hood earlier that day: Maj. Nidal Malik Hasan, a licensed Army psychiatrist, had gone on a mass shooting rampage and killed

242

twelve soldiers and one civilian. He also wounded thirty-eight people at the Fort Hood Army post in Texas. The story made me sick. I was glued to the news, watching events unfold. I felt I should do something regarding my story, but I didn't know what to do. Maybe I should share it, but with whom? Would anybody care? Who is going to listen to someone that was fired? Where would my credibility be?

A couple of weeks prior, Lt. Col. Becker called to ask me if I would be her date to the Marine Corps Officers Birthday Ball. Her husband wasn't able to attend, and she really wanted me to go with her. My first thought was *No way*, but then I thought about it some more and thought it would be fun. Plus I loved being around the Marines and missed them terribly. It'd be fun to go to a ball. I'm glad I did because it was amazing. The Marines do such a wonderful job of celebrating their accomplishments and their birthday, which is on Veteran's Day. The civilians dress in formal attire, and the Marines get all spruced up in their dressy blue. Lt. Col. Becker picked me up at my office, where I did a quick change for the evening. I had convinced myself that I had nothing to worry about; this was the officer's ball, for officers and their guests. We went to the general's reception first. As soon as we walked in, the very first person we saw was Lt. Col. Rowe (Barbara's POC that hung up on me). My heart stopped. I had my stupid impulsive reaction to smile and said hello. Why do I always have to act so civil and nice? He didn't deserve a hello from me. He said hi back, and that was that. That brief encounter was the only negative part of the evening. The rest of the night was awesome! People kept coming up to me to talk and say hello. I felt like a true celebrity. Some would thank me, others would apologize for what happened, and some didn't know why I left and just asked questions. Almost everyone told me that he had really benefited from the proactive program and felt its absence.

A few days later, I received a very disturbing article, which was forwarded to me by a Marine officer. The source was Salon. com and the article was called: "Camp Lejeune Whistle-Blower Fired."[15] The story was about a psychiatrist named, Dr. Kernan Manion who was hired to treat Marines coming home from war with acute mental health issues at Camp Lejune, North Carolina, the largest Marine base on the East coast (best known for the water contamination scandal that led to numerous cancer and birth defects among the marine families that lived there). Manion repeatedly warned the base about the mishandling of Marines that were displaying violent acts and committing suicides at record amounts.

> Manion describes a frustrated Marine punching a telephone pole with his bare fists outside a treatment clinic, then storming around, cursing, with a piece of lumber with a nail in it, though nothing was done to ensure he didn't hurt himself, again, or others. In another case, a severely homicidal and suicidal Marine pounded his fists into a table and stormed out of treatment. Yet the hospital, Manion complained to his superiors, made no efforts to discuss these cases or how to better handle similar events in the future.[16]

Rather then come up with plans of how to handle the situations before they become problems, the emotionally wounded marines would end up in an over burdened health care system that often harassed men and women from getting help.

Manion was successful at getting a Marine into treatment that had been feared "to lose it" by two of his colleagues. Instead of being praised for preventing another potential Fort Hood Masacre, Dr. Manion was warned to stop making trouble. He did not stop. He continued to bring attention to the massive gaps in caring for the Marines. He wanted to help set up protocols for handling intense situations, like having military police ready to intervene if things got bad, or to quickly hospitalize potentially violent patients. Within a few days of his complaints, "the contractor fired Manion 'effective immediately,' according to his termination e-mail. The note provides no reason for the firing. Manion was directed to clean out his office the next day, under the watchful eye of a chief petty officer, and have no further contact with his patients."[17]

I was so disgusted after reading the article, I decided to contact Kernan Manion myself. I was grateful that he accepted my phone call and agreed to be interviewed. He shared with me that just prior to getting fired, he had appealed to a series of military inspector generals in a written complaint. He warned them about immediate threat of loss of life and/or harm to service members or others, if conditions did not improve. He told me that the Navy had called his contractor to have him fired, but never said *why* they were terminating him. The contractor only revealed that they were acting on the Navy's request. After being fired, Manion filed a fourteen-page complaint with the Department of Defense inspector general warning the Navy's Bureau of Medicine and Surgery of "serious mismanagement of post-deployment mental health services that was both endangering patient, staff and community safety as well as severely compromising the quality of care for returning Marines." He didn't stop there. Manion also wrote to President Obama stating that "In my more than twenty-five years of clinical practice, I've never seen such immense emotional suffering and psychological brokenness—a relentless stream of courageous, well-trained and formerly strong Marines deeply wounded psychologically by the immensity of their combat experience."

His story only gets worse. Manion asked his Rep. Walter Jones, R-N-C to help him investigate. The Navy reported back to Rep. Jones that Manion was fired because of a pattern of non-compliance, including absenteeism and unprofessional conduct. *Salon.com* investigated the story and requested the internal Navy documents. To Manion's surprise, the documents clearly showed evidence of unfavorable doctoring. His good performance records were altered after he blew the whistle on them. Manion was fired on September 3. A lieutenant commander filled out his final performance review, called an "exit PAR," and signed it on Nov. 10, 2009. The document, obtained by *Salon.com*, evaluates Manion as "satisfactory" in every applicable performance category, including his judgment, ethical conduct and ability to work with peers.[18]

On Manion's new tampered evaluation, his professional judgment, ethical conduct and ability to work with peers had been changed from "satisfactory" to "unsatisfactory." Manion explained that the new document had a comment stating that, "Dr. Manion demonstrated poor ethical conduct and professional judgment." He added that he had "disruptive relationships with his superiors and peers that had a negative impact on patient care and clinic process." Manion sounded frustrated and exacerbated. He has since hired an attorney.

Manion's Camp Lejeune story to me is an example of what happens to those who blow the whistle on conditions for military personnel with mental problems. I felt like I understood how Manion felt. He was trying to do the right thing, and yet he got fired for "making waves." It sounded a little too familiar. I didn't know this man well, but I did know one thing: he felt that there was wrongdoing and he was vocal about it. At least when he looked in the mirror, he knew that he had done what he could. What had I done? Absolutely nothing. I went into hiding and fell silent. I continued feeling extremely disappointed and stuck. I was so disgusted at the whole situation.

I was ready to try to do something. Telling my story will most likely fall on deaf ears, just like Kernan Manion. How I can I show people that they need to change their viewpoints from a reactive model to a proactive one? Could I effectively describe the internal dysfunction that goes on? What if I made an attempt at starting a proactive counseling program? Or what if I could lobby to inspire turning existing military programs into having more of a preventative slant. After all, how would I really know if a formalized proactive counseling program would really work if I didn't at least try? I had two big questions I needed answered. First, how did I really know that the Marines would want it? I knew I had positive feedback, but what if they were just being nice to me? How could I be sure that if I put forth the energy the program would be well received? Second, if I decided to formalize and write the program, how would I get the funding to try a pilot program on a base? I decided to—take things one step at a time.

I needed to survey the drill instructors to find out what they really wanted. This was going to be very tricky. I had been off the base for seven months. Many of the drill instructors I worked with had already left. Another problem was that I had very few e-mail addresses. How was I going to get the surveys out to them? If they did get the survey, would they even remember me? Lastly, even if I could reach them, these were drill instructors, some of the busiest men on the planet. They hated paperwork. The likelihood that they would fill out my survey was very slim.

I didn't know how I was going to do it, but I was finally ready to try.

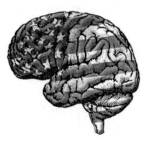

MARINES EXPRESS
THEIR SUPPORT

S
even months after my last day working on the depot, I wrote two online surveys—one for the drill instructors and one for the command leadership. I tried to make them as brief as possible. I didn't want to use the MFLC name and potentially get in trouble. Due to my lack of e-mails, I decided the best way to hopefully get some returned surveys was to send them to the top. I sent a letter to the four battalion commanders asking for assistance in distributing the surveys.

Lt. Col. Becker, cc'd me on this e-mail that she sent to her command.

From: Becker Lt. Col. Linda A.
Sent: Monday, November 23, 2009 10:48
Subject: FW: A few minutes of your time?

Leaders,
Please take the time to answer and forward to your Marines if you/they had any direct or periphery inter-action with Marjorie when she was the Depot Military Family Life Consultant.

No pressure to complete.

As you know mental health for service members has been and continues to be a hot topic. Some of the Marines who saw Marjorie as a group with pick-up or on an individual basis have since moved on, and some may still be on deck who were here before April 2009 and have an opinion.

I can say from my perspective that her proactive approach had contributing impact as the number of legal issues were reduced. Some out there may feel the same or may feel otherwise, so here is your opportunity to provide feedback. I took the command survey and it took less that 5 minutes.

Links to the surveys:

- Drill Instructors Survey
- Command Survey

Lt. Col. Becker

Lt. Col. Linda A. Becker, USMC
Commanding Officer, Support Battalion
Recruit Training Regiment
Marine Corps Recruit Depot
San Diego, CA

I was happy to see Lt. Col. Becker's e-mail. Unfortunately it was followed by another e-mail from a battalion commander who told me that the new colonel (Colonel Chester had since rotated out to another base) would not let them send out the surveys. He was Colonel Chester's replacement and got there after I left; he knew of me, but we had never met. He was afraid it might be a "phishing" scam and was adhering to a strict policy to not distribute "outside" surveys.

This was going to make it extra tough to get the surveys filled out. To my complete astonishment, by the end of the first week over one hundred Marines had filled out the surveys. Twenty-five command surveys and eighty-five drill instructors surveys had been completed. I honestly have no idea how they reached that many, from the few I had emailed out. I had only sent the link to a handful of people. What was even more amazing than the numbers was the results!

On the officers' survey, I asked seven multiple-choice questions.

1. Did you find that Marjorie's proactive counseling services were helpful and beneficial service for your Company/ Battalion?

    •   95 percent said "yes" and 5 percent said "indifferent"

    •   Comments: It was great and the Marines responded to it.

2. Did you receive feedback of command climate from Marjorie after she worked with your Marines?

    •   100 percent said "yes"

    •   Comments:

        1. Always.

        2. I received valuable info related to my command's climate without regards to specific names or issues.

        3. I am unsure of the total benefit of the command climate feedback. I think good command climates usually were already aware, and poor command climates tended to resist and make excuses. I found it very useful to confirm my own assessment of my command climate through Marjorie's feedback.

3. Did you ever feel that a Marine's confidentiality was jeopardized during her conversations with you?

    •   100 percent replied "no"

- Comments:

  1. Never.

  2. Confidentiality was NEVER compromised.

4. Did you notice an improvement in company camaraderie after they completed a group with Marjorie?

   - 83 percent said "yes"

   - Comments:

     1. N/A

     2. Hard to tell sometimes due to the confidentiality.

     3. Marjorie appears to give us an excellent picture of the company camaraderie as an observer rather than as a facilitator. Her perspective was valuable and unattainable without her.

     4. *Absolutely* beneficial to the working environment and self esteem of each Company.

     5. Camaraderie was high to begin with, but received positive after-action comments from the Marines.

5. Do you think it is beneficial for Marines to have ongoing periodic counseling on a regular basis?

   - 100 percent said "yes"

   - Comments:

     1. The issue isn't counseling, but rather conversation. We all need to be talking to our Marines.

     2. It was very beneficial.

     3. I don't think periodic counseling is necessary for all Marines. However, I do believe it can be a beneficial tool for Commanders who have or think they have Marines with issues that need professional assistance.

4. This is an important program and was executed with genuine care and concern.

5. I think it is beneficial to have unfettered access, periodic visits that open the door for contact of the Marine's choosing.

6. Do you have any comments or feedback that could shed insights into how you think mental health services are perceived, utilized, and delivered?

- Marjorie took the stigma out of counseling and got Marines to open up about their challenges. They learned to deal with some very difficult issues and emerged better people.

- The stigma is still there...the more Marines are able to talk about their experiences and have someone mediate it with their peers the more likely they are to heal or seek help in the future.

- Marjorie was approachable and personable. A leader must be personable and approachable. Counseling, communicating, and connecting with your people is critical. Margie helps give us a critical outside perspective on my company's climate.

- There is a gulf between the "services" provided by Family Support Servicesand those provided by private Mental Health Care professionals like Ms. Morrison. Marines will engage with someone like Marjorie before they would ever consider going to Family Support Services. As a result, they are unlikely to seek and receive the services they need/desire.

- I feel the mental health services are perceived by many as an under utilized service that can provide great benefits to all that take advantage of this service. The service that Marjorie provided made many of the Marines feel they were being listened to and that their issues were very confidential with her. Marjorie made herself available to the Marines no matter the location. The privacy of mental health services is a big reason many took advantage of this service. I am not sure of the usage of this service since the departure of Marjorie. She was a very well liked and respected provider.

- Until counseling can be viewed as sustainment training, it will continue to carry a stigma with it. We should continue to provide more services to the Marines in a variety of forms.

- Mental health services have been frowned upon, and Marines who have used MHU have been joked about afterward. I have had to personally counsel my unit as a whole and crush this pre-existing culture. I feel that MHU is an awesome asset and it is in place for many significant purposes beyond the support of recruits.

- Mental health services are perceived by some as a sign of weakness. I personally know this isn't the case.

- The Marines responded in an OUTSTANDING manner and built genuine rapport with Marjorie. Marines that would have earlier refused to speak with someone about their problems or concerns were extremely comfortable speaking with Marjorie.

- The current system doesn't work well enough. By the time Marines are seen, it is too late-usually after an incident. The reason Marjorie was so successful with my company was that it was the first time Marines could talk about their problems with someone outside the chain of command without fear of command interference or retribution. Marines will not openly talk to anyone if they believe that the command is going to find out about what was said.

- A proactive approach is beneficial because many Marines do not feel comfortable seeking psychological help. They would be much more willing to talk to somebody with whom they have already established a rapport.

- Mrs. Marjorie Morrison (while acting as an MFLC Representative) provided a discreet and powerful platform for identification/resolution of latent issues within the training company chain of command in a way that no other outreach program was able to. She expertly immersed herself into each training company schedule as they executed the recruit training matrix and was able to master the intricate details that emerge during each segment of training. In my opinion, she achieved unprecedented milestones as a civilian in terms of the professional relationship that she was able to establish within the Company HQs, coupled with the additional capability that she was able to bring about that ultimately improved command climate/stability. Her primary success accrued from the fact that the DIs were comfortable talking to her because she made her services readily available to all hands, for the right reason and at the right time. The Marines instinctively gravitated toward her because they trusted her as a bona fide outlet to vent their grievances and complaints. Further, she was extremely adept with the focus groups that she was able to implement throughout the critical phases of recruit training. Speaking as a training Company Commander, she was definitely a good piece of gear to have around while performing my duties in the caldron of recruit training environment.

- All too often the individual seeking counseling is looked at as a sort of outcast. With Mrs. Morrison, it was given to everyone in a group and individual setting which allowed help and provided a sense of anonymity.

- Current MFLC is constantly changing personnel contracts making rapport and trust building nearly impossible. There is no command climate evaluation from an unbiased source. Marjorie provided a combination of building trust and involvement both with the Marines and with the commands. She also provided a source for commanders to reference as a subject matter expert in psychology and human behavior. From a command perspective the current system is a resource utilized once something has already gone wrong. Any element that is proactive in nature is usually completely hidden from command view. Marjorie provided service with command involvement in a manner that protected confidentiality.

- Proactive, confidential counseling that is available to provide the opportunity for a Marine to speak to someone (one-to-one) in a non-attribution environment about their challenges (as long as the counselor understands the demands of military service) would be a tremendous asset that would receive favorable reception by the individual and benefit the organization.

The drill instructor surveys were even more staggering:

The following charts represent approximately eighty-five drill instructors:

Although your one-on-one meetings with Marjorie were some what mandatory, did you feel comfortable sitting with her and talking?

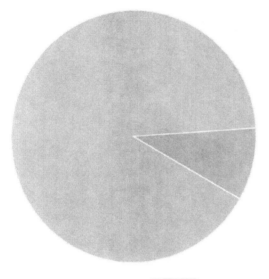

 Yes. I was comfortable.

 At first I was uncomfortable, but got used to it.

 No. I was uncomfortable the whole time.

Did you find Marjorie easy to talk to about personal things?

YES

NO

Comments:

1. She was only part of the depot for a little while, like she came here just to get credentials and left.

2. It was good when she was here, but she left and never came back.

3. I only met with her once but I had some things that I was going to talk to her about, but then she never came back.

Did you trust that what you shared with Marjorie would remain confidential?

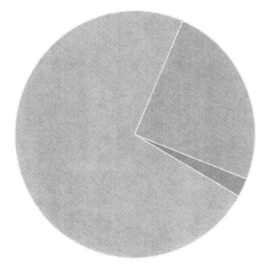

 YES. I trusted that she would keep our conversation to herself.

 CAUTIOUS. I wasn't quite sure I could trust her.

 NO. I was afraid she would tell my command whatever I told her.

Did you feel meeting with Marjorie, proactively for 15 minutes, was a good use of your time?

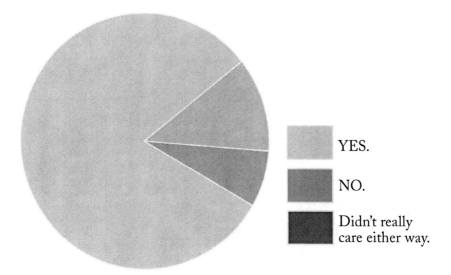

YES.

NO.

Didn't really care either way.

If you had an issue that you needed assistance with, did you find that meeting with Marjorie helped give you the tools you needed to solve your problems?

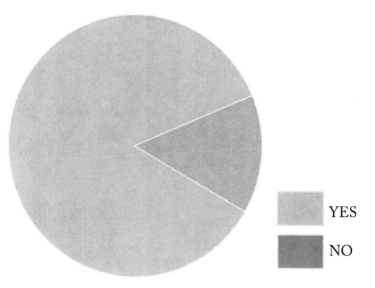

YES

NO

Comments:

1. No issues discussed.

2. She always gave me resources that I would be able to use if I needed to.

3. She taught me how to stop my mind racing so I could fall asleep at night. I use that every night now.

4. I learned how to talk to my wife without starting a fight. My wife says she saved our marriage.

If you needed help in the future, would it be easier to ask for help after having your one-on-one meetings with Marjorie?

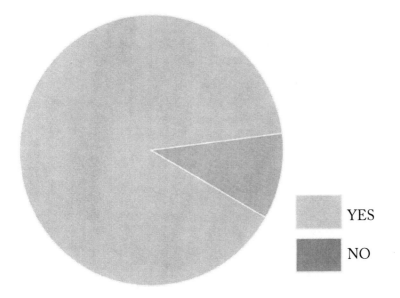

YES

NO

Comments:

1. Does not apply.

2. I wouldn't ask for help.

3. Yes, I went and saw her during my cycle to help me with a work issue.

4. Before I met her I would not have gotten help but after I met her, I asked her for help a few times.

Was it helpful to see the same counselor during every pick-up and throughout the cycle?

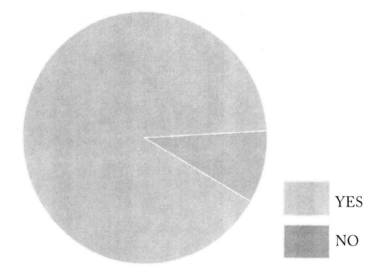

YES

NO

Comments:

1. As time goes on you get comfortable with people. As did I with Marjorie.

2. Yes. I guess there is a new MFLC, but they are like everybody else. I don't know who they are and they are always changing. Marjorie was the only one that actually cared.

3. I wouldn't care if the people changed if they understood what it meant to be a Marine. Most of the

counselors treat us like animals and not warriors. Marjorie treated us with respect and dignity. She was as solid as they come. The depot did us a disservice by replacing her.

Overall, was it a positive experience for you to meet with Marjorie privately every three months?

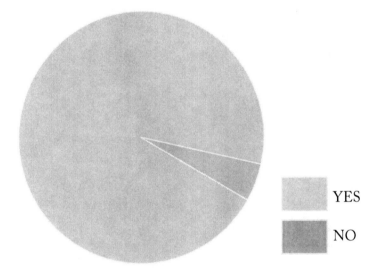

YES

NO

Comments:

1. We only met twice, I have been on the depot for two years.

2. It wasn't consistent. I haven't seen her in a really long time.

3. Best program the Depot has ever run.

4. Good idea because like me, Marines won't get help but if it is there, they'll talk.

In regards to groups:

Did you get to know personal things (i.e. names of spouse's and children) about your fellow drill instructors better after the group?

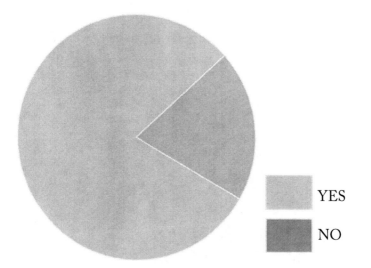

Were the group meetings to be a good use of your time?

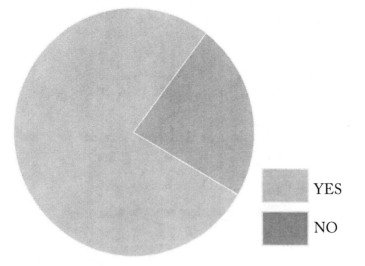

Comments:

1. Sometimes.
2. She helped our company work out some of our issues.
3. I learned that other drill instructors had the same issues as me.

And the final question:

Would you like to see this type of program continue?

- Over 90 percent said "Yes."

I took the next month to do research. Maybe there was a proactive counseling program in the military that I didn't know about. I spent every extra hour I had researching the existing military mental health system. I found very little information in regards to preventative programming. How different is it from getting an annual physical with your doctor? It is the one thing insurance companies will pay for with no copays. The health care system knows that preventative medicine provides you with early detection and, in turn, ends up saving the insurance company millions of dollars. Why can't we view mental health the same way?

I began the process of formalizing my proactive counseling program. I broke down exactly how the mandatory individual sessions will work:

They will occur every three months with the same counselor. The counselor will preserve the same anonymity and confidentiality as the MFLCs. Unlike the MFLCs, these counselors will be well trained and will not rotate out every six weeks. The program will utilize an assessment tool that the military members fill out in the counselor's presence. The military members will not need to put any identifying information on the questionnaire.

In fact, when they leave the session, they will take it with them. The assessment will show individuals what type of coping styles they most likely exhibit when exposed to stressful situations, i.e., alcohol use, anger, anxiety, PTSD, and potential suicide. It will also delineate how well they are handling their work stress and personal stress, including marital, family, and children.

Depending on the results of each individual, the counselor will provide psychological education and provide useful resources and tools to help with the issues. If the results are extreme in any one area, i.e., danger to self or others, then the counselor will make sure the military member gets immediate help.

In the program, the groups will have a format that focuses on building cohesion and creating a safe environment to share feelings with one another. The outcome will be focused on building a strong network within the company, so that they can rely on each other during difficult times. It will also create a safe environment for service members to reach out to their comrades, if they have concerns about them. Who doesn't benefit from knowing they are not alone in how they are feeling? On the other hand, the counselor will be well trained on how to make sure the groups do not become "bitch" sessions. On the contrary, they will be an opportunity to fix problems together while deepening the bonds of brotherhood.

The counselors will know exactly how to perform their job and will have a clear understanding of what their purpose is on that base. They will have support and ongoing training from their contractor. There will be an extensive interview process, so that the right counselors are put in the right places. After learning about all the effort that goes into training recruits to become marines, I know at very least, they deserve a well-trained support staff.

A few weeks later, I went back to MCRD (Marine Corps Recruit Depot) for the Bravo Company change of command. Driving over there, I decided to call Gary, the MFLC who replaced me for my first rotation out. I liked keeping in touch with him from time to time. He told me he had some depressing news about MCRD. I drew a deep breath—now what? Family Support Services had decided to keep the MFLC program and Gretchen had been promoted to oversee it. She was the new POC for it! It's gone back to the original way where every six weeks a new MFLC rotates out and a new one comes in. Gary reminded me that he still took part in the current weekly MFLC phone conference calls. He laughed when he told me that every week the MCRD MFLC would comment that Gretchen wouldn't let him or her do anything or go anywhere. They were only allowed to work with cases that she assigned and that they were her glorified assistants. How pathetic; the cycle continued. What a broken system! I couldn't imagine that this was what the MFLC program was devised to do.

I was discouraged by the news but not very surprised. As I pulled onto the depot, I realized that I wasn't nervous coming back this time. It was a rainy day and the ceremony had been moved from the outside parade deck to the "Moment of Truth" classroom. This is where the young recruits take their initial vows when they begin recruit training on their journey to become Marines. As I walked down the corridor, a few drill instructors stopped me to shake my hand. They remembered me and wanted to say hello. I walked a little farther and had to chuckle to myself. Here I was going to the Bravo Company change of command. I reflected back to when I started. They were the only company that had initially given me opposition when the program was started. Now, almost a year later, the current company commander had wanted me to attend his change of command.

I was anxious to meet the new RTR colonel (Colonel Chester's replacement). I knew he had somewhat of an idea of who I was because he was the one who prohibited my surveys from being sent out. I didn't blame him; he had never met me and most likely did not understand why I was asking for the information. Besides, in spite of that, I still received over one hundred surveys returned, which gave me more than enough data. The ceremony was beautiful. I love how the military takes the time to acknowledge a beginning and an end. It is such a nice way to reflect on what you have accomplished and how you have grown. Despite religious events and holidays, I can't think of anything in the civilian world that comes close to matching these ceremonies.

After it was over, I made my way up to the new colonel to introduce myself. He was a really nice man, and we talked for a while. He asked me when I left the depot. I replied, "I was let go last May."

He smiled and said, "It doesn't look or sound like any of the Marines ever let you go." That comment meant a lot.

I smiled back at him and said, "Thank you sir."

I took a good look at the room before I walked out. There I was, standing in the "Moment of Truth" classroom. I couldn't help but wonder how the young recruits felt when they stood in my exact spot. I imagined that they were afraid of the unknown but also excited about what their potential future held. In my mind's eye, they were very scared and unsure of how everything was going to turn out. At the same time, they knew they had come too far and turning back was no longer an option. I knew just how they felt.

I came home and felt inspired. I decided to get on the computer and research alternatives and solutions. The information I found was surprising! The site I stumbled on was *Veterans Today*, and it was in relation to the latest Department of Defense contract announcements. [19, 20]

I recognize that the Internet is not always a credible source and that comments found are not always accurate, so I've decided not to include what I read, (although it was a tough decision because they are so powerful). It turns out that there are at least a dozen practitioners that have publicly commented regarding their negative experiences with the MFLC program. One anonymous MFLC shared that "they feared their job security if the public knew that most MFLCs get paid $10,000.00 a month for working around four hours a day". One medical doctor stated "Some of the internal supervisors and managers inside HWM are working closely with some bullies in the military bases to protect their own jobs and lucrative contracts." A social worker that fulfills a lot of MFLC contracts explained that "there is not adequate training nor supervision for MFLC's to learn and address the severe needs that our soldiers and their families are facing". She also suggested that when the DOD was investigating the MFLC contract, she was bullied by her team lead to not share the truth because they would all lose their jobs. She chose to keep silent but said, "my conscious and the fear of losing potential assignments tormented me." Another MFLC wrote in and said, "What's most troubling is that no one seems to give a damn about the situation...If the DOD really knew how HWM treats its consultants, I think HWM would have some real problems. But no one cares and all the consultant are afraid of getting 'black listed' if they dare say anything."

Later that day I called my congressman's office to schedule an appointment in hopes of sharing my proactive counseling program with him. I didn't want to go after HWM; that was a fight I couldn't endure. I wanted to advocate for preventative psychology in the military. I didn't know what I could accomplish alone, but I was ready to try.

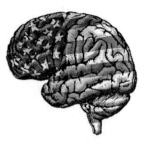

LOBBYING FOR MILITARY MENTAL HEALTH

I spent the next couple of months preparing for my first ever lobbying trip in Washington. I pulled all my contacts together and set up as many meetings as I could with members of Congress. I found out that most people that do this type of lobbying are asking for a specific favor. My goal was to lobby on behalf of proactive and preventative military mental health. I was curious if there would be support and/or funding for a pilot program. If there was, how could I go about getting one started? I was out of my comfort zone, having never done anything remotely like this. Thankfully, I had lunch with a friend who is a professional lobbyist, who helped me come up with an outline, explaining to me how the process works. I learned that at first I would meet with a staffer and I would explain to them what I was there for and brief them on the purpose of my meeting. The staffer would then take me into the Congress member's office where the meeting would be held. He told me I'd have about five minutes of their time and if I didn't grab them in the first thirty seconds, they probably wouldn't listen to anything after that point. I was nervous. I had taken the week off work (which translated to loss of income), booked a hotel and rental car, and scheduled the days with back-to-back meetings. I didn't know how my mission would be received, but I was excited.

The U.S. Capitol can be an intimidating place, but it's also an awesome place. Surrounding the Capitol is a bunch of office buildings. They are all connected underground, so once you enter a building you can travel from one place to another place without going outside. I got there early because I didn't know how hard it would be to find my way around. Getting through security was easier than I thought, which helped calm my nerves a little. My first meeting was with Rep. Duncan Hunter, Jr. He is a member of the Armed Services Committee and is the youngest member of Congress who most recently "took his uniform off." He is a former Marine and conducted his congressional campaign while deployed in Iraq.

Exactly as I was told, upon arrival the staffer took me to a small table and asked me to fill him in on why I was there. He was very nice and commented that the congressman would be very happy to meet me. The whole experience went much better than I could have ever expected. When I walked in the congressional room, Rep. Hunter was sitting in a large leather chair, and asked me to take a seat on the couch. After introducing myself, the first thing out of my mouth was, "With all due respect, sir, I'm feeling a little role reversal. You see, I'm used to being the one in the chair and talking to the person on the couch." I was a little nervous, and tried humor to lighten the mood. Luckily, he laughed and asked if I'd like us to switch places. He was a wonderful listener and spent over a half hour with me (much longer than the five minutes I was expecting).

I told him all about the program at San Diego Marine Corps Recruit Depot, how it worked, and why I thought it should be replicated in other bases. I told him a little about the bureaucracy on the base and about the MFLC program, (which he had never heard of). He liked the proactive program, liked the overall concept, and said he was there to offer or provide any help that he could. His only two objections were whether or not the mandatory sessions might only be seen as a "check in the box," meaning that people would do it because they had to, and wouldn't be honest to get the most of it. (I knew having conducted the program myself that it works and service members will take it seriously.) The other concern was whether or not the success of my program was personality driven. I interpreted it as; I was good at my job, but what if someone else did not have the same success. I knew this could be handled effectively because of how well Gary was able to pick up the program where I left off. Deidre, my second replacement, had a harder time conducting it, but whoever was running the program would have to make sure that they took time in their selection process and emphasized training. I told Congressman Hunter and his staffer, who stayed in the room, that I would come back and see them again at the end of the week before I left to go home.

My next meeting was with Rep. Brian Bilbray, who is a member of the House VA (Veteran Affairs) Committee. He is my congressman from home, and although I had never met him, I felt a connection to him from the beginning. He also appeared enthusiastic and eager to support my proactive military counseling cause. He shared with me a story about how service members used to need their commander's approval in order to get married. Due to a shift in philosophy through the years, service members are now given the right to wed whenever they feel ready. His commentary was that he didn't think the current, more independent liberating ways were benefiting our service members. New, young military members don't make enough money to support a family and although they are strong people, they don't always know what is best for them. He valued the concept of proactive military counseling. He asked me whom else I had met with. I explained that so far I had only spoken to Duncan

Hunter Jr. He announced that he'd like to start a campaign with Rep. Hunter in support of preventative counseling and that the two could team up together in support. Somebody should have probably pinched me because the whole experience was too good to be true.

The next couple of days went equally well. Nobody I met with gave me a hard time about my cause and the concept I was selling. The idea of proactive military counseling seemed to make sense to everyone. It was bipartisan, and everyone seemed to genuinely care about our military.

The meeting that stood out to me the most was with Rep. Susan Davis. She is a member of the Armed Services Committee and the chair for the House Military Personnel Subcommittee. That subcommittee is responsible for all of the military health programs; therefore, if anyone could really institute effective change it would be her. She listened to my speech thoroughly, which I was now becoming well versed at giving. She asked me hard questions, which showed me she understood it from a deeper level and tracked me throughout our conversation. I learned that her husband was a military psychiatrist who worked at Walter Reed Hospital. She profoundly understood the issues. She was open-minded to the idea of starting a pilot program at Camp Pendlelton. She wanted me to contact the folks at TriWest Health Alliance. TriCare,which is responsible for handling the military's health system, is broken up into three regions. TriWest handles the western portion of the country, including twenty-one states. It covers 2.26 million square miles, stretching from Missouri to Hawaii and serves 2.9 million military members, retirees and their families. She told me about an embedded pro-vider program that TriWest was involved in, and how it might be somewhat similar in its preventative nature. She reassured me that we could continue our conversations in San Diego and that we should meet again.

A few of the congress members I was scheduled to meet with were unable to attend our meeting due to unscheduled congress votes. The one that was the biggest disappointment to me was Rep. Bob Filner. He was chairman of the VA committee, and I was very curious as to how he would feel about my agenda. The reason why I was optimistic that he'd be supportive of the cause was because in the VA community, they see the service members after they get out of the military. Taking care of their mental health while they are still on active duty, could considerably affect the potential mental health services they may need when they get out. Not able to meet him was one of the very few disappointments of my week.

Another highlight was a visit to Military OneSource. I met with their senior vice president and the executive staff. I was given the opportunity to tour the facility and learn about their different military support programs and witness firsthand the amazing work they do.

When I boarded the plane to head back to San Diego, I felt whole again. If nothing else came of my work thus far, I spoke my piece. I never badmouthed HWM nor spoke about my conflicts with the Family Support Services folks. I focused on the cause and advocated on behalf of our militaries mental health.

When I arrived back at work, a letter from Congressman Filner was waiting for me in the mail.

Marjorie Morrison, MFT
May 28, 2010

Dear Marjorie:

Thank you for meeting with my Legislative Director, Sharon Wagener, to discuss the "Proactive Military

Counseling" program. I am sorry that I was unable to personally meet with you due to votes in the House.

I have reviewed the printed materials that you delivered. I wholeheartedly agree—this approach to mental health counseling makes sense and should be implemented by the Department of Defense for all soldiers.

I understand that you are working with Susan Davis, Chair of the Armed Services Subcommittee on Military Personnel. Please let me know what I can do to help!

Sincerely,

Bob Filner
Member of Congress

BF/sw
2542037

It felt so good to find my message hadn't fallen on deaf ears.

In the following months, I continued my lobbying efforts and began consulting for some large government contractors. I have earned a reputation as *a prevention expert* in the military mental health community and am hired to consult with several contractor mental health agencies. I was able to assist in writing program proposals for the Navy, Air Force, National Guard, and Reservists instituting and incorporating proactive techniques. I was beginning to feel more optimistic and starting to recognize new trends in prevention, which the military labels resiliency.

After six months, I returned to Washington for more lobbying. I again attended a number of positive and productive meetings. The most encouraging one was with Congresswoman Susan Davis where she again expressed her support of a pilot proactive military counseling program at Camp Pendleton. Her biggest objection was about the wording "mandatory sessions" because the service members shouldn't be forced to do it. I explained how it was done at MCRD and that it wasn't actually mandatory because if someone did not want to participate, they didn't have to. I discussed my concerns to her as well, explaining that I am a clinician not an administrator. I shared how I felt about the myriad of services available and how the multitude of programs were almost polluting the system. It is a fragmented organization, and I wanted to make it better, not contribute to it. In addition, I didn't want to run a program alone. I knew firsthand what it was like not having support. This time around I wanted to do it differently. We talked about doing a joint venture with TriWest Health Care Alliance. I promised her I would get in touch with them. One of the challenges that we came up against was that it was the end of November. The election had just taken place, and all of the staffers were in transition, so she couldn't give me a contact person to communicate with. We agreed to reconnect in the beginning of January.

Nothing ever ends up being as easy as it sounds. I got in touch with TriWest, and they were supportive and enthusiastic about collaborating with me on a pilot program. On the other hand, the economic climate had changed in the past year which greatly affected new program funding. Federal budgets were being cut, military spending was reduced, and funding for new programs was temporarily suspended. Although I was confident a pilot program could potentially happen, the obstacles and objections that I was facing overwhelmed me.

A few weeks later, I received a phone call from a sergeant major that I used to work with at MCRD. He is now a sergeant major at the Wounded Warrior Battalion working with the Marines that have come back from the current wars wounded. He had no idea what I was doing in regards to trying to get an official pilot program set up at Camp Pendleton, he wanted to know if there was any way I could operate the same type of proactive program at the Wounded Warrior Battalion that I did at MCRD. The wounded warrior battalion was located in Camp Pendleton. I shared with him my efforts and encouraged him that progress was slowly being made. I listened to his stories and tried to truly understand what was currently going on with our returning Marines. The only positive thing I derived from our conversations was his fond recollection on how the proactive counseling program prepared him and his marines for the stressors that they later had to face.

It seemed I had everything lined up—congressional support and Marine support. It still didn't seem to be enough. How was this program going to get funded? As I started searching for alternative ways to raise funds, I became discouraged. It seems that large corporations and universities were the ones getting the financial support. On a positive note, I was noticing a new trend of preventative type programs that were beginning to pop up. None of them seemed be as simple and foolproof as the program I was involved in, but nevertheless they were targeted at hitting the issues before there was a problem. I was giving up hope that my proactive programs would come to fruition in the near future.

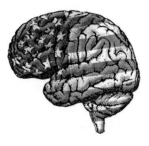

PREVENTATIVE PROGRAMMING TRENDS

The buzzword these days in the military is "resilience." It is exciting for me to see the new emphasis on prevention evolve. In January 2011, *USA Today* released an article titled "Study: Proactive Counseling Stems Troops' Mental Ills."[21] The article is based on a study the Army conducted with over 20,000 soldiers during a troop surge in Iraq. They concluded that there was a staggering 80 percent reduction in soldiers developing behavioral health illnesses when proactive efforts were put in place to counsel and educate soldiers about mental illness. The well instituted study was published in the *American Journal of Psychiatry*, which showed that the number of soldiers sent home for mental health issues declined nearly 70 percent. "We're excited about what this study shows," says Maj. Gen. Patricia Horoho, Army deputy surgeon general. "It is the first direct evidence that a program (of more aggressive screening and treatment) is effective in preventing adverse behavioral health outcomes."[22] It was concluded that doctors were able to better determine who was fit for combat and identify those who needed more attention from counselors. If the questions asked raised concern, a psychiatrist or mental health worker immediately saw the soldiers. When comparing the control group of 10,353 soldiers to the non control group, the positive results were highly note worthy. In general, one in eight soldiers developed symptoms after a six month combat, but in the group that received more intense mental health screening, only 1 in 35 developed psychiatric conditions. The soldiers contemplating suicide were down significantly as was the number of those experiencing general stress of being deployed and separated from family.

It gives me such pleasure to read an article like this and have credence given to proactive practices. It was the impetus for me to realize that I was going to need to begin a journey of researching programs that encompass these concepts. If I was to do this effectively, I had to delve into these existing services a lot deeper. There was a lot to learn. It is one thing to gather information off the Internet and read about what these programs state their missions are, but another to meet and talk with the program staff directly. I wanted to interview them myself to get a true understanding of their missions, obstacles, and successes. The process of finding which programs to research was completely daunting. There is no shortage of services, and I couldn't find one resource or directory that organizes everything all in one place.

I started with the Director for the MHS (Military Health Systems) Office of Strategic Communications. I appreciated the time he took to help me out. He explained that the main goal of MHS Communications is to provide health care from the time a person joins the military through his/her deployments to final separation. After describing the systems in more detail (that is a book in itself), he referred me to the DCoE (the Defense Center of Excellence for Psychological Health and Traumatic Brain Injury). They are a relatively new organization started in 2007. I was really excited to connect with them because I had been a follower of the DCoE on both Twitter and Facebook over the past year, and have loved the information that they put out. I learned that DCoE is considered "the integrator and authority for the DOD (Department of Defense) on all information regarding psychological health and traumatic brain injury. Some of the subordinate organizations of DCoE provide clinical care to patients, but the headquarter of DCoE does not."[23] The media relations representative I spoke to explained that the

> DCoe seeks to identify promising practices and quality standards for suicide prevention and psychological health concerns, combat stress and traumatic brain injury (TBI) for service members. They lead the collaborative efforts that includes Department of Veterans Affairs (VA), civilian agencies, community leaders, advocacy groups, clinical experts and academic institutions that are dedicated to expanding the state of knowledge of psychological health and TBI.

The DCoE falls under the purview of the DOD (Department of Defense) Military Health System. It maintains a 24/7outreach center staffed by transition/outreach consultants who provide psychological health and TBI resources for service members, veterans and their families. One of the programs the outreach center supports is DCoE's Real Warriors Campaign, a multimedia public education initiative designed to break down the barriers to psychological health and TBI care. I wanted to learn more about what they do and got connected with their deputy program manager. She explained that the Real Warriors Campaign (RWC) has three goals: The first is to encourage service members to reach out for care and to help them cope with mental health issues, including PTSD. It provides practical tools and resources to help them and their families reintegrate into society when returning from combat. The second is to educate service members, veterans and their families to understand the different stages of the deployment cycle. The third is to educate the country so that civilians better appreciate all that our service members are doing for us. The campaign reaches service members and their families through web marketing, conferences and events and AFRTS (American Forces Radio Television Service), which broadcasts to 1.5 million military members every day. It was very impressive talking with her and learning about all of the time, effort and money that had gone into their campaign.

DCoE also manages the inTransition program. It was developed by the Defense Department, to help ensure that service members who receive psychological health care do not "fall through the cracks" when moving from one duty station to another. A personal coach, along with resources and tools, assists them during the transition period and empowers them to make healthy life choices. Coaches are available 24/7 via toll-free call. Having learned from my individual sessions with Marines, transitions can be difficult for the families and therefore, I imagine these services are a very valuable resource.

From a firsthand perspective, I can attest that the DCoE stays true to their rhetoric. For the year I have been following their social media efforts, I've been impressed with their ability to disseminate preventative information to service members. I now understood that this is accomplished through their five-component centers:

1. *Center for Deployment Psychology (CDP).* Their mission is to provide care necessary to address the deployment-related psychological health needs. CDP offers one and two-week training programs, military treatment facility based training, mobile training teams, two- to three-day intervention workshops, and online training and education services.

2. *Center for the Study of Traumatic Stress (CSTS)*. Its mission is to provide knowledge, leadership, and applications for preparing, responding to, and recovering from the consequences of disaster and trauma. The center focuses on: military psychiatry, disaster psychiatry, children and family, family violence, neuroscience, and public education.

3. *Defense and Veterans Brain Injury Center (DVBIC)*. Congress established DVBIC in 1992 to integrate specialized traumatic brain injury (TBI) care, research, and education across the Departments of Defense and Veterans Affairs. Its mission is to serve active-duty service members, their dependents, and veterans with TBI through state-of-the-art medical care, clinical research initiatives and educational programs.

4. *Deployment Health Clinical Center (DHCC)* is to improve deployment-related health by providing caring assistance and medical advocacy for military personnel and families with deployment-related health concerns. DHCC serves as a catalyst and resource center for the continuous improvement of deployment-related healthcare across the military system. It includes, what I believe to be the largest proactive military program currently in place, called RESPECT-Mil. I had the opportunity to talk with the folks there and get a more detailed account of their program and hear about its success thus far. I learned that "RESPECT-Mil is a system of care in which military primary care providers screen service members for depression and post-traumatic stress disorder (PTSD) and then offer treatment for these conditions. The way they explain it is, "service-members experiencing psychological trauma symptoms might not step forward to seek care because they may be intimidated by the stigma attached to

PTSD or because they simply believe they can work through the issues by themselves." They believe that by relying on primary care providers to screen, evaluate and when appropriate, treat service members rather than waiting for them to seek care, is an effective model to use. RESPECT-Mil has bright plans for the future. There electronic case management tracking system, First-Steps, is set to provide advanced outcome measurement and metrics reporting. A tri-service effort is underway to pilot Re-Engineering Healthcare Integration Programs (REHIP), a model that blends the Army, Navy, and Air Force approaches to behavioral health and primary care. The pilot program at six tri-service military sites began in early 2011. I love what they are trying to do. They're "out of the box" thinkers and look to approaching mental health issues from a different angel.

5. *National Center for Telehealth & Technology* is most widely known as T2. I spoke with a public affairs officer for the program who explained that the mission of T2 is to develop telehealth and technology solutions for psychological health conditions and TBI. He was very enthusiastic about this program, which is the only component of DCoE that functions outside of Washington, DC. It emphasizes the use of smart phones as a means of promoting mental health. T2 psychologists along with tech experts and researchers are working on designing, developing, and piloting web and mobile applications as virtual reality therapy tools, which is now called telehealth. They have created a number of smart phone applications to accompany Prolonged Exposure (PE), the gold standard for PTSD treatment. They call this app the PE Coach. It puts resources for prolonged exposure therapy in the hands of the patient. You don't have to be in

the military to download these applications to their phones, anyone can do it. I put MoodTracker on my phone and can personally attest to the ease of its use, if one wants to take the time to use it.

T2 has also figured out ways to use virtual reality exposure therapy for PTSD. It requires the patient to activate the memory of their trauma during treatment. He explained that following combat deployments, many soldiers are emotionally detached and have difficulty with this aspect of treatment. VRET enhances the patient's ability to revisit the trauma memory with a sensory-rich environment that includes computer-generated sights, sounds, vibrations, smells, and naturalistic devices that give users a sense of participating in an alternative environment, relative to their actual physical location. The VRET was described as a game-like video walk though experience that can help soldiers feel more comfortable with the idea of therapy. T2 has also come up with new ways to bring psychological services to service members who do not have easy access due to working in remote or not heavily accessed areas. The TTU (transportable telehealth units) are an example of this. They are transportable space solutions that expand PH/TBI health care.

I was fascinated to learn about the BioFeedback Facilitation, which is a device that monitors, measures, and reports physiological functions to help diagnose and treat a range of ailments. T2 is developing software tools that sense and record data and make it available for evaluation and interpretation on a mobile device via a Bluetooth connection. They have developed the base software necessary to gather data from a single device that collects heart rate, respiration rate, skin temperature, and physical orientation. A service member can wear the device while working with a clinician at a remote off site location. The provider can receive the biofeedback, which will enhance their ability to provide quality care.

In addition, they host theAfterDeployment.org website launched in August 2008. Afterdeployment.org offers a wide range of behavioral health resources in support of service members, veterans, families, and health care providers serving the military community. In 2010, the site underwent a major refresh. Expansion included six new topical libraries and seventeen additional self-assessments, along with video-based personal stories obtained from service and family members. The site established a social media presence on Facebook and Twitter, and introduced podcasts highlighting warriors' deployment challenges. It also provides a portal that offers health care workers client guides, practice guidelines, links to continuing education opportunities, instruction concerning the site's self-assessments, and quick facts about diagnosing and treating PTSD and TBI.

I was very impressed with everything I had learned thus far. However, the more I learned, the more frustrated I became that I never knew about any of this information while I was working with Marines. Clearly, programs are in place, but it makes me wonder how the information is being disseminated to both the military and provider communities? I couldn't find anyone that could answer those questions effectively. The common answer always seemed to be, "yes, that is a challenge we are having and we continue to work on solutions." It sure seems like a giant waste, if those that need help don't know about the programs supplying it.

I continued my research further. Because I had done the majority of my work with Marines, I was very interested in learning more about what the Marine Corps has implemented on their own in regards to proactive measures and resilience building. The Navy presides over the Marine Corps, so I started with the Navy Bureau of Medicine and Surgery (BUMED), which is the headquarters command for Navy Medicine. I interviewed a well informed media representative, that like everyone I had encountered, was eager to share information about his programs. BUMED personnel deploy with Sailors and Marines worldwide. They also furnish civilian health care to professionals that are providing care for uniformed services, their family members and retirees at military treatment facilities.

One of the key preventative BUMED programs in naval mental health prevention is the Naval Center Combat & Operational Stress Control (NCCOSC). Their purpose and goal is to improve the psychological health of Marines and Sailors through comprehensive educational programs that are designed to build resilience for the treatment of combat and operational stress injuries. I was excited for the opportunity to meet with their director, Captain Scott L. Johnston. I interviewed him at the NCCOSC facility located inside the San Diego Navy hospital property. Captain Johnston was an impressive man. He not only has had an impressive Navy career, he also is a trained clinical psychologist. This puts him in a powerful position of truly understanding all sides of the complex issues.

NCCOSC is divided into four components:

1. Research Facilitation to provide fleet clinicians with comprehensive and innovative programs of collecting and analyzing data. They have some very interesting research projects they are currently working on. One that particularly fascinated me was a computer-based, attention-retraining program designed to reduce symptoms of anxiety in military personnel.

2. Their Programs Department staff work with military leadership, health care providers, service members, and families to implement psychological health treatment and care management systems through the Psychological Health Pathways (PHP). PHP has been designed to support the return of service members to optimal health in a timely manner.

3. Strategic Communications Department is responsible for internal and external relations to supply information to communities, media, and public affairs. Their emphasis is to help service members and their families become more resilient and optimistic and find creative solutions to their problems. He explained that the NCCOSC goal is to ensure that their communication products provide timely and accurate information, as well as being a resource to educate, dispel myths, and decrease stigma surrounding psychological health issues.

4. The knowledge management department is the center's information hub. Its staff supports data collection, analysis and database development, as well as maintaining internal and public websites. The department administers the Care Management Registry (CMR), a web-based tracking tool designed to support effective wounded, ill and injured service member case management.

Last spring I attended the NCCOSC annual conference. It was a very informative and educational agenda focusing on important combat and operational stress issues. After talking with Capt. Johnston for a significant period of time, I was relieved to learn how much they emphasis and value prevention. He reminded me that 85 percent of the most elite fighters have some sort of reaction to war. NCCOSC recognizes that if most people are going to experience symptoms, we have to help them cope with potential issues right from the start. Resilience building is part of the culture there and one of the key elements of what they are striving to accomplish.

Another one of BLUMED (Navy Bureau of Medicine and Surgery) programs is National Intrepid Center of Excellence (NICoE). They are a facility dedicated to the research, diagnosis, and treatment of service members and veterans experiencing psychological health conditions and TBI.

In addition to all the programs mentioned so far, the DOD (Department of Defense) Psychological Health Programs also sponsors:

- *The Yellow Ribbon Program* (YRP): This program assists reserve component members and their families to connect with local resources before, during and after deployments; especially during the reintegration phase that occurs in the months after service members return home. Yellow Ribbon events take place in large conference settings where service members and families can access information on health care, education/training opportunities, financial and legal benefits.

- *U.S. Army Comprehensive Soldier Fitness* program uses individual assessments, virtual training, classroom training and embedded resilience experts to provide skills for soldiers, families and Army civilians.

- *U.S. Army Resiliency Training program* (formerly Battlemind) is a program which offers positive psychology tools to soldiers, leaders, and families helping them grow and recover from adversity.

- *U.S. Air Force Landing Gear Program* launched in 2010. This program was designed for airmen who were considered at elevated risk for post-traumatic stress disorder (PTSD). It consists of a thirty- to sixty-minute class conducted by a mental health care provider. Landing Gear is primarily a resiliency program but does cover PTSD, traumatic brain injury (TBI) and normal stress reactions.

- *National Guard Resiliency Program* is online training designed to help National Guard soldiers develop mental toughness to thrive in basic training and throughout their military career.

- *National Resource Directory* is a website for connecting wounded warriors, service members, veterans, and their families with those who support them. The National Resource Directory provides access to more than 10,000 services and resources at the national, state and local levels that support recovery, rehabilitation and community reintegration.

What disappoints me still is that with all of this comprehensive programming that exists, never once in my years of being both a MFLC or a Military OneSource provider, have I ever been offered or exposed to any of this information. The clinical training, reference materials and referral giving potential, would have helped me out immensely. The services are in place, and yet as an "outside" military mental health provider, I would have never known about them. For example, now that I know about T2, I always have my military clients download it to their smart phones. Now that I know about DCoE, I have signed up for a free conference to gain additional skills and learn about the new research and growth in resiliency studies. Every TriCare, MFLC, Military OneSource provider, etc., should be included in receiving the plentiful information that these programs provide.

The initiatives that have come out of the Department of Defense are profound. They are attacking the problem from every angle, and for that I give them a lot of credit. It also feels good to see that others share my beliefs on the need for proactive counseling and appreciate the inherent benefits that come from dealing with issues before they turn into problems. On the other hand, I'm left feeling very troubled. Although it appears the DOD government run military mental health programs are very effective, I don't believe they are being utilized to their fullest potential. The primary reasons seem to revolve around the fact that military members don't entirely trust the government. I reached out and talked to over 50 Marines to help me gain a deeper understanding of the situation. This is a very complicated issue to explain and I heard a lot of varying opinions from them.

One common reason that came up multiple times is still the continual fear that accessing help may hurt their military careers. Another is that some service members feel these programs are comprised of propaganda and they will be brainwashed to view things in a military benefiting way. I personally don't believe either to be true, but time and time again service members report to me that they are reluctant to entrust government programs. The most common issue I heard was regarding the complexity of services offered. It's hard for people to figure out where to turn, who to go to for help and how to find them. One Marine described it as "a giant web of information that works like a maze. You get referred from one place to another and then end up at a dead end."

I recently sat in on a military mental health round table meeting. Leaders and key players were present to discuss concerns and areas of deficit with regards to military mental health services. The two main issues that kept popping up were, (1) the need for a counselor or mental health coach to provide ongoing, routine proactive counseling and (2) the need for counselors to reach out via Skype or other technology to military members in distress that live in remote locations. Of course I empathized with the proactive counseling piece but I knew it wasn't a quick fix. With regards to remote therapists, I was optimistic I could offer assistance. I was excited to share what I had recently learned about T2 and the tele-health advances that had been made. Everyone in the room was interested in hearing about the new technology, yet equally frustrated that they had never heard of it and had no idea how to access it. After leaving the meeting, I called T2 with hopes of making a connection from them to the military leaders that were requesting services. I was surprised to learn that T2 doesn't do any direct service work, not to individuals nor to specific branches in the military. They are "reliant on the highest levels of leadership to become aware of their products and then to distribute that information through their own channels. The information flows from T2 to the DOD (Department of Defense) to the different military branches and then down to the treatment facility level." When I asked the person I was speaking to if he felt the information about their products was getting disseminated effectively, he replied "I think there is so much saturation with different products and programs right now, that those at the top don't know what to push down, so instead they aren't doing anything." I interpreted that to mean; the DOD has a need, they create organizations (such as T2) to develop state of the art treatments and solutions, the organizations deliver back what they are asked to provide, and it ultimately gets stuck somewhere up at the high levels of the government. At the same time, our military members living all over the world are struggling with mental illness and help is limited. When I asked my contact at T2 what their annual operating budget was, he couldn't give me an answer and that it wasn't public information. I probed a little as to why not if it is a government contract, but his answer was vague. I do know that it is in the multi millions. I do not fault T2 in anyway. They were asked to do a job and they were outstanding with fulfilling that task. The problem is there are a bunch of men and women that need help and there is an awful lot of money being spent on providing it, there just appears to be a large deficit in the middle. It makes me wonder if the people at the top have any idea what is going on with the people on the ground.

The for-profit insurance companies or corporations that fulfill a lot of the military mental health contracts don't appear to be providing the solutions either. Through all of my research looking into government run programs, everyone I spoke with appeared to have the service members' best interest in mind. I cannot say the same for the for profit contractors.

I recently looked up the HWM earnings statement. I found it very disturbing on how much emphasis was put on streamlining costs and projected revenue. Like all for-profit companies, when they present themselves to their shareholders, the emphasis is on earnings. Simply put: the more money they take in and the less they spend, the more money the company makes. I have a hard time understanding where a company's incentive is to provide a high quality of care, if their primary goal is earnings. That's not to say that they can't furnish strong services, it just doesn't appear that they are. Perhaps the reason is simply because as a country we are not making it a priority, or it could be that those organizations that are awarded the contracts may be earning the business for the wrong reasons.

We live in a changing technological world where everyone in accountable for their words and actions. Another thing that bothers me is that the DOD programs all have a fairly extensive social media presence. Anyone can go on and see the efforts and energies that are being extended. As a result, one can see how much interaction they are having with service members and their families. I now follow all of the programs mentioned above and am quite impressed with the level of outreach and dissemination of information that occurs. I am hopeful that eventually that will help effectively circulate information to the military communities and providers. On the contrary, with regards to the government programs, neither the MFLC (military family life consultant) nor Military OneSource, both operated through for profit contractors, have social media sites. It makes me wonder where their public accountability is?

As my research came to a close, I was left with mixed emotions. The programs are abundant and the need for them is even greater, but all of it appears so complicated. The little program that evolved at MCRD seemed to work so well, and yet at the same time it was so simple. On the other hand, I now knew more than ever that the system is far more complex than I ever imagined. I spent months trying to figure out the military mental health web. I have yet to find one person who truly knows about all the different programs that exist. If I'm confused, I can most definitely understand why the military members don't know where to turn. I was however hopeful that a shift in attitudes was occurring and somewhat optimistic that slowly things will get better. On an endnote, out of all of the government people and programs that I spoke to and interviewed, no one person had ever heard of the $500 million MFLC program!

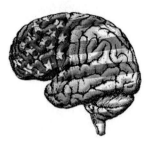

SLOW PROGRESS

As a sheer coincidence, the other day when I was searching military mental health trends on the Internet, I came across a document containing "minutes" taken from a MCRD support council meeting discussing the MCCS (Marine Corps Community Services) programs. (it still amazes me how much one can find on the Internet). The meeting took place approximately one year after I was abruptly removed from the depot. It began with General Burns, the new commanding general (who was not there when I was a MFLC). He stated,

> Commanding General: "I believe it is important that we meet and express concerns and issues. These programs are near and dear to me, I am interested in supporting Marines and their families."

> (The MCCS lieutenant colonel that hung up on me when I called for answers) spoke next and did an overview of the new MCCS programs (it did not include the MFLC program). After the CG (commanding general) gave his comments, they opened it up to the attendees for a general Q&A. The very first question was from the Second Battalion commander:

2nd Bn Lt. Col.: MFLC program…used to be very beneficial for the people. The current system is with a new person, they meet with families and drill instructors, rotating in and out every 45-90 days, it's a problem for us is to establish rapport… Right now the way it is working isn't efficient, sometimes the professionals don't know what we do, don't understand the rigors of training, DIs don't feel they understand. There is no continuity.

MCCS Lt. Col.: All I can tell you is that this is an OSD (Office of the Secretary of Defense) program, they have rules, there were some issues, and they are very strict on change over.

Chief of Staff: This is not an entitlement program, this is a something for nothing program.

Commanding General: Can we offer feedback?

MCCS Lt. Col.: Yes, they can get feedback.

Chief of Staff: if we were able to ask location to change from 45 days to 90 days would that ease your mind?

2nd Bn Lt. Col.: 90 days would be more effective, if they rotate the same people that would be ideal, but not sure they can do that…

Chief of Staff: not sure they can, but if you want to send an e-mail, we can put it out and see the feedback. [24]

To me this brief dialogue says everything! This conversation happened one year after I left the Depot and the Marines were still discussing the loss of not having the program anymore. A once incredibly useful program was replaced with a useless program. To add insult to injury, when I read the roll call of members in attendance for that meeting, no one from Family Support Services was there.

The Marine Corps isn't the only one grumbling. I also found that the Army had put in a request to have the MFLC program renegotiated. "The Army has asked that the MFLC support longer rotations (beyond the present maximum of 90 days) be considered."[25] It doesn't sound to me that the current model is working the way it was hoped.

I was still feeling uneasy. At minimum, a few times a week I continue to hear from Marines in distress. They rarely request the counseling for their own personal reasons, it's typically for help dealing with one of their subordinates. They have someone in their company or platoon that is showing signs of distress and they are not sure the best measures to handle it. Of course they have taken numerous mandatory classes on suicide prevention, but it doesn't seem to prepare them for the times when they need it. I call these times the "gray" area. These are the in-between cases when things are not so clear cut. The majority of the questions I field from the Marines are how to develop deeper dialogue when talking to their subordinates. They need help with the type of questions they should ask, in order to elicit information out of their men and women without putting them on the defense. In addition, they often need referrals to find out where the safest resources are, places that they can trust that their issues will be properly taken care of.

The military is comprised of leaders at many different levels. To complicate the problems even more, since the wars in Iraq and Afghanistan, officers of lower and lower rank are in charge of making major decisions. These well-meaning junior active-duty leaders do not have the know-how or experience to help their subordinates deal with the stress and trauma they are confronted with. I have come to the sad realization that until larger attitudes shift, leaders are going to need to take the proactive counseling piece in their own hands. Leaders need to recognize how important it is to personally get to know the men and women who serve under them. They need to push past the awkwardness and work on becoming comfortable eliciting open and honest conversations. With the duration of these wars, the situation is more urgent than ever.

Despite the multitude of available mental health programs, if service members don't access them, they are of no use. It is going to take a long time for stigmas to change and for our military to trust outsiders. If the change takes place from the inside first, progress will come faster. The paradigm needs to shift and the leaders themselves are going to need to take the first step in that change. When leaders are able to discuss mental health issues openly, it will remove all the stigma and barriers. The role modeling that can occur will effect future generations for years to come.

This has been a hard conclusion to come by, especially because I have been so focused on providing proactive services from a clinical standpoint. I've come to recognize what a complicated issue it is, and how many variables get in the way from accessing and receiving quality services. I'm beginning to realize that real trust comes from inside. As I observed watching recruit training, I witnessed firsthand how service members are taught to rely on their leaders and do as they are told.

Don't get me wrong, I'd love nothing more than to see every service member go through on going proactive counseling, but in the meantime I'd like to see more service members take an active role in learning these skills. This would include improving meaningful dialogue with subordinates and helping their men and women learn what they have a propensity toward while under stress. There is a difference between violating someone's personal space and getting to know them personally. Teaching them the difference is imperative. I found a valuable leadership toolkit resource through the NCCOSC (Naval Center Combat Operational Stress Control) website. It states: "Think of emotional resilience as armor for the mind, push-ups for the brain. Emotional resilience helps to protect a person from the debilitating effects of trauma and high-stress situations. Some people may seem more naturally resilient than others, but resilience can be developed and strengthened." [26] They state facts, strategies, and tools to help leaders attain this. I included their leadership tools as a reference in the back of the book because I found them very helpful for everyone that may come in contact with a service member.

Life has gone back to a new normal. My private practice is busier than ever and I enjoy doing some military work on the side. Unfortunately, the company that held the Military One Source contract when I signed up to be a provider, was not awarded it again during a recent rebid process. Now a new company has the contract and they chose not to take on the existing providers. What this essentially means is, a whole new group of clinicians are providing these services and those of us that used to be Military One Source providers no longer are able to. It makes it difficult on me if a Marine I know, or a Marine that was specifically referred to me, calls seeking mental health services. My typical response is to encourage them to call the Military One Source referral line, explaining that all providers are good and that getting the help is more important than who is providing the help. The other day I experienced an exception to the norm.

It was a typical Monday morning and I was back to back with patients all day. I did not have an opportunity to listen to my messages until the end of the day. There was a message from a Staff Sergeant who was calling me in regards to one of his fellow Marines. He described the Marine as severely depressed and was afraid he may be suicidal. The Marine had gone on base for help but they simply gave him a bunch of psychotropic medication to take and put him on a wait list to see a therapist. I immediately called the Staff Sergeant back and got the phone number for the suffering Marine. I was glad the Staff Sergeant in distress answered his phone. He didn't appear overly depressed during our conversation and when I asked him if he felt suicidal he answered "no". I couldn't fit him in the next day, but scheduled him for Wednesday, two days later. I leave a percentage of my practice open for pro bono military work, and he would fall into that category. Wednesday afternoon he did not show up for his appointment. I called his cell phone and my heart dropped when a sobbing female answered it. Staff Sergeant James had committed suicide by hanging himself the day before! I felt horrible! What if I had scheduled him a day earlier, could I have saved him? There is nothing that anyone can say at a time like that to make you feel better. He was so close to getting help, but yet it was too late.

I sat there dazed knowing that as bad as I felt, it paled in comparison to those that loved and knew Staff Sergeant James. I tried to make myself feel better by thinking about all the Marines I had helped over the years. I remembered the time a company commander called me about one of his Marines that had been acting odd and irrational over a few day period and then hadn't shown up for work. He was worried about him. He had called him multiple times and there was no answer. I told him he needed to go to his apartment and make sure he was okay. After minimal prodding, the commander agreed to go. He found his young Marine in the bathtub with a shotgun in his hand. That Marine was saved in the nick of time, but it didn't make the pain of Staff Sergeant James any less.

I try to stay positive and believe that things are getting better. It's hard to do when you continue to hear stories like the recent US soldier who killed 16 Afghan civilians in a violent shooting spree. The atrocities feel like they are getting worse every day. Although at times I have a heavy heart, I smiled when I read the email below.

From: Major Aaron R. Granada
Sent: April 18, 2012
Subject: Request for conversation

Marjorie:

I received your contact from a fellow Marine after we talked about your successes (and challenges) at MCRD.

We have had a similar situation developing here at Camp Pendleton with a program to proactively counsel staff at the Wounded Warrior Battalion.

If you have a few moments to bounce ideas, I'd love to tell what has happened here, compare situations to MCRD, and get your input on issues to consider as I fight the battle to continue to get proactive counseling for the staff here.

My numbers are below; I hope we can connect!

Regards,

Major Aaron R. Grananda
Camp Pendleton, CA 92055

Change is happening slowly. I now understand more than ever that no one can change the system alone. Collectively we can make a difference. Encouraging movement is happening, but if people remain silent as long as I did, it's going to happen at a snails pace, and that is too late! We need to change the societal culture of how we view mental health. We need to demand quality of care and use a common sense approach to deliver it. We cannot sit back and hope the problem goes away, it won't! Perhaps the reason that no one is doing what they really need to, is because all parties are acting complacent. That goes from the government right down to the military themselves and everyone in between. The Marines have a saying that I love "complacency kills." I can't think of a more fitting time to use it.

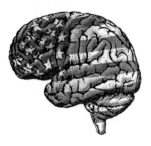

FINAL THOUGHTS

In conclusion, I strongly believe there is tremendous value in discussing mental health issues from a preventative standpoint. Learning what an individual has a propensity toward while under stress will help mitigate issues down the road. Whether this is done by mandatory sessions, military leaders or in-group settings, the shift from reactive to proactive must occur.

I also do not think it is in our military's best interest to have companies deliver mental health services when their primary goal to report positive revenue to shareholders, there is an inherent conflict. To me that states: Get the most money as you can from the government to run the program and then spend the bare minimum on the operating costs, yielding a large profit margin. My view of the mentality at the inception of the MFLC program was: If we can spend a lot of money on this program, then it will show need and the government will increase our spending ceiling.

According to the HWM investor relations statement,

> In 2007, HWM was awarded a five-year contract, the Military Family & Life Consultant Program ("MFLC"), to develop, administer and monitor the non-medical counseling program for service members. Services under the MFLC began on April 1, 2007 and will end in 2012, subject to an early termination provision which is based

on a funding ceiling of approximately $542.5 million over the term of the contract. The funding ceiling was recently raised by $242.5 million over its originally estimated limit of $300 million. The program is designed to deliver short-term situational problem solving counseling, primarily with regard to stress factors inherent in the military lifestyle. Revenues for the MFLC subcontract for the year ended December 31, 2009 were $210.4 million and were $353.7 million since the contract's inception. [27]

That contract nearly doubled from when it was first incepted in the early 2000s. The new contract, expected to begin in early 2012, is estimated at $1.2 billion!

For the sake of this book, I chose to stick only to my story and the issues that I was presented with. I was not able to address the multitude of other problems that are currently going on in the military. I focused only on active duty concerns and did not delve into the equally important subjects including military families, kids, spouses, veterans, sexual abuse/rape, etc.

In summary to date, more than 2.2 million troops have served in the post-9/11 wars. According to the American Psychiatric Association,

> People who serve in the military and veterans can face unique challenges. There are many emotions involved with being at war, separated from loved ones, as well as the stressors that are inherent in multiple and extended deployments. The stress encountered in service abroad can also play a role and cause mental health issues, including anxiety, posttraumatic stress disorder, depression and substance abuse.
>
> In addition to these mental health issues, the war has exposed many soldiers to traumatic brain injury or mul-

tiple concussions from exposure to IEDS (improvised explosive devices).[28]

An American Psychiatric Association survey highlights the issues that soldiers and their spouses cope with: More than one-third self-report frequently experiencing feelings of anxiety (military member 38 percent, military spouse 39 percent), depression (military member 40 percent, military spouse 33 percent). In addition to stress caused by worry for their loved one serving in the military, spouses reported a lot or a little stress from handling domestic issues alone (60 percent), single parenting (54 percent). More than 60 percent of military members think that seeking help for mental health concerns would have at least some negative impact on their career.[29]

Sadly, it isn't only our military in combat that are at risk of suffering severe mental health issues. Of the 112 guardsmen who committed suicide last year, more than half had never even left American soil. At a Senate hearing in June 2010, Army Vice Chief of Staff General Peter Chiarelli said, "a look at the previous four months data showed that soldiers with one or no deployments represented 79 percent of all suicides and first termers represent 60 percent of all suicides."[30] Shortly after, ABC News reported,

> It's difficult to assess what pressures are leading to the increase in suicides among Guard and Reservists who have not been mobilized because it is not as simple as saying previous combat experience has increased their mental stress when they return to their civilian lives. For example, in April 2010, of the seven confirmed suicides on the reserve side, five had never been deployed overseas. In the month of June, four of the eleven military who

committed suicide had never deployed, and five had at least one deployment.[31]

Vice Chief of Staff General Peter Chiarelli told the *Army Times*, "If you think you know the one thing that causes people to commit suicide, please let us know because we don't know what it is."[32]

Currently the National Institute of Mental Health (NIMH) is conducting a $50 million research project attempting to identify categories of soldiers most at risk for suicide. According to the first round of preliminary data from an Army study, the suicide rate for female soldiers triples when they go to war. Suicide rates among men increase from 15 per 100,000 to 21 per 100,000 when they deploy to Iraq or Afghanistan. Soldiers of Asian descent have dramatically higher suicide rates than other racial groups. Their risk is double or triple that of other soldiers, and four times higher in the war zone.[33]

It isn't only those suffering from long-term mental health issues who are at risk of suicide. According to Dr. Prudence L. Gourguechon, past president of the American Psychoanalytic Association,

> Most of the military personnel who attempt or commit suicide are not suffering from long-term mental illness. They are often depressed, yes, but they don't necessarily have the biology for life long mental illness. What they are is profoundly hopeless, and emerging from an experience where the meaning of life, both theirs and others, has radically shifted on its axis. They suffer a crisis of meaning and connectedness and often they panic. Suicidal acts are frequently undertaken in a state of temporary, extreme panic, when the mental doors shut down; the individual

can not see any alternatives and cannot stand the agony of
the panicky, despairing state.[34]

If the government is spending large amounts of money providing
goods and services in every capacity imaginable for our military,
why do we still have a problem? Why are we seeing these disturbing statics continually rising? In February 2011, The Joint Mental
Health Advisory Team comprised of members from Office of
the Surgeon General, United States Army Medical Command
and Office of the Command Surgeon HQ, USCENTCOM
and Office of the Command Surgeon U.S. Forces Afghanistan
(USFOR-A) put out an extensive report of the latest findings:
The report states that the decline in individual morale is significant: 46.5 percent of troops said they had medium, high or very
high morale, compared with 65.7 percent who said that in 2005.
Only about one in seven soldiers—and one in five Marines—
reported high or very high morale.

Acute stress rates are significantly higher than rates from
2009 and 2005. Rates of combined psychological problem measure (acute stress, depression, or anxiety) significantly higher than
2005. Soldiers on their third/fourth deployment report significantly more psychological problems and use of mental health
medications than Soldiers on their first or second deployment.
The rate of Marines reporting psychological problems (acute
stress symptoms, depression or anxiety) is significantly higher in
2010 than in 2006 or 2007. Marines report dramatic increase in
combat exposure relative to 2006 and 2007 in Operation Iraqi
Freedom (OIF).

There has been a significant increase in the percentage of
Marines who report high or very high concern about not getting enough sleep. Sleep disruption is primarily due to poor sleep
environment (e.g., too hot, noisy, etc.). Marines on three or more

deployments report lower morale than those on first deployment. Multiple deploying Marines also show increased psychological problems.[35]

These discouraging statistics aren't the only issues of concern. We must also look at the pervasive problems facing our vets. More than 10,000 Iraq and Afghanistan veterans are homeless or in programs attempting to keep them off the streets. This number has doubled three times since 2006, according to figures released by the Department of Veteran Affairs.[36] The VA blames the rise on a poor economy and the nature of the current wars, where a limited number of troops serve multiple deployments. Half or more of those surveyed said they had killed the enemy, and 75-80 percent described the death or wounding of a buddy. Half also said that an improvised explosive device detonated within fifty-five yards while they were on foot patrol. The VA study's researchers also found evidence of physical wear-and-tear with a third of the force experiencing chronic pain.[37] In May 2011, military.com reported an average of eighteen veterans a day were committing suicide. A federal appeals court earlier that same month ordered the Department of Veterans Affairs to dramatically overhaul its mental health care system. In the strongly worded ruling, the Ninth U.S. Circuit Court of Appeals said, "it takes the department an average of four years to fully provide the mental health benefits owed veterans".[38]

A 2008 Rand Institute study found that 18.5 percent of soldiers returning from those countries were diagnosed with PTSD, and the study concluded 300,000 troops currently deployed suffer from it or major depression. It reviewed the appeals court case illustrating that it often takes weeks for a suicidal vet to get a first appointment. The "unchecked incompetence" in handling the flood of post-traumatic stress disorder and other mental health claims is unconstitutional, the court added. The study also stated, "one of every three service members returning from Iraq and Afghanistan has been treated by the VA for mental health issues, including post-traumatic stress syndrome."[39]

If that is not depressing enough, there is the disturbing new trend of sexual assaults and rapes that are occurring both overseas and at home. Representative Jane Harman stated, "A female soldier in Iraq is more likely to be raped by a fellow soldier than killed by enemy fire." [40] According to *Time Magazine* 3/8/2010, "Sexual Assaults on Female Soldiers: Don't Ask, Don't Tell,"

> The fight over 'Don't ask, don't tell' made headlines this winter as an issue of justice and history, and the social evolution of our military institutions. We've heard much less about another set of hearings in the House Armed Services Committee regarding women and sexual assault. Maybe that's because too many commanders still don't ask, and too many victims still won't tell, about the levels of violence endured by women in uniform.[41]

The Pentagon's latest figures show that nearly 3,000 women were sexually assaulted in fiscal year 2008, up 9 percent from the year before; among women serving in Iraq and Afghanistan, the number rose 25 percent. When you look at the entire universe of female veterans, close to one third say they were victims of rape or assault while they were serving. That is twice the rate in the civilian population.

The problem is even worse than that. The Pentagon estimates that 80 to 90 percent of sexual assaults go unreported, and it's no wonder. Anonymity is all but impossible; a Government Accountability Office report concluded that most victims stay silent because of "the belief that nothing would be done; fear of ostracism, harassment, or ridicule; and concern that peers would gossip." [42] More than half feared they would be labeled troublemakers. Women worry that they will be removed from their units for their own "protection" and talk about not wanting to undermine their missions or the cohesion of their units. And then some just do the math: only 8 percent of cases that are investigated end in prosecution, compared with 40 percent for civilians arrested for sex crimes. Astonishingly, about 80 percent of those *convicted* are honorably discharged nonetheless.

In May 2011, the Pentagon released its report on sexual assault in the military, stating that for FY2010, there were 3,158 total reports of sexual assault in the military. The DOD estimates that this number only represents 13.5 percent of total assaults in 2010, making the total number of military rapes and sexual assaults in excess of 19,000 for FY 2010. "This latest report clearly shows that the military's response to rape and sexual assault within its own ranks has been both inadequate and ineffective," said Anu Bhagwati, former Marine Corps captain and executive director of the Service Women's Action Network. "This crime continues to see massive amounts of underreporting because victims do not feel the climate is safe to report, and perpetrators are not being brought o trial in sufficient numbers."[43]

Along with the *Annual Report*, the DOD also released its *2010 Workplace and Gender Relations Survey of Active Duty Members*, which surveys service members every two years about sexual assault and sexual harassment in the workplace. This report indicates that the military's climate of fear and intimidation around sexual assault reporting still exists. The survey reveals that 67 percent of women are "uncomfortable" with reporting, 54 percent "fear reprisal," and 46 percent of both men and women in the military believe that sexual assault was "not important enough" to report at all. Sexual assault: VA regulations require that all potential felonies be reported to the inspector general, but the GAO study found that the office did not learn of forty-two rape cases.

During this study investigators visited five VA medical centers and found panic alarm systems that did not work, closed-circuit surveillance cameras that were not being monitored and under-staffed police offices.[44] It sounds to me like a mixed message.

Addiction to prescription medication is yet another alarming concern for our troops. According to the Army Surgeon General, hospitalizations and diagnoses for substance abuse doubled among members of U.S. forces in recent years. Nurses and case managers at Army wounded care units report that one in three of their patients are addicted or dependent on drugs. For nearly five years, a Green Beret general has quietly been hooked on narcotics he has taken for chronic pain. In going public about his drug dependency during interviews with *USA Today*, Fridovich, 59, echoes the findings of an Army surgeon general task force last year that said doctors too often rely on handing out addictive narcotics to quell pain. "The abuse is getting higher and higher and more and more," Fridovich says, "and that leads to a very dark, deadly, dangerous place."[45]

An internal Army investigation report revealed that 25 to 35 percent of about 10,000 soldiers assigned to special units for the wounded, ill, or injured is addicted to or dependent on drugs, according to their nurses and case managers. Doctors in those care units told investigators they need training in finding other ways to manage pain besides narcotics.[46]

From 2005 to 2009, the Pentagon reports that the number of troops diagnosed with substance abuse disorders jumped 50 percent to nearly 40,000 each year. Substance abuse hospitalizations increased from 100 troops per month in 2003 to more than 250 per month in 2009.[47]

There is also grave concern in regards to our military families. They too have high risk factors. The *Huffington Post* reported on 7/11/11,

Children with one or more parent on long-term deployment in Iraq or Afghanistan have a higher chance of
mental health problems, according to a new study. Recent
estimates suggest that more than 44 percent of active duty
members have kids. Using data from more than 300,000
children who had at least one active-duty U.S. Army parent between 2003 and 2006. Researchers found that the
length of deployment played a significant role in overall
mental health. Nearly 17 percent of the military children
studied were diagnosed with at least one mental health
issue during the study period, including conditions such
as depression and anxiety. The likelihood of a mental
health diagnosis increased with the length of deployment,
particularly among boys and girls whose parents were
deployed for more than 11 months.[48]

To make matters worse, there have been scores of reports recently
stating that there are not nearly enough mental health providers to meet the ever growing needs. *Time Magazine* 8/22/10
"Invisible Wounds, mental health and the military" reports that
"Army Lieut. General Eric Schoomaker, the surgeon general
who oversees the mental and physical well being of the nation's
soldiers, concedes he doesn't have the doctors and therapists he
needs. 'We're in uncharted territory in respect to the strain on
the force,' Schoomaker said recently. Translation: he needs help.
According to the Army's estimates of its needs, 414 psychiatrists are 20 percent less than Schoomaker should have. A study
released by the Army on July 29, 2010 concluded that 'numerous
critical shortages of care providers including behavioral health'
personnel are hurting its efforts to curb suicides. 'The Army
has been criminally negligent,' says Captain Peter Linnerooth,
an Army psychologist, "the service has had a difficult time find-

ing psychiatrists to care for combat vets, which puts even more pressure—'and way too much burnout'—on those who stay." [49]

"Going to a psychiatrist is still seen as a sign of weakness in the Army; the chief fear is that it will work against promotion. That may be the reason only about half of those needing help seek care," according to a 2008 Rand Corp. study. And only half of those—25 percent of the total who need help—get "minimally adequate treatment," the Rand study found. Repeat deployments deepen the crisis. One in every 10 soldiers who has completed a single combat deployment has a mental ailment; that rate jumps to 1 in 5 with a second deployment and nearly 1 in 3 with a third. That means that more than 500,000 troops have returned home to the U.S. in the last decade with a mental illness. [50]

The article continues stating, "the Army has spent $7 million building at Fort Campbell what it calls its first behavioral-health campus (soldiers call it "the mental-health mall") with a half-dozen new clinics filled with the latest technology for diagnosing and treating post traumatic stress disorder (PTSD) and traumatic brain injury." The fort's mental-health staff has grown from 31 in January 2008 to 95 today. Yet suicides continued to rise. "The way Fort Campbell deals with the soldiers are why there's so many suicides there," Sergeant James Kendall, now studying to be an Army nurse at Fort Sam Houston in Texas, says. "Pretty much everyone who went to mental health said the same thing I did—they're just shoving them out the door." Kendall, a medic in the 101st, returned from Afghanistan in March 2009 and says he was brushed off when he initially sought help. It was only after he downed a full bottle of Army-prescribed Vicodin, he says, that the Army took his worries seriously.[51]

Can the Army's mental-health corps heal itself? It doesn't look anytime soon. Some 100 physical-health jobs have shifted to mental-health billets, and combat tours for some medical specialists, including psychiatrists, have been cut from 12 months to six. But the Army has been forced to hire regular civilians to help, many who know little about the military and its culture. The Rand Corp study states that, "one soldier walked out on a civilian therapist who thought an RPG—a rocket-propelled grenade, one of which killed his buddy—was a small car."[52]

If everything that is being done thus far isn't helping, it's hard to imagine what will happen once more vets come home coupled with the problems that will incur with the upcoming budget cuts. Nine months after the tragic shootings occurred in Fort Hood where an Army psychiatrist was charged with fatally shooting thirteen soldiers and wounding thirty, *USA Today* reported,

> "Fort Hood the nation's largest Army post can measure the toll of war in the more than 10,000 mental health evaluations, referrals or therapy sessions held every month. About every fourth soldier here, where 48,000 troops and their families are based, has been in counseling during the past year, according to the service's medical statistics. And the number of soldiers seeking help for combat stress, substance abuse, broken marriages or other emotional problems keeps increasing...
>
> A common refrain by the Army's vice chief of staff, Gen. Peter Chiarelli is that "far more soldiers suffer mental health issues than the Army anticipated." Nowhere is this more evident than at Fort Hood, where emotional problems among the soldiers threaten to overwhelm the system in place to help them. Counselors are booked. The 12-bed inpatient psychiatric ward is full more often than not. Overflow patient-soldiers are sent to private local clinics that stay open for 10 hours a day, six days a week to meet the demand. "We are full to the brim," says Col. Steve Braverman, commander of the Carl R. Darnall Army Medical Center on the post. That doesn't

even count those soldiers reluctant to seek care because they are ashamed to admit they need help, or the hundreds who find therapy outside the Army medical system, Braverman and other medical officials say. Officials' worry the problems may worsen—for the military and the country...

"If Fort Hood is representative of the Army—and 10 percent of the Army is assigned to Fort Hood—then if you follow the logic, our numbers should be scalable to any other post in the country," says acting base commander Maj. Gen. William Grimsley. "I worry that if we don't see this through the right way over the long haul ... we're going to grow a generation of people 10 or 15 years from now who are going to be a burden on our own society," he says. "And that's not a good thing for the Army. That's not a good thing for the United States."[53]

Statistics provided to *USA Today* by Fort Hood commanders showed the explosion of mental health issues there. They confirmed that counselors meet with more than 4,000 mental health patients a month. Specifically it was reported that last year, 2,445 soldiers were diagnosed with post-traumatic stress disorder (PTSD), up from 310 in 2004. On average, 585 soldiers are sent to nearby private clinics contracted through the TRICARE health system because Army counselors cannot handle more patients. They go on to state that hundreds more see therapists "off the network" because they want their psychological problems kept secret from the Army. A free clinic in Killeen offering total discretion treated 2,000 soldiers or family members this year, many of them officers. Last year, 6,000 soldiers here were on anti-depressant medications and an additional 1,400 received antipsychotic drugs.[54]

General Peter Chiarelli says in response to the staggering statistics, "I don't think we fully understand the total effect of nine years of continuous conflict on a force this size," The even larger concern is what will happen when these soldiers leave the military. It's feared that there are not enough counselors in the system to take care of them. Braverman stated in the *USA Today* article, "Every time more counselors are hired here, their schedules immediately fill up with patients. It's almost like a *Field of Dreams*," referring to the famous line from the baseball field movie film "If you build it, they will come." The story continues by stating, "Despite the increase in mental health resources, there have been 14 confirmed or suspected suicides among Fort Hood soldiers this year. That figure outpaces 2009 and matched each of the three worst years for suicides in recent base history, 2006-2008. In June, the Army recorded 32 suicides overall, the highest monthly total since it began keeping records."[55]

The future for our returning military is looking very grim. It's as though everyone is holding his or her breath waiting to see what the future holds. The *New York Times* reported on 7/27/11,

> "Though the withdrawal of American military forces from Iraq and Afghanistan will save the nation billions of dollars a year, another cost of war is projected to continue rising for decades to come: caring for the veterans...
>
> Though there is currently strong bipartisan support for veterans programs, some budget proposals have called for trimming benefits for veterans and military retirees. In a recent hearing before the panel, Heidi Golding, an analyst with the Congressional Budget Office, testified that the annual cost of caring for veterans from the Iraq and Afghanistan wars would nearly triple or more in the next decade. With an annual budget of more than $125 billion, the Department of Veterans Affairs runs a nation-

wide health care system that cares for more than eight million people who have left military service, of which about 700,000 are from the current wars.

More troops today are surviving injuries. But that also means that more troops are coming home with complex and severe wounds. Although not all seek help, a significant percentage is expected to receive care from the veterans system, in part because of efforts to reduce the stigma of mental health problems in the military.

Linda Bilmes, a Harvard academic who has done extensive research on the impact of the wars, said all those factors together suggested that "the actual cost over 30, 40 or 50 years will be even higher than we projected—And with life expectancy getting longer," she said, "the cost will probably peak later than in past wars."[56]

We can only guess what lies ahead for our men and women in uniform as these wars wind down. Can we comprehend what over a million service members look like? That is the approximate number of men and women that will be returning. How many of those will require mental health services is anyone's best guess? *Huffington Post* reported on May 16, 2011

> With the anticipated drawdown from Afghanistan and Iraq, we'll have around 1.2 million returning warriors, 30 percent of whom are likely to have some kind of combat stress (and that's not taking into account the *moral injury* all troops suffer, from the grief, shame, guilt, woulda-shoulda-couldas and personal crises that exposure to war imposes on everyone). Thirty percent of 1.2 million is around 360,000 service members returning to this country with PTSD... To make matters worse, these returning warriors will also be suffering the loss of their cohort of fellow war fighters — those they fought with, who feel

closer to them than family, the only ones who totally get what they've been through and how it's changed them. This loss is huge and comes at the worst time.[57]

Yet simultaneously as government cuts back programming, private sector donations are also shrinking. *USA Today* reported on November 22, 2010,

> "The largest individual donation ever made to charities supporting Iraq and Afghanistan troops, veterans and their families has run out: $275 million given from 2005 through 2009 by Californian David Gelbaum. Dozens of non-profits now face drastic reductions in services ranging from mental health treatment to care packages mailed to far-flung combat outposts. The National Military Family Association says it may slash spaces for 7,500 children for its Operation Purple camps next year unless emerging funding arrives.
>
> The Association says Gelbaum's donations of $17 million over four years covered nearly 100 percent of its budget for the Operation Purple program of summer camps for children of deployed or wounded troop and camps for military families struggling emotionally to reconnect after war.[58]

In summary, the number of soldiers forced to leave the Army solely because of a mental disorder has increased by 64 percent from 2005 to 2009, which now accounts for one in nine medical discharges. Soldiers discharged for having both a mental and a physical disability increased 174 percent during the past five years from 1,397 in 2005 to 3,831 in 2009. According to the U.S. Army, the June 2010 statistics for military suicides look as grim as ever. Despite all of the prevention programs being studied and implemented, thirty-two soldiers reportedly took their own life.

That is more than one soldier per day.[59] On a final note, today the *New York Times* 4/14/2012, came out with a new article which states, "An American soldier dies every day and a half, on average, in Iraq or Afghanistan. Veterans kill themselves at a rate of one every 80 minutes."[60]

To quote Debbie Ford, imagine if

> We can create a new reality for all the men and women that serve our country. Imagine if every man and woman pre and post war understood who they were, how they tick and why they do what they do. Imagine these people having the programs, processes and exercises to address their experiences. Imagine each of these remarkable individuals receiving emotional education that would allow them to come home from where they are stationed in better shape than when they left, with more skills, with an inspiring vision, feeling a part of something bigger and greater than themselves. Imagine if these men and women know that they are loved and valued by all they protect, that they are important to us, and that we are willing to give them the emotional education and the tools they need to live vibrant and productive lives.

I will never pretend that I have all of the answers, but I do believe in a common sense approach. My dream would be that a proactive counseling program could exist every US military base in the world. Realistically, I recognize that it's going to be a long time before attitudes will shift in that direction. It will be a process, but we must start somewhere. Everyone can make a difference if we collectively make it a priority. I have recently started an organization called Proactive Military Counseling. This is a place where civilians can get involved and make a difference in their home communities or on a national level. Everyone has something they can offer, services they can contribute, or talents they can share. My hope for sharing my story is that we can begin the conversation where I have left off. Please join me at www. OperationHelpOut.org. Let's find a way together to give back to the men and women that have given up so much for our safety and freedom.

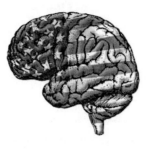

COUNSELING AND LEADERSHIP TOOLS

Below are leadership skills that I took from the NCCOSC website. [61] Truly, anyone who comes into contact with a service member that needs some help can employ these tools.

I replaced "sailor" with "warrior" because this was written for the Navy, but I feel it can be used in all military branches.

> *Resilience*: It is always better to PREVENT a stress injury than to treat a stress injury. The best prevention of a stress injury is RESILIENCE.

> *Resilience:* The capacity to prepare for, recover from and adjust to life in the face of stress, adversity, trauma or tragedy.

> Resilience is armor for the mind, push-ups for the brain.

> Resilience can be built in anyone.

Even in situations where a service member has no control over what is happening, he or she can learn to exert control over his or her response to what is happening. This is resilience.

Factors That Promote Resilience:

Scientific research has shown there are six factors that consistently are identified as resilience builders and stress resisters. They are:

- Active coping style means learning to face fears. It involves working to solve a problem and accepting the emotions that stress brings.

- Physical exercise releases endorphins and other hormones that lift moods and increase the brain's ability to learn from, and adapt to, stressful situations.

- Positive outlook and a good sense of humor help put negative events into perspective and increase a person's ability to recognize that hardships are temporary.

- Religious beliefs or spirituality help an individual attach a sense of meaning, purpose and value to experiences. It provides a moral compass and encourages finding fulfillment by helping others.

- Strong social support systems increase feelings of self-worth and trust and help to keep problems in perspective.

- Cognitive flexibility is finding the good in the bad. It is a trait that allows a person to see an event or situation from a variety of perspectives.

How To Promote Resilience In Your Warriors

- Provide tough, realistic training and drills that build confidence.

- Set high standards for physical fitness and give warriors time for fitness training.

- Make certain warriors get adequate sleep, rest and restoration to allow recovery from stress between periods of challenge.

- Learn ways to get a restful night of sleep and how to manage insomnia.

- Build positive relationships within the command through open and frequent communication, both with warriors and their families.

- Make certain warriors know why the mission is important and how their duties fit into the big picture.

- Help warriors maintain a realistic work-life balance and offer opportunities for both personal and professional improvement.

- When possible, provide stable routines to maximize opportunities for off-duty education and family time.

- Provide mentoring opportunities to all warriors.

- Encourage a positive outlook and a good, appropriate sense of humor.

- "De-glamorize" alcohol use.

- Conduct after action briefs.

- Set a good example: Effectively manage your own stress.

Q: How Do I Know If A Warrior Is Having A Stress Problem?

A: Meet OSCAR

Operational Stress Control Assessment and Response

This is an evaluation tool that can be used to gauge the level of stress in a fellow warrior.

Observe: Actively know your warrior. Learn their usual behaviors.

Example:

SN Carter usually is an optimistic and upbeat guy who does his job well. Recently, he has become irritable and short-tempered. He looks really tired and is showing up late for work.

State observations: If a Warrior seems to be acting "different," tell him or her that you are concerned something may be troubling them.

"Carter, you seem to be off your game and cutting some corners on the job. Let's talk about it."

Clarify your role: Say why you are concerned.

"I'm worried that you are not as interested in your job as you used to be. You also seem to be rude with a lot of the other guys. This is starting to create a tense atmosphere in the unit."

Ask why: Try to understand the other person's perception.

SN Carter tells you his girlfriend broke up with him and she is not going to pay back $500 she owes him. He's obsessed with how he's going to make rent.

Respond: Discuss desired behavior.

"Let's get you in touch with the command financial planner. Maybe Navy Relief can help, too. The unit needs the 'old' Carter back!"

Every leader should know the 7 C's

- Check
- Coordinate
- Cover
- Calm
- Connect
- Competence
- Confidence
- Scenario

While on a response team in Iraq, LTJG Harper witnesses a team member killed by an IED. Harper was near the explosion but was unhurt.

You begin to notice:

- Harper is not sleeping well.
- He seems unfocused during briefs.

- He misses meetings and has visited "doc" because of headaches and blurry vision.

- He looks tired and is jumpy. He appears very anxious and agitated.

This goes on for a couple of weeks. What do you do?
Check

Tell LTJG Harper that you are concerned about his appearance and his behavior and ask him how he feels.
Coordinate

You plan with the unit doc and chain of command to get Harper help.
Cover

Take Harper to a quiet place so you can talk. Actively listen to him.

Why? This promotes a sense of safety and reduces the effects of stress on the body.
Calm

Give LTJG Harper some relaxation techniques—such as deep-breathing exercises—to reduce his anxiety. Assure him you want to help.

Why? Reducing anxiety helps support sleep and promotes better decision-making.
Connect

Engage unit support, such as getting Harper to a chaplain and to medical to further evaluate for symptoms of TBI.

Why? Support is related to better emotional well-being and recovery. It leads to normalizing reactions and experiences. It reminds us we are not alone.

Competence

After a few visits to the chaplain and medical, you start to get LTJG Harper back on task and engaged in his job.

Why? Competence restores the ability to manage daily activities. It increases our trust in our capabilities.

Confidence

LTJG Harper is performing well again and has reintegrated with the unit.

Why? Self-confidence improves post-trauma outcomes. Expressing your confidence in Harper shows him and the unit that the LTJG is valued. This helps to reduce any stigma of asking and receiving help.

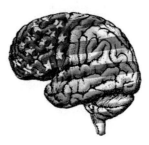

ACKNOWLEDGMENTS

First and foremost, I'd like to thank every one of our military members that have suffered from mental illness or have committed suicide. This book took me two and a half years to write and was the hardest thing I've ever done. It pales in comparison to what you have been through. Every time I wanted to quit, I thought of your suffering. This was written for you.

They say it takes a village to raise a child and I'd say the same thing about writing a book.

I owe a huge thank you to Debbie Ford who sat intently and listened to my every word while crying as I told her my story. She made me promise I'd write about it and gave me a timeline to adhere to. Debbie, if it weren't for you, this book may have never happened. You are truly an amazing person. Your intellect, passion and courage inspire me daily. I'm indebted to you for life.

To my mom, Marlene Sorosky Gray, who nagged me to no end to finish this book. You believed in it (and me) from the beginning and never let me quit. You have incredible work ethic and have been a wonderful role model. Thank you.

To Julie Dubick who has unconditionally always been there for me. The day I met you was truly one of the luckiest days in my life. You're an extraordinary friend and mentor and your constant support will never go underappreciated. Thank you for always finding the time for me.

The remarkable Marines and Drill Instructors from MCRD, thank you for believing in me and allowing me to enter into your world. You always had an open door and trusted me with your personal and your marine's mental health care. I am forever grateful.

Sgt. Major Mark O' Laughlin, words cannot express how much I value our friendship. You are an incredible Marine and I have learned so much from you. Thanks for always being there and providing unwavering support. We still have lots of work to do; I know our future is bright.

The Charlie Company "head shed" Major Derrick Oliver and 1st Sgt. (ret) Robert McDermott. You guys are two of the most passionate men I've ever known. The Marine Corps is truly a better place because of you. Thanks for everything, every step of the way. I know I have friends for life with the two of you.

Lt. Col Eric Peterson, your initial support will forever be imprinted on my heart.

Lt. Col Melanie Mercan, you are an amazing woman and I feel important just being in your presence. The women (and men) in the Corps are lucky to have you as a leader. Thanks for consoling me. I am so grateful for how hard you fought for me.

Lt. Col. Mike Cromwell, another phenomenally brilliant Marine. I love your authenticity and honesty. Thank you for everything.

Major Animea Utok, you are one of the most heartfelt Marines I know. You have been a true friend and I always enjoy every opportunity I get to spend with you.

A special thanks to: Gunny Sgt. Robert Alexander, Capt. Nick Borrelli, 1st Sgt. Martin Brewer, Capt. James Brobyn, Lt. Col. John Covazos, Capt. Michael Cragholm, Capt. David Dalby, S.Sgt Ryan Dunn, Col. Rob Gates, Col. Gregg Habel, 1st Sgt. Ryan Hermance, 1st Sgt. Lance Harrell, Lt. Col. Hezekiah

Barge, Andrew Hybel, Sgt. Major Brian Jackson, Capt. Glen Jenson, Sgt. Major Brian Link, Col. Patrick Looney, Lt. Col. George Malkasian, Capt. AJ Mallo, Sgt. Major (ret) Allen Mark, Lt. Col. John Meade, Capt. Nate Osbrach, Lt. Col. Roy Paul, Chaplain Robert Peters, Sgt. Major Terry Petersen, Capt. Luke Prigg, 1st Sgt. Juan Quijada, Sgt. Major Christopher Reed, Gunny Sgt. Joseph Restivo, 1st Sgt. Reymond Moore, Sgt Major Harry Rivera, Capt. Ricardo Scalise, Lt. Col. (ret) Rob Scott, Sgt. Major Karl Simburger, Capt. Joe South, Capt. Kevin Stepp, Chaplain Wayne Tomasek, Major Tom Warren, and Chaplain Matthew Weems, for always supporting me by reading and/or responding to my endless emails and providing me information and assistance when needed.

Thanks to all the countless people that helped me gather and make sense of the endless data I collected.

Congresswoman Susan Davis, thank you for your genuine passion and forward thinking vision. A special thanks you to Daniel Hazard, who always went the extra mile and spent the additional time to help me out.

Michael Kilpatrick, thank you for always taking my calls and guiding me in the right direction.

To all the staff at DCoE, thank you for being so gracious with your time and resources and allowing me to conduct so many different interviews. I greatly appreciate the passion you put into preventative military programing.

A special thanks to Terry Mizell, I'd pass the baton to you any day.

I never could have done this without all of my incredible friends, thank you for allowing me to vent and teach you about the military and their pervasive mental health issues. Jessica Vizcaino, life would be a perfect place if everyone had a friend like you. You are the bestest friend a girl could ever ask for. Rabbi David

Kornberg, thank you for allowing me to be myself and accepting me just the way I am. Clarence Perry, thank you for always being my rock. Your sound clinical direction is always appreciated.

Publishing a book is a complicated endeavor, I am grateful to everyone that helped me along the way. Thank you to all of the staff at Tate Publishing, especially my editor Sheridan Irick, for helping me get through this tedious process and to Melanie Harr-Hughes and Stephanie Mora for their brilliant creative input. Thank you Elaine Ratner, my first editor who encouraged me from the beginning. To Gideon Weil, who always took the time to listen, I greatly appreciate all of your publishing advice.

To my father Arthur Sorosky, the most insightful person (and psychiatrist) I've ever known. You raised me to believe I could accomplish anything I set my mind to. I miss you but I carry your spirit and memory deep within my soul.

Most importantly I want to thank my family. My husband Michael, who had to endure my late night writing and endless ranting about the military injustices, thanks for filling in the holes at home and always being there for me. Every mom thinks their children are the best, but my three kids; Jacob, Lindsey & Charlie truly are the most amazing. Thank you so much for putting up with me. Thanks for allowing me to take time away from you to complete this project. I hope I make you proud and pray you never fear speaking up when you witness wrongdoings. I love you very much.

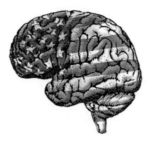

ABOUT THE AUTHOR

Marjorie Morrison

In more than a dozen years as a clinician, public speaker, and mental health consultant, licensed psychotherapist Marjorie Morrison has brought an innovative approach to mental health therapy to individual clients and organizations ranging from the San Diego Unified School District and San Diego's Children's Hospital to the United States Marine Corps.

In 2005, she was offered the opportunity to become a Military Family Life Consultant, and began accepting short-term contracts that took her to Army, Navy, Air Force, and Marine bases in the U.S. and abroad. In May 2008 that program placed her at San Diego's Marine Corps Recruit Depot for a three-month assignment that grew into a yearlong project and kindled both a deep respect for Marines and a determination to improve their mental health services.

The successful preventative-counseling program for Drill Instructors she created and implemented at the Recruit Depot has become a model for a proactive approach to military mental health therapy that is now attracting attention and gaining active support in military circles and the U.S. House of Representatives.

Marjorie Morrison has a Masters degree in Counseling Psychology, is a Licensed Marriage Family Therapist, a Licensed Professional Clinical Counselor and holds a PPS credential as a School Counselor and Psychologist. She divides her time between her overflowing private practice and a burgeoning career as a military mental health consultant and advocate. In addition to her work with the military, she has a deep passion for woman's issues. She recently launched a revolutionary working woman's work/life balance group combining group therapy coupled with a psycho education.

Marjorie lives in San Diego with her husband and three children.

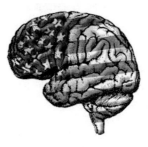

REFERENCES AND BIBLIOGRAPHY

1   Gregg Zoroya, "Army suicides linked to risky behavior, lax discipline." *USA Today*, July 30, 2010.

2   Gregg Zoroya, "Army efforts don't stem Fort Hood suicides." *USA TODAY*, Jamuary 6, 2011.

3   Belleruth Naparstek, "Who Gets Better from Combat Stress (And How)." Huff Post Healthy Living, May 16, 2011.

4   The DCoE Blog, http://www.dcoe.health.mil/blog, "Continuity of Care Heals the Wounded and Builds Trust." January, 8, 2010.

5   Thomas E. Ricks *Making The Corps*, 1997 (A Touchstone Book Published by Simon & Schuster).

6   Jeanette Steele, "Panel to Look at Suicide Prevention in Military: Stigma of Asking for Help Often Hinders Soldiers." *San Diego Union Tribune*, 10/6/2009.

7   Joe Klein, "Giving Back to Vets." *Time Magazine*, July 3, 2008.

8   Vanesa Williamson and Erin Mulhall, "Invisible Wounds Psychological and Neurological Injuries Confront a New Generation of Veterans." *IAVA: Iraq and Afghanistan Veteras of America*, Issue Report, January, 2009.

9   On the USMC website, http://www.usmc-mccs.org/leaders-guide/Emotional/MHProblems/generalinfo.cfm "Mental Health Problems." *Leaders Guide For Managing Marines in Distress*.

10 U.S. Army Sexual Assault Prevention, //www. sexualassault.army.mil /content /policy_restricted_unrestricted_reporting.cfm, "U.S. Army Sexual Assault Prevention & Response Team."

11 U.S.M.C. website http://www.usmc-mccs.org/LeadersGuide/ Emotional/MHProblems/generalinfo.cfm"Why Marine May Not Seek Help." *Leaders Guide For Managing Marines In Distress.*

12 HWM website, https://www.HWMgs.com, Military Family Lile Consultant (MFLC) Program.

13 Barbara Schading with Richard Schading U.S.M.C & Major Virginia Holeman, US Army RET, *A Civilian's Guide To The U.S. Military: A Comprehensive Reference to the Customs, Language, & Structure of the Armed Services.* 2007 (Writer's Digest Books, 237-239.

14 Barbara Schading with Richard Schading U.S.M.C & Major Virginia Holeman, US Army RET, *A Civilian's Guide To The U.S. Military: A Comprehensive Reference to the Customs, Language, & Structure of the Armed Services.* 2007 (Writer's Digest Books), 237-239.

15 Mark Benjamin, "Camp Lejeune whistle-blower fired: A psychiatrist who tried to prevent Fort Hood-style violence among Marines about to "lose it" instead loses his job." *Salon.com,* November 15, 2009.

16 Mark Benjamin, "Camp Lejeune whistle-blower fired: A psychiatrist who tried to prevent Fort Hood-style violence among Marines about to "lose it" instead loses his job." *Salon.com*, November 15, 2009.

17 Mark Benjamin, "Camp Lejeune whistle-blower fired: A psychiatrist who tried to prevent Fort Hood-style violence among Marines about to "lose it" instead loses his job." *Salon.com*, November 15, 2009.

18 Mark Benjamin, "Navy Supervisor doctored whistle-blower's records." *Salon.com,* January 31, 2010.

19 VT Veterans Today "US Department of Defense Announces Latest Contract Awards." www.veteranstoday.com, February 19, 2010.

20 VT Veterans Today "US Department of Defense Announces Latest Contract Awards." www.veteranstoday.com, March 26, 2010.

21 Greg Zoroya, "Study: Proactive Counseling stems troops' mental ills." *USA Today*, January 19, 2011.

22 Greg Zoroya, "Study: Proactive Counseling stems troops' mental ills." *USA Today*, January 19, 2011.

23 DCoE website, http://www.dcoe.health.mil.

24 http://www.mccsmcrd.com, "support council meeting 26 March 10.pdf"

25 Army Posture Statement, http://pentagon.mil/https://secureweb2. hqda.pentagon.mil/vdas_armyposturestatement/2010/informa-tion_papers/Military_Family_Life_Consultants_%28MFLC%29_ Program.asp, "Military Family Life Consultants (MFLC) Program." October 8, 2010.

26 Naval Cneter Combat & Operational Stress Control website, http:// www.med.navy.mil/sites/nmcsd/nccosc/leadersV2/infoAndTools/ Pages/default.aspx. "Leaders Info & Tools."

27 HEALTH NET INC Form 10-K Filed 2010-02-26, www.inves-torscopes.com/HEALTH-NET-INC/10-K/9794448.aspx.

28 American Psychiatric Association, http://healthyminds.org/More-Info-For/Military.aspx. "Healthy Minds. Healthy Lives."

29 American Psychiatric Association, http://healthyminds.org/More-Info-For/Military.aspx. "Healthy Minds. Healthy Lives."

30 ABC News, http://abcnews.go.com/blogs/politics/2010/07/junes-record-number-of-army-suicides/ "June's Record Number of Army Suicides." July 15, 2010.

31 ABC News, http://abcnews.go.com/blogs/politics/2010/07/junes-record-number-of-army-suicides/ "June's Record Number of Army Suicides." July 15, 2010.

32 Army Times, http://www.armytimes.com/news/2011/01/army-guard-reserve-suicide-rate-sees-big-spike-011911w/. "Guard, Reserve suicide rate sees big spike." January 19, 2011

33 NIMH (National Institute of Mental Health), http://www.nimh.nih.gov/science-news/2009/evidence-based-prevention-is-goal-of-largest-ever-study-of-suicide-in-the-military.shtml, "Evidence-Based Prevention is Goal of Largest Ever Study of Suicide in the Military." July 16, 2009.

34 Dr. Prudence L. Gourguechon , http://www.huffingtonpost.com/dr-prudence-l-gourguechon/closing-the-hope-gap-pres_b_813679.html, "Closing the Hope Gap: President Obama as Psychoanalyst-in-Chief." *Huffington Post,* February 2, 2011.

35 Joint Mental Health Advisory Team 7 (J-MHAT 7) Operation Enduring Freedom 2010

Afghanistan 22 February 2011, Office of The Surgeon General United States Army Medical Command and Office of the Command Surgeon HQ, USCENTCOM And Office of the Command Surgeon US Forces Afghanistan (USFOR-A)

36 Gregg Zoroya, http://www.usatoday.com/news/military/2011-07-25-homeless-veterans_n.htm. "Recent War vets face fear of homelessness." *USA Today,* July 26, 2011.

37 U.S. Department of Veterans Affairs Internet Search Results "Invisible Wounds of War: Psychological and Cognitive Injuries, Their Consequences, and Services to Assist Recovery."

38 Military.com News, http://www.military.com/news/article/appeals-court-blasts-va-mental-health-care-system.html. "Appeals Court Blasts VA Mental Health Care System." May 11, 2011.

39 RAND Center for Military Health Policy Research: A Joint Endeavor of Rand health and the Rand National Security Research Division. "Invisible Wounds of War: Psychological and Cognitive Injuries, Their consequences, and services to assist recovery." Published 2008.

40 Time Magazine, http://www.time.com/time/magazine/article/0,9171,1968110,00.html, "Sexual Assaults on Female Soldiers: Don't Ask, Don't Tell." March 8, 2010

41 Time Magazine, http://www.time.com/time/magazine/article/0,9171,1968110,00.html, "Sexual Assaults on Female Soldiers: Don't Ask, Don't Tell." March 8, 2010.

42 Department of Defense Annual Report on Sexual Assault in the Military Fiscal Year 2010.

43 About Face: A Community Supporting Military Women, http://servicewomen.org/2011/03/pentagon-releases-2011-report-on-military-sexual-assault/, "Pentagon Releases 2011 Report on Military Sexual Assault." March 18, 2011.

44 Department of Defense Annual Report on Sexual Assault in the Military Fiscal Year 2010

45 Gregg Zoroya, http://www.usatoday.com/news/military/2011-01-27-1Adruggeneral27_CV_N.htm, "General's Story A Warning About Use Painkillers." USA Today, January 27, 2011.

46 Greg Zoroya, http://www.usatoday.com/news/military/2011-01-26-soldieraddicts26_ST_N.htm, Up to 35% of wounded soldiers addicted to drugs." USA Today, January 26, 2011

47 Gregg Zoroya, http://www.armytimes.com/news/2011/01/gannett-army-david-fridovich-opens-up-about-battle-with-narcotics-012611/, "3-star opens up about battle with addiction." Army Times, January 26, 2011.

48 Catherine Pearson, http://www.huffingtonpost.com/2011/07/11/military-children-long-de_n_890476.html, "Military Children: Long Deployments Linked to Mental Health Problems." Huffington Post, July 11, 2011.

49 Gareth McConnell, http://www.time.com/time/magazine/article/0,9171,2008886,00.html, "Invisible Wounds: Mental Health and the Military." Time Magazine, August 22, 2010.

50 Rand Corporation, www.rand.org/news/press, "One in Five Iraq and Afghanistan Veterans Suffer from PTSD or Major Depression." April 17, 2008.

51 Mark Thompson, http://battleland.blogs.time.com/2010/11/12/as-we-were-saying/, "As We Were Saying…" Time Magazine: Battleland, November 12, 2010.

52 Mark Thompson, Time Magazine, "Invisible Wounds: Mental Health and the Military." August 22, 2010.

53 Gregg Zoroya, http://www.usatoday.com/news/military/2010-08-23-1Aforthood23_CV_N.htm, "Thousands Strain Fort Hood's Mental Health System." USA Today, August 23, 2010.

54 Gregg Zoroya, http://www.usatoday.com/news/military/2010-08-23-1Aforthood23_CV_N.htm, "Thousands Strain Fort Hood's Mental Health System." USA Today, August 23, 2010.

55 Gregg Zoroya, http://www.usatoday.com/news/military/2010-08-23-1Aforthood23_CV_N.htm, "Thousands Strain Fort Hood's Mental Health System." USA Today, August 23, 2010.

56 James Dao, http://www.nytimes.com/2011/07/28/us/28veterans.html, "Cost of Treating Veterans Will Rise Long Past War." New York Times, July 27, 2011.

57 Belleruth Naparstek, http://www.huffingtonpost.com/belleruth-naparstek/who-gets-better-from-comb_b_853073.html, "Who Gets Better From Combat Stress (And How)." Huffington Post, May 16, 2011.

58 Gregg Zoroya, http://www.usatoday.com/news/military/2010-11-22-militarycharities22_ST_N.htm, "Donor's Millions for Military Causes Drying Up." USA Today, November 22, 2010.

59 Cilla McCain, http://www.huffingtonpost.com/cilla-mccain/a-frightening-public-heal_b_1074115.html, "American Society in Crisis: Non-Hostile Deaths are Overtaking Veterans." *Huffington Post*, November 7, 2011.

60 Nicholas D. Kristof, http://www.nytimes.com/2012/04/15/opinion/sunday/kristof-a-veterans-death-the-nations-shame.html?_r=1, "A Veteran's Death, the Nation's Shame" *New York Times*, April 14, 2012.

61 http://www.med.navy.mil/sites/nmcsd/nccosc/leadersV2/infoAnd-Tools/Pages/default.aspx "Leader Information and Tools." NCCOSC.

CPSIA information can be obtained at www.ICGtesting.com
Printed in the USA
LVOW070232261112

308759LV00009B/942/P